Rommel's Greatest Victory

ROMMEL'S GREATEST
VICTORY

The Desert Fox and the Fall of Tobruk,
Spring 1942

Samuel W. Mitcham Jr.

PRESIDIO

Published by Presidio Press
505 B San Marin Drive, Suite 300
Novato, CA 94945-1340

Library of Congress Cataloging-in-Publication Data

Mitcham, Samuel W.
    Rommel's greatest victory : the Desert Fox and the fall of
Tobruk, spring 1942 / Samuel W. Mitcham Jr.
      p. cm.
    Includes bibliographical references and index.
    ISBN 0-89141-656-0
    1. Tobruk, Battles of, 1941–1942. 2. Rommel, Erwin, 1891–1914.
I. Title.
D766.93.M58   1998
940.54'23—dc21   98-12169
                             CIP

Printed in the United States of America

This book is dedicated to:
Don and Wanda Pounds of Nashville, Arkansas
When it comes to in-laws, God gave me the best.

Contents

List of Maps

List of Tables

Acknowledgments

First of all, I would like to thank my lovely and long-suffering wife Donna for all of her help. I would also like to thank Frank Tugwell for his assistance with computers, Dr. Gene Mueller of Henderson State University for his advice, and Friedrich von Stauffenberg for giving me his papers shortly before his death. As usual, thanks go to the United States Military History Institute at Carlisle Barracks, Pennsylvania, the Still Photo Branch of the U.S. National Archives, and the staff of the Bundesarchiv/Kolbenz for providing materials and/or photographs. Appreciation is also extended to Ms. Donna Glaze of the Computing Center, Northeast Louisiana University, for her help in preparing this manuscript. Last but certainly not least, thanks go to the extremely capable Melinda Matthews, interlibrary loan librarian at Northeast Louisiana University, for the fine job she did in locating and obtaining materials.

Table of Equivalent Ranks

U.S. Army	German Army
General of the Army	Field Marshal *(Generalfeldmarschall)*
General	Colonel General *(Generaloberst)*
Lieutenant General	General of (Infantry, Panzer Troops, etc.)
Major General	Lieutenant General *(Generalleutnant)*
Brigadier General*	Major General *(Generalmajor)*
Colonel	Colonel *(Oberst)*
Lieutenant Colonel	Lieutenant Colonel *(Oberstleutnant)*
Major	Major *(Major)*
Captain	Captain *(Hauptmann)*
First Lieutenant	First Lieutenant *(Oberleutnant)*
Second Lieutenant	Second Lieutenant *(Leutnant)*

*Brigadier in British Army

CHAPTER I: Enter the Desert Fox

THE ROUT OF THE ROMANS

World War II began on 1 September 1939, when Adolf Hitler's Wehrmacht (armed forces)—spearheaded by a handful of vaunted panzer divisions—invaded Poland. True to their treaty obligations, the British declared war on the Third Reich on 3 September, and the French followed suit a few hours later. As was the case in World War I, however, Italy found a pretext not to enter the war on the side of Germany. For the next nine months, Benito Mussolini and his Fascist cronies watched in fascination, horror, and envy as Hitler's legions smashed country after country. Poland was conquered in five weeks, Denmark in a few hours; every major city in Norway fell within two days, Luxembourg lasted less than a day, the Netherlands was overrun in six days, and Belgium surrendered within three weeks of being invaded by the Reich. The Nazi onslaught seemed invincible, and a new word was coined to describe it—*blitzkrieg*: German for lightning warfare. By the last days of May 1940, even the stubborn British Expeditionary Force had been smashed and was desperately trying to escape the European mainland before Hitler could finish it off, while the French Army—rated by the experts as the best in the world prior to 1939—had been decisively defeated in less than three weeks and was clearly on its last legs militarily. All of this was enough to convince the ambitious Mussolini—called Il Duce (the commander, the leader) by his followers—that Nazi Germany had already won World War II. On 26 May, he cornered two of his top generals, Marshal Pietro Badoglio, the Army chief of staff, and Air Marshal

Italo Balbo, in the hall of the Palazzo Venezia in Rome. "If Italy wants to sit at the Peace Conference table when the world is to be apportioned, she must enter the war and enter it fast," the dictator declared.

Balbo, the Italian commander in chief, North Africa, and governor of Libya, exchanged negative glances with Badoglio, the conqueror of Ethiopia.[1] Mussolini noticed their exchange and tried to nip any argument in the bud by pompously declaring that Italy would invade France on 5 June.

Badoglio tactfully asked Mussolini if he understood the implications of this order. Italy was completely unprepared for a war from the military point of view, he declared. Only 20 percent of her divisions were at war strength, more than 70 percent of her armored divisions did not have a single tank, the soldiers did not even have enough shirts, the colonies were completely unprepared for war, and the merchant fleet was scattered all over the high seas. Badoglio tried to continue, but Mussolini cut him short. "History cannot be reckoned by the number of shirts," he snapped.[2]

Italy declared war on the Western Allies on 10 June, and France surrendered eleven days later. Although Hitler refused to grant a disappointed Mussolini any of the vast territorial concessions he sought, the French capitulation did greatly improve Italy's military position in North Africa, for Rome no longer needed to worry about an invasion of its Libyan colony from French Algeria, which had been neutralized by the German victory. With his western flank thus secured, Mussolini was now in a position to turn east, where Egypt, the Suez Canal, and possibly even the Middle Eastern oil fields seemed to be within his grasp. Numerically the odds were stacked heavily in his favor. Balbo had 250,000 men in Libya, and the Duke of Aosta commanded another 300,000 in Ethiopia and East Africa. Most of Aosta's troops were natives, however, and they would prove to be ineffective in a confrontation with the British, although no one yet realized how useless they would be. Balbo, on the other hand, seemed to grasp how helpless his predominantly nonmotorized (or "marching") forces would be in a war of maneuver against the British, but he did not live long enough to convince Mussolini. On 28 June 1940, this world-famous aviation pioneer was shot down near Tobruk by his own trigger-happy antiaircraft gunners. He was succeeded by Marshal Rudolfo Graziani, the fifty-eight-year-old veteran of the East African and Ethiopian campaigns. He was nicknamed "the Breaker of the Natives" because, while he was in charge of the pacification campaign in Libya, he had native chiefs tied hand and foot and then tossed out of airplanes from an altitude of several hundred feet, right into the camps of the indigenous warriors.[3] He had later used poisonous gas and extermination in his efforts to pacify Ethiopia. Like Balbo, however, Graziani had serious reservations about the Duce's proposed invasion of Egypt; also, Graziani was still suffering from the effects of gunshot wounds he had suffered in Marseilles on 9 October 1934. (He had been seriously wounded in the same terrorist attack that killed King Alexander I of Yugoslavia and Louis Barthou, foreign minister of France.) Mussolini, however, pointed out to the marshal that he outnumbered the British forces in the Western Desert almost ten to one, and insisted that he "cross the wire" into Egypt.[4]

While the Italians in Libya put up an illusion of great strength, the British in North Africa seemed to be very weak indeed. Most of the British Army was in England, preparing for a Nazi invasion of the home islands, and few men could be spared for the defense of Egypt. The Western Desert Force (later redesignated XIII Corps) under Lt. Gen. Sir Richard O'Connor consisted of only two partially ready and understrength divisions: Maj. Gen. Sir Michael O'Moore Creagh's 7th Armoured and Maj. Gen. Sir Noel Beresford-Picrse's 4th Indian.[5] Together they numbered about 30,000 combat effectives.

Numbers are frequently misleading, and nowhere is the truth of this statement better illustrated than by the example of the North African theater of operations in 1940. The Italian Army was one of the worst in Europe. Its weapons (including many of its rifles) dated from World War I, it had little artillery and few antitank guns, and what little it did possess was obsolete—just like the rest of its equipment. Its tanks were called "self-propelled coffins" by the soldiers and were in no way equal to even the poorest British tanks. The Italian Army's greatest weakness, however, was its lack of mobility. More than was the case in any other theater of operations, mobility in the desert was absolutely essential not only for victory, but for mere survival. The

Italian soldiers, however, walked everywhere they went. As a result, the individual soldier's morale was understandably bad and his self-confidence was pitiful. He knew that he would be fighting a European-style war, but his leaders had armed and equipped him for a colonial conflict. The average Italian soldier in Libya rightly looked to the future with a sense of foreboding.

Marshal Graziani suffered from none of the delusions of grandeur which afflicted Mussolini. He did not want to drive on Cairo, and only crossed the frontier after the Duce threatened to relieve him of his command if he did not advance within two days. On 13 September, Graziani's strike force—the Italian Tenth Army under Gen. Mario Berti—crossed the wire into Egypt. On 16 September its spearhead, the 1st Blackshirt Division, reached the village of Sidi Barrani, sixty-five miles inside the border. Here, to the surprise of the Allies, it halted, never to advance again. As the Italians rested, built up their supplies, and erected a number of defensive camps east and south of Sidi Barrani, they completely surrendered the initiative to the British.

Meanwhile, O'Connor and his superior, Gen. Sir Archibald Wavell, the C in C, Middle East, prepared to deal the Italian Army a devastating blow. Erwin Rommel, the "Desert Fox," later remarked that Wavell was the only one of his opponents who showed a touch of genius. Wavell liked to do the unexpected. "Never let yourself be trammeled by the bonds of orthodoxy," he once said. "Always think for yourself . . . and remember that the herd is usually wrong."[6] He ordered O'Connor to launch a surprise attack on the Italian concentration at Sidi Barrani on 9 December. The British spearheads, however, were discovered early that morning by Lt. Col. Vittorio Revetra, the chief of the Italian fighter forces in Libya, who was on a routine patrol/reconnaissance flight. He immediately signaled Graziani that he had spotted "an impressive number of armored vehicles." To his shock and bewilderment, Graziani calmly replied: "Let me have that in writing." Graziani later claimed that he notified his subordinates of Revetra's report, but this is highly doubtful.[7]

Sir Richard struck Camp Nibeiwa, the forward Italian position south of the town, at 7:00 A.M. on 9 December, and took the Italians completely by surprise. Less than an hour later, the battle was over.

General Pietro Maletti, the garrison commander, was dead (shot through the lung while firing a machine gun), and his 4,000 men were prisoners. Twenty-three tanks and several artillery pieces were also captured.

O'Connor then turned on the other forward Italian camps and on Sidi Barrani itself, attacking with 31,000 men and 275 tanks. General Gallina, the commander of the Libyan Group of Divisions, met him with 81,000 men and 125 inferior tanks. The British were seized by a sense of euphoria, as if it were impossible for them to do anything wrong. The 1st Royal Fusiliers, for example, advanced on one of the camps, kicking a soccer ball in front of them. One British captain's truck broke down, so he had it towed into battle backwards, with himself and his orderly sitting imperturbably in the front seat.

To the north, Lt. Col. Eustace Arderne of the 1st Durham Light Infantry prepared to attack Camp Maktila, the northern (coastal) anchor of the Italian defenses. A Durham machine gunner fired two bursts; then an officer shouted to Arderne: "There's a white flag, sir!"

"Nonsense!" the colonel snapped. But it was true. Inside the fortified camp, the Durhams found 500 Italians in parade formation, standing rigidly at attention, a brigadier general in front of them, awaiting the arrival of the first British officer to surrender to.[8]

Few had it as easy as Colonel Arderne, but, by the end of the day, the Italian Tenth Army was smashed. The 1st Libyan, 4th Blackshirt, and 2d Libyan Divisions and the Maletti Group (the equivalent of an armored division) had dropped their weapons and marched off to the prisoner-of-war camps, along with most of the 64th Catanzaro Division and parts of the 2d Blackshirt. Only the 63rd Cirene Division escaped intact; General Gallina was among the prisoners. By 12 December, O'Connor had taken 39,000 prisoners—more than the total strength of the Western Desert Force. One British battalion commander contemptuously reported capturing an estimated "five acres of officers, 200 acres of other ranks."[9] An astonished Wavell at once saw an opportunity to deal the Italian empire in Africa a devastating blow. He expanded the scope of his operations from a five-day, limited-objective offensive into a full-scale blitzkrieg of his own (see Map 1, p. 6). Relying largely on captured Italian supplies, he overran the Italian forces at Fort Capuzzo, on the Libyan-Egyptian

WAVELL'S CONQUEST OF CYRENAICA

border, on 16 December and took several thousand more prisoners. The Western Desert Force's losses were minimal.

The Italian Tenth Army quickly deteriorated into a disorganized rabble. Men threw away their weapons and streamed to the rear in droves, seeking safety in the coastal fortresses of Bardia and Tobruk, which Graziani ordered to be held at all costs. At this point O'Connor was forced to halt temporarily, because the 4th Indian Division had been sent to Sudan, to operate against the Duke of Aosta. O'Connor besieged Bardia but did not assault it until 3 January 1941, after the Australian 6th Infantry Division arrived from Palestine to join the fighting.

Mussolini and the Italian people put a great deal of hope in the defense of Bardia, which was generally considered to be the most strongly fortified town in Libya. It was held by Lt. Gen. Annibale "Electric Whiskers" Bergonzoli—an officer famous for his toughness—and the 1st Blackshirt, 2d Blackshirt, 62d Marmarica, and 63d Cirene Divisions. It fell in two days, yielding another 38,000 prisoners, 462 guns, 127 tanks, and 700 trucks. Total British casualties numbered about 500. The Australians had taken the defenders so lightly that they entered this battle singing the theme song from *The Wizard of Oz*.

After the Bardia garrison collapsed, the Italians were staggered. If the British could not be stopped at Bardia, then where could they be stopped? Suddenly resistance collapsed everywhere as panic spread throughout the Italian colony of Libya—or what was left of it. Tobruk, an excellent fortress, fell in two days and yielded another 25,000 prisoners. Among them were Gen. Pitassi Manella, the commander of the XXII Corps, his staff, and the entire 61st Sirte Infantry Division. More than 200 guns and 87 tanks were captured.[10] Sollum and Derna also collapsed, and the 60th Sabratha Division surrendered, as defeat after defeat was heaped upon the heads of the latter-day Romans. Benghazi fell, and, at Beda Fomm, 3,000 British and Australian soldiers, supported by only thirty-two tanks, destroyed the 17th Pavia Artillery Regiment, and the last surviving Italian armored group, completing the destruction of the Tenth Army. Its commander, General Tellera (Graziani had recently sacked Berti) was mortally wounded at Beda Fomm and died the next day.[11] This time, no one escaped. Wavell and O'Connor captured 20,000 Italians, along with 216 field guns and approximately 100 tanks. The Allies suffered fewer than fifty casualties. "The police in Tel Aviv gave us a better fight than this," one Australian snorted in contempt.[12] In commenting on the effect of this campaign on Mussolini's legions, General Rommel observed: "The Italian troops had, with good reason, lost all confidence in their arms and acquired a very serious inferiority complex, which was to remain with them throughout the whole war . . ."[13]

General O'Connor finally reined up at El Agheila on 8 February, within striking distance of Tripoli, the last major seat of Italian resistance in Libya. In less than two months, the Italian Tenth Army had been destroyed, along with all of its divisions, including the 1st, 2d, and 4th Blackshirt, the 1st and 2d Libyan, the 60th Sabratha, 61st Sirte, 62d Marmarica, 63d Cirene, and 64th Catanzaro Infantry Divisions and the Maletti Armored Group. The Italians had lost 130,000 men, 1,300 guns, 400 tanks, and 150 aircraft, while inflicting only 2,000 casualties on the attackers. All that remained to defend Tripoli was a reinforced artillery regiment at Sirte and a makeshift garrison of four divisions, holding a twelve-mile perimeter around the city, under the command of Gen. Italo Gariboldi's Fifth Army.[14] Clearly they could have been gobbled up as well, had not the Allies involved themselves in a futile military adventure on the European mainland. With Hitler massing 600,000 men in the Balkans in an obvious preparation for the invasion of Greece, Churchill acidly rejected Wavell's advice (that O'Connor continue the offensive to Tripoli), and sent his most experienced soldiers and many of his air units from the desert to the mountains of Greece. In doing so, he violated one of the cardinal maxims of Frederick the Great, who said: "He who defends everything defends nothing." Sir Winston also threw away his best chance for total victory in North Africa in exchange for another disastrous defeat on the mainland of Europe, for Hitler's blitzkrieg overran Yugoslavia in a week and Greece in less than a month.

Meanwhile, on 3 February, Adolf Hitler told his staff officers at the Führer Headquarters at Staaken that the loss of North Africa was not important from the military point of view but would have a strong psychological effect on Italy. It would also free a dozen British divisions in the Mediterranean, which they could use "most dangerously. . . . We must make every effort to prevent this . . ."[15] He had therefore decided to send military aid to his fellow dictator in the form of an "Afrika Korps" of one panzer and one light division. Initially, the High Command of the Army (Oberkommando des Heer, or OKH) selected the commander: Maj. Gen. Baron Hans von Funck, a veteran cavalry and panzer officer who had most recently led the 5th Light Division.[16] Hitler, however, was very much unimpressed by the aristocratic von Funck and was annoyed by the fact that he had undergone a scandalous divorce; he therefore voided Funck's appointment and filled the vacancy with one of his favorites: Lt. Gen. Erwin Rommel, the commander of the 7th Panzer Division. OKH then handed command of the 7th Panzer over to von Funck, as a sort of consolation prize.

THE DESERT FOX

Erwin Johannes Eugen Rommel, the future Desert Fox, was born at Heidenheim in Swabia, a district in the former kingdom of Württemberg, on 15 November 1891. His strict father (also named Erwin) was a schoolmaster, like his father before him, and the thing Rommel remembered best about him was that he was always asking educational questions, much to the annoyance of his less-than-interested son.[17] Young Erwin, however, had a reasonably happy childhood, despite the fact that he was weak, sickly, and lethargic. He spent most of his time daydreaming and had no interest in hobbies, games, athletics, or girls. It was, however, obvious early in his life that he could get things done when he applied himself. Once in primary school, a teacher asked young Erwin how to spell a certain word. The clearly disinterested Rommel had no idea but made a half-hearted attempt and missed badly. Amidst general laughter, the teacher announced that he would declare a holiday if Erwin ever did well on a spelling exam. Ignoring his giggling peers, Rommel sat upright in his seat and stared at the teacher, whom he had taken quite literally. The next day, he correctly spelled every word on the list.

When the promised holiday did not materialize, however, he promptly lapsed back into his policy of doing the bare minimum to get by. So went his so-called formative years. Then, as a teenager, he suddenly shook off his lethargy. He began a program of exercise and self-improvement, systematically developing physical strength and stamina. He biked, worked out, ran, became a gymnast, played tennis, skied, and learned how to skate. He also developed many of the characteristics considered typical of a Württemberger—self-reliance, toughness, stubbornness, pragmatism, loyalty, and thrift. He was an open and somewhat unsophisticated person and remained so until the day he died. Material possessions were of little or no interest to him, and, in later years, when his first book became a best-seller, he was embarrassed by his wealth and the size of his royalty checks. Even so, Rommel developed a great interest in practical things, new inventions, and innovative ideas—traits which he exhibited throughout his life. When he was fourteen, for example, he and a friend built a full-scale glider in a field near Aalen, and the thing actually flew— but not very far. Still, it was a remarkable accomplishment for a teenager, especially when one considers that the year was 1906: only three years after the Wright brothers' famous flight.[18]

At an early age, and strictly on his own, Erwin Rommel decided to become a soldier. What prompted this decision is not known. Except for his father, who had briefly served as a reserve lieutenant in the artillery, there was no military tradition in his family. In addition, the Prussian aristocrats dominated the German Army and always had. The best young Erwin could hope from such a career was retirement at the relatively low rank of major (if he was lucky) and a modest pension. His father opposed his career choice and tried to talk him out of it, but, when he saw that Erwin was determined, he did all he could to help him, including paying for a minor operation and his initial upkeep. He also bought his *Fahnenjunker* (officer cadet) uniforms.[19] Young Erwin enlisted in the 124th (6th Württemberg) Infantry Regiment at Stuttgart on 19 July 1910. He was promoted to corporal three months later, and to sergeant in early 1911. In March 1911, he entered the War School at Danzig, to begin officer training. He was not the top candidate in his class, and was even considered somewhat awkward, but he impressed his officers with his conscientiousness, enthusiasm, and willpower, as well as with his intelligence, the firmness of his character, and his strict sense of duty.[20] He graduated from the War School and returned to the 124th Infantry at Stuttgart, where he was commissioned *Leutnant* (second lieutenant) on 27 January 1912.[21] (See page xi for a table of equivalent ranks.)

While at Danzig, Rommel met and romanced the only love of his life: Lucie Maria Mollin. She was a very attractive young lady with dark hair, a nice figure, and an outgoing temperament.[22] Rommel quickly fell hopelessly in love with her. Lucie at first considered the young cadet to be too serious, but Rommel managed to change her mind, and soon she returned his affections. The couple were deeply in love and considered themselves engaged by the time Erwin returned to his regiment. They were married in Danzig on 27 November 1916. Rommel, a faithful husband and companion, remained completely and unconditionally devoted to her until the day he died.

Meanwhile, World War I erupted in August 1914.

Until this point, Rommel's life and career had been absolutely undistinguished. They centered around the dull routine of garrison life in a nonelite infantry unit in an out-of-the-way corner of Imperial Germany and were characterized by endless drills, parades, and training exercises. His private life seemed boring to many of his peers. He never smoked or drank and never took part in the after-dark amusements of the other bachelor officers, who considered him friendly but altogether too serious. Instead, Rommel immersed himself in his profession and spent his nights studying the literature of war. On the job, he was businesslike and impersonal. His already strong will grew even stronger. He had a hard streak in him, and he exhibited no tolerance for the lazy or inefficient.[23]

The battlefield transformed this serious young second lieutenant into a warrior of the first class. "From the moment he first came under fire," Brigadier Desmond Young wrote later, "he stood out as the perfect fighting animal: cold, cunning, ruthless, untiring, quick of decision, [and] incredibly brave." A fellow officer commented later, "He was the body and soul of war."[24]

Rommel fought in Belgium and France, at Verdun, and in the Argonne. Near Varennes he was wounded in the upper leg—shot down by a French infantryman during a bayonet attack. He spent three months in various hospitals but was back in action in January 1915, commanding the 9th Company of the 124th Infantry Regiment. Again he did exceptionally well, earning the Iron Cross, 1st Class, and a promotion to first lieutenant (*Oberleutnant*) while engaged in trench warfare on the western front. Then, in September 1915, he was transferred to the Württemberg Mountain Battalion, an elite unit being formed to handle the most dangerous tasks in the most difficult terrain. In some indefinable way, Rommel's spirit and zeal permeated the entire battalion, even though he only commanded the 2d Company. "Everyone was inspired by his initiative, his courage, his dazzling acts of gallantry," Lt. Theodor Werner recalled.

Anybody who once came under the spell of his personality turned into a real soldier. However tough the strain he seemed inexhaustible. . . . He had an exceptional imagination, and it enabled him to hit on the most unexpected solutions to tough situations. When there was danger, he was always out in front, calling on us to follow. He seemed to know no fear whatever. His men idolized him and had boundless faith in him.

Rommel and his men trained in the Austrian Alps and then were sent to the Rumanian front. Here, with fewer than 200 men, Erwin Rommel captured 400 Rumanians in a single, well-coordinated attack in January 1917. Later that year, the Württemberg Battalion was sent into action in the Italian Alps, where young Rommel's performance was nothing less than astonishing. During the battle of Mount Matajur, in fifty hours of continuous movement and fighting, Erwin Rommel led his command (now enlarged to six companies—about 600 men) through enemy lines without being detected. He then proceeded to overrun the Italian artillery positions and ambushed the 4th Bersaglieri Brigade, the Salerno Brigade, and several smaller enemy units, forced them all to surrender, and seized the decisive, 7,000-foot heights of Mount Matajur for the Central Powers. In the process, he took 9,000 prisoners (including 150 officers) and captured 150 pieces of artillery. For this incredible feat of arms, he was promoted to captain and awarded the *Pour le Mérite,* a medal roughly equivalent to the Medal of Honor of the United States when awarded to someone of such relatively junior rank.[25]

Rommel was ordered home shortly thereafter and—much to his distaste—spent the rest of the war in staff assignments. After the armistice was signed in November 1918, Rommel returned home to his wife, his parent unit (the 124th Infantry), and the routine of garrison duty. He spent the next twenty-one years in more or less normal, peacetime soldiering and enjoying the quiet domestic life with Lucie and their only child, Manfred, who was born in 1928, on Christmas Eve. He spent fifteen years as captain and did not reach field-grade rank until 1933.

One of the turning points of Erwin Rommel's career occurred in the years 1929–1933 when, as a tactics instructor at the infantry school at Dresden, he wrote *Infantry in the Attack*. Based upon his World War I experiences, it was adopted as a textbook by the Swiss Army and became a best-seller in Nazi Germany, which was in the process of rearming. In 1936, Adolf Hitler (who had become chancellor in 1933) read it and decided to meet its author, who was now a lieutenant colonel. Rommel was attached to Hitler's escort during the Nuremberg Party Rally of 1936 and commanded the ad hoc *Führergleitbataillon,* Hitler's personal bodyguard battalion, during the Sudetenland crisis (1938), the occupation of Czechoslovakia (1939), and the invasion of Poland (1939). He was promoted to major general (*Generalmajor*) on 23 August 1939, eight days before World War II began.

While attached to Führer Headquarters, Erwin Rommel did not socialize with the Nazi elite and did not care to associate with most of them, although he did get along well with Joseph Goebbels, the minister of propaganda. Rommel was, however, impressed with Adolf Hitler and remained under his almost hypnotic spell until November 1942.

The Führer (leader) whom Rommel guarded in 1938 and 1939 was a far cry from the physical and mental wreck who, almost totally insane, cowered in his Berlin bunker and finally shot himself in the head on 30 April 1945. In 1939, Hitler (though already addicted to drugs) was still capable of rational thoughts and actions. He was certainly not yet the monster he later became. Rommel was treated to none of the fits, temper tantrums, rages, or psychotic behavior which Wilhelm Keitel and other generals experienced—not yet, anyway.[26] Rommel's main headache during the Polish campaign was Hitler's constant desire to go forward into the combat zone and to be right up front with the fighting soldiers. The German leader went so far as to expose himself to Polish sniper fire and observed the storming of a river line by German infantry and combat engineers—a contested crossing at that. This was a trait which Rommel could admire. "I had a great deal of trouble with him," he recalled later. ". . . He seemed to enjoy being under fire."[27]

In Poland, Rommel had the chance to observe the blitzkrieg firsthand, with its emphasis on speed, surprise, shock action, rapid movement by motorized formations, deep-thrusting armored spearheads, command from the front, and air power. Although he had been in the infantry for twenty-nine years and had probably not seen the inside of a tank before 1936, he decided that his future lay in the panzers.

After they got home from Poland, Rommel approached Hitler and asked for a command.

"What do you want?" Hitler asked.

"Command of a panzer division," Rommel replied, without batting an eye.

Much later, Rommel told his chief of staff that this request had been an "immoderate" one.[28] This it certainly was. There were many officers senior to him with much better credentials for such a post; indeed, Rommel was not even a member of the panzer branch at the time. The Führer, however, both liked and respected the young general and thought him capable of great things. On 5 February 1940, Rommel succeeded Lt. Gen. Georg Stumme as commander of the 7th Panzer Division.[29]

Rommel's new command hardly fit the propaganda ministry's description of an elite armored striking force. It was a recently converted light division,[30] outfitted largely with foreign equipment; in fact, more than half of its 218 authorized tanks were nine-ton Czech T-38s, which had simply been incorporated into the German Army after the occupation of Prague in 1939. They would be of little use against the much heavier tanks of the Western Allies. The British

Matilda (Mark II), for example, had three inches of frontal armor, making it invulnerable to the standard 37mm German main battle gun. Indeed, none of Rommel's tanks weighed more than twenty-three tons, and he had only a handful of these.

Despite his poor equipment, Rommel proved himself a master of panzer tactics during the conquest of France in 1940. He conducted an assault crossing of the Meuse, broke through the French Ninth Army, destroyed the 1st French Armored Division and the 4th North African Division, burst through the Maginot Line Extension, secured the critical Sambre River crossing near Le Cateau, and turned back the most important Anglo-French counterattack of the campaign near Arras on 21 May. Later he helped surround the First French Army at Lille, seized a railroad bridge intact and crossed the Somme, overran the 31st French Motorized Division at Fécamp, and captured the French ports of Saint-Valéry and Cherbourg. He was approaching the Spanish frontier when the French surrendered.

During a breathtaking six-week campaign, Rommel's division had suffered 2,594 casualties, including 682 killed. According to one source, 7th Panzer suffered a higher casualty rate than any other German division in the campaign.[31] During the process, Rommel's men inflicted a disproportionate amount of damage to the enemy. They took 97,468 prisoners, shot down 52 aircraft, destroyed 15 more on the ground, and captured a dozen airplanes intact. They captured Admiral Abrial, the commander of the French Atlantic fleet, and four other admirals, a French corps commander, the commander of the British 51st Infantry Division, about twenty other generals, and a number of headquarters and supply staffs. They also bagged 277 field guns, 64 antitank guns, 458 tanks and armored cars, 4,000 to 5,000 trucks, 1,500 to 2,000 cars, a similar number of horse and mule wagons, 300 to 400 buses, and about the same number of military motorcycles.[32] A delighted Adolf Hitler personally decorated Rommel with the Knight's Cross of the Iron Cross.

Rommel spent the rest of 1940 training his division and in occupation duties at Bordeaux. He also cooperated with Dr. Goebbels in the making of the propaganda film *Victory in the West* and started writing another book, this one chronicling the exploits of the 7th Panzer Division during the French campaign. Rommel had an almost American sense of public relations; unlike the typical German general, he recognized its value and used it both as a weapon and as a means to advance his own career. Thanks to Goebbels and the propaganda ministry, Rommel's name was already a household word when Hitler summoned him to Staaken in early February 1941, promoted him to lieutenant general, and gave him command of the Afrika Korps.

THE BIRTH OF A LEGEND

Erwin Rommel arrived in Tripoli on the morning of 12 February 1941, reported to Marshal Italo Gariboldi (who had recently replaced the hysterical Graziani as commander in chief of the Italian Army in North Africa),[33] and almost immediately made his presence felt. Initially, the forces he had were very weak: the X Italian Corps, consisting of the 27th Brescia Infantry Division, the 17th Pavia Infantry Division, and the 25th Bologna Infantry Division (all unsteady and of low quality), and elements of the excellent 132nd Ariete Armored Division, which was just arriving from Italy. It had only sixty tanks—all completely obsolete.[34]

Rommel had been ordered by Field Marshal Walter von Brauchitsch, the commander in chief of the German Army, and Col. Gen. Franz Halder, the chief of the General Staff, not to launch an offensive until both of his German divisions (the 5th Light and 15th Panzer) had disembarked in North Africa.[35] This would not occur until the end of May. Rommel, however, soon realized that the Western Desert Force (now redesignated the Cyrenaican Command) had been significantly weakened by Churchill's Greek adventure. He therefore decided to disregard his orders and assumed the offensive on 31 March. Within a matter of days he had recaptured Benghazi and annihilated the British 2nd Armoured Division in a daring campaign of unrelenting pursuit. He also captured the famous General O'Connor and four other British generals.[36] (Map 2, p. 17, shows Rommel's First Cyrenaican campaign.) His spectacular advance sent shock waves throughout the Western world and gave birth to the legend of the Desert Fox. The legend would grow to incredible proportions over the next two years.

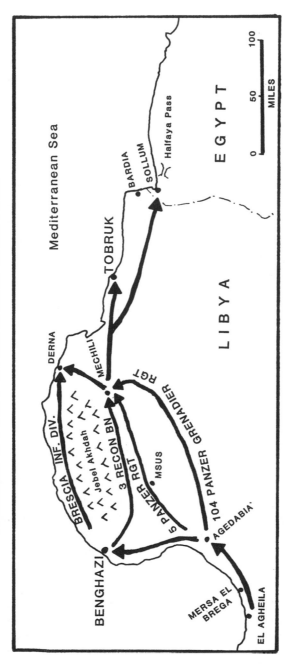

ROMMEL'S FIRST CYRENACIAN CAMPAIGN

Rommel hoped to swamp the entire British Army in Libya by cutting off the Australian 9th Infantry Division before it could retreat into the fortress of Tobruk. This phase of the campaign misfired, however, and Rommel was forced to mount a hasty attack on the fortress. This failed, so Rommel launched a prepared assault on 30 April. When this also failed, Rommel had no choice but to lay siege to the place. It was to last 242 days. Despite this check at Tobruk, Rommel had nevertheless succeeded in pushing the Allies back 1,000 miles, and the Axis foothold in Africa was no longer in imminent danger of collapse. For his victories, Rommel was given command of the newly formed Panzer Group Afrika, which included the Afrika Korps, the X and XXI Italian Infantry Corps, and the 90th Light Division, a partially motorized German formation which was activated in North Africa during the fall of 1941. The Italian XX Motorized Corps was later added to his command.

The British Eighth Army made two major efforts to relieve the fortress but were twice defeated by Rommel, who demonstrated considerable tactical brilliance in the process. As a result, Churchill relieved Wavell of his command and replaced him as commander in chief, Middle East, with a Scot, Gen. Sir Claude Auchinleck.[37]

Auchinleck has been described as "a most attractive personality; he detested all forms of pomp, display, and self-advertisement." Even Maj. Gen. Shahid Hamid, his former private secretary, said: "There is nothing dominating or overbearing in his character at all."[38]

Sir Claude grew up in the army. His father, Lt. Col. John C. A. Auchinleck, was an Indian Army soldier and an officer in the Royal Horse Artillery. He died when Claude was eight, which qualified his son for a foundation place at Wellington College. His mother, however, was financially hard-pressed to pay even the reduced fee of ten pounds per year. Claude grew up in strained financial circumstances and accustomed to hardships. He developed a lifelong indifference to personal comfort. He decided to make the army his career as a matter of course. He graduated from Sandhurst in 1903 and was commissioned into the 62d Punjab Infantry Regiment. Most of his service in the next forty-four years was in India, and much of that was on the troubled frontier. In 1932 (as a brigadier) he became commander of the Peshawar Brigade and led it in two campaigns against the Upper Mohmands. In 1936 he was promoted to major general and deputy chief of the General Staff of the Indian Army. Here he played a key role in the modernization of the Indian Army and in replacing British officers with Indians. In January 1940 he was ordered home (an unusual step) to raise, train, and command the IV Corps. This assignment was interrupted on 5 May, when Auchinleck (now a lieutenant general) was named GOC in C (General Officer Commanding-in-Chief) of the Anglo-French military forces, Norway. He did well here, taking Narvik from the German mountain troops and then evacuating it, on orders from London. He also irritated Winston Churchill (then First Lord of the Admiralty) by insisting upon the provision of essential supplies.[39] On 14 June he assumed command of V Corps in southern England, and on 19 July he succeeded Sir Alan Brooke (now Chief of the Imperial General Staff [CIGS]) as GOC Southern Command. Had Hitler launched Operation "Sea Lion," he would have been a key commander responsible for repelling the German invasion.[40] Four months later, after the threat of invasion had receded, "the Auk" (as he was called) was promoted to full general and named C in C, India.

Sir Claude Auchinleck was a solid professional officer and a competent general, but one who lacked Wavell's touch of genius. He was, however, endowed with a bulldog tenacity, and he immediately began building up for another attempt to break the Siege of Tobruk. Just as feverishly, Erwin Rommel prepared his army to meet it. By the fall of 1941, his men—like those of the Württemberg Mountain Battalion before them—had been thoroughly permeated by his spirit and had boundless confidence in him. They did not have much else, however. Operating out of the island-fortress of Malta, British air and naval forces were able to virtually sever the Mediterranean supply lines and strangle Rommel's command. More than two-thirds of the supplies sent to Libya were sunk en route. With the Afrika Korps in danger of literally starving to death, Adolf Hitler transferred Field Marshal Albert Kesselring's Second Air Fleet from the Russian front to Sicily, from whence it was able to temporarily neutralize Malta. This came too late to help Rommel in his next battle, however. During November 1941, Allied ships, submarines, and aircraft sank 77 percent of the supplies bound for Panzer Group Afrika. On 18 November, the

British Eighth Army launched Operation "Crusader," which was called "the Winter Battle" by Germans. Rommel went into it with only 15 percent of the supplies he needed to fight it.

General Sir Alan Cunningham's Eighth Army attacked Panzer Group Afrika with a massive array of 748 tanks.[41] Cunningham also had 200 tanks in reserve and another 236 en route to Egypt aboard British convoys. Rommel met the onslaught with only 249 German and 146 Italian tanks, with nothing in reserve except 50 tanks in the repair shops.[42] The battle that followed was one of the most complex and fluid of World War II. Despite his lack of food, fuel, and ammunition, and in spite of odds of three to one against him, Rommel was able to check the Allied advance by defeating the piecemeal and uncoordinated British thrusts one at a time. Then he became overly impressed by local successes and launched his famous "dash to the wire," hoping to cause the collapse of the Eighth Army. This raid was a miserable failure. General Auchinleck sacked General Cunningham[43] and replaced him with Gen. Sir Neil Ritchie, who used the respite furnished by Rommel's absence to reorganize and repair many of his damaged tanks. When Rommel returned to the Tobruk sector with his armor, the tide of the battle had already turned against him. The Desert Fox nevertheless put up a fierce resistance and, by 2 December, had claimed the destruction of 814 enemy tanks and scout cars. The Afrika Korps, however, was down to a strength of 80 operational tanks. By the time he was finally forced to retreat to the east on 7 December (after abandoning the siege of Tobruk during the night of 4/5 December), Rommel had lost 386 of his 412 tanks. He also lost all three of his German divisional commanders, and 38,300 men were killed, wounded, and captured—32 percent of his original force.

Following their victory during Operation "Crusader," the British generals believed they had won the war in North Africa and that one more push would give them Tripoli. On 12 January, for example, Auchinleck signaled London that "indications of weakness and disintegration" were multiplying on the Axis side.[44] Thinking there was no danger of a German resurgence, the British scattered their forces all over Egypt and eastern Libya while they finished off the trapped German-Italian garrisons at Bardia, Sollum, and the Halfaya Pass, repaired their tanks, built up their supplies, and prepared for their final offensive. All they had in the forward areas were elements of the 1st Armoured Division and the 201st Guards (a motorized brigade), with parts of the 4th Indian Division in reserve at Benghazi. The Allied military leaders had grossly underestimated their opponent. With Malta temporarily devoid of offensive capability, the Italians were able to send a major convoy to Africa, and Rommel was reinforced with 55 new panzers, 20 armored cars, and large quantities of fuel and other supplies. Soon his two panzer regiments, the 5th and 8th, had 111 tanks each. The Italian Ariete Armored Division had 89 tanks, and there were 28 panzers in reserve.[45] Early in the morning of 21 January 1942, Erwin Rommel wrote to his wife: " . . . I've decided to take the risk [and strike again]. I have complete faith that God is keeping a protective hand over us and that He will grant us victory."[46] Two hours later he unleashed a major offensive and achieved complete surprise all along the line. This was Rommel's most brilliant campaign. In a three-day running battle with the Afrika Korps and the 90th Light Division, the British 1st Armoured lost 100 of its 150 tanks, as well as thirty-three pieces of artillery and thousands of men. The divisional staff was taken prisoner, and another 30 battleworthy Valentine tanks were seized in a rear-area supply depot.[47] Colonel Friedrich Wilhelm von Mellenthin, Rommel's chief intelligence officer, recalled that "the pursuit attained a speed of 15 miles per hour, and the British fled madly over the desert in one of the most extra-ordinary routs of the war."[48] By 26 January, the British had lost 299 tanks and armored vehicles, 147 guns, and 935 prisoners. Rommel reported a total loss of only 3 officers, 11 enlisted men, and 3 tanks.[49] At noon on 29 January, Rommel reentered Benghazi, the capital of Cyrenaica. Another 1,000 prisoners (these from the 4th Indian) surrendered when the city fell. Hitler—who had upgraded Rommel's command to panzer army status on 21 January, was so pleased that he promoted Rommel to colonel general (*Generaloberst*), the second-highest rank in the German Army.

The remnants of General Ritchie's forces retreated to the area around Gazala, where they rallied and were reinforced with the 1st South African Division and the 32d Army Tank Brigade. Rommel reached this sector on 6 February but decided he was too weak and lacked the supplies to attack it. As a result, he fell back into the desert to the west, and a lull descended on the North African front as both sides prepared for the next campaign, like a pair of battered boxers getting ready for the next round. It would be a very interesting one indeed.

CHAPTER II: Preparing For Action

THE BATTLEFIELD

General von Ravenstein called the desert "the tactician's paradise and the quartermaster's nightmare." The "Western Desert," where Rommel and his opponents fought, is somewhat ill defined but refers to the wasteland extending westward from the edge of the Nile River valley to the rainier foothills of the Atlas Mountains, near the Libyan-Tunisian border.[1] It is bounded on the north by the Mediterranean Sea and to the south by the Great Sand Sea, about 150 miles inland. Extending along the sea is a coastal plain, which varies in width from less than a mile to about twenty-five miles. One of the most important tactical features in the desert lies at the southern edge of the coastal plain. Here, the escarpment, a rise of the ground, extends sharply upward to the Libyan plateau, about 500 feet above the plain. The escarpment, which generally parallels the coast, is quite steep in most places and is generally not negotiable by either wheeled or tracked vehicles. In some places, up to three such abrupt rises in the escarpment make travel across it even more difficult.

The plateau does not fit the common misconception of what a desert is. It is dark brown in appearance and is generally covered with low scrub vegetation and rocks. Water is so scarce here (outside of a handful of oases) that the area is virtually uninhabited. However, if one is careful, it is possible to drive a vehicle almost anywhere on the desert—except from the interior plateau across the escarpment to the coastal plain. Of the desert, Strawson wrote:

of the traditional soft burning sand of the Sahara, they had found little, save in the Great Sand Desert far to the south. But there were vast stretches of hard sand and of stony ground riddled with black basaltic slabs; there were bony ridges and ribbed escarpments and deep depressions; there were flat pans which held water after the rains, where gazelles cropped the coarse grass in midsummer. There were wadi-fed flats which sprang overnight into flowery glory in spring; there were endless undulating sand and gravel dunes whose crests marched in rhythm, like waves at sea.[2]

The much smaller coastal plain, on the other hand, is mostly sand and—unlike the plateau—generally conforms to the typical American's concept of a desert. Here the small population of the region, which consisted of native Arabs and colonial immigrants, concentrated in the coastal towns. The bulk of the fighting, however, took place on the uninhabited coastal plateau.

Communications in the desert are extremely limited. The only paved road was the Via Balbia, or Coastal Road, which was built by Marshal Balbo in the 1930s. In the interior, however, vehicles followed trails (called *trighs*) or crossed the wasteland navigating by compass, like ships at sea.

The climate of the desert is harsh. It is extremely hot in the summer and is sometimes very cold in winter. In all seasons, there is a sharp drop in the temperature at night. In Libya, the rainfall comes mainly in the winter and decreases from the escarpment inland. Typically, the summer of 1942 was a dry one.

One of the most unpleasant features of the desert is the ghibli (called the *khamseen* or *khamsin* by the Arabs and the British), which is a hot wind blowing from the Sahara, bringing huge clouds of dust which clog the mechanisms of vehicles and weapons and bring all movement to a halt. Of his first ghibli, Erwin Rommel recalled:

> Immense clouds of reddish dust obscured all visibility and forced the car's speed down to a crawl. Often the wind was so strong that it was impossible to drive along the Via Balbia. Sand streamed down the windscreen like water. We gasped for breath

painfully through handkerchiefs held over our faces, and sweat poured off our bodies in the unbearable heat.[3]

Ghiblis and smaller sandstorms are likely to occur at any time. In addition, the region is plagued by flies and sand fleas in all seasons. All in all, it is a harsh, unpleasant environment, made worse for the Axis side by horrible rations and periodic shortages, usually caused by the British forces on Malta.

STRATEGIC PLANNING, 1942

When the British lost in western Cyrenaica in January 1942, they lost the airfields that were supplying Malta as well. Without these airfields, it was not possible to supply the island adequately. Without proper provisions, it was no longer possible for the fortress to intercept Rommel's convoys; and the longer Malta starved, the stronger Panzer Army Afrika became. It was therefore essential, from the British point of view, to recapture western Cyrenaica as soon as possible.

As we have seen, the Gazala position was weakly held initially, but Auchinleck ordered that it be made as strong as possible, in order to preserve Tobruk as a base for a new offensive. If Rommel struck first, Auchinleck ordered, he was to be checked in the Gazala Line. In the event the Gazala Line were lost, Auchinleck insisted, Ritchie was not to allow Tobruk to be invested again; rather, he was to retreat to the general lines of Sollum–Fort Maddalena–Jarabub—in other words, to the Egyptian frontier. Admiral Sir Andrew B. Cunningham, the Royal Navy's commander in chief, Mediterranean, fully agreed with this policy, as did Air Chief Marshal Sir Arthur W. Tedder of the RAF and his deputy, Air Marshal R. M. Drummond. The decision not to risk a second siege of Tobruk was communicated to London as early as 19 January. Neither the War Cabinet nor the Chiefs of Staff challenged this decision or even commented on the matter.

On 7 February, after Rommel had ended his pursuit, the C in Cs (Auchinleck, Cunningham, and Tedder) instructed General Ritchie to organize a striking force and prepare for an offensive. His objectives were to regain the airfields in the Derna-Mechili-Martuba area and reoccupy Cyrenaica. He was told that he might expect to have three armored divisions, two armored brigade groups, one army tank brigade, and three infantry divisions for the offensive. Most of this force would be equipped, trained, and available by the middle of April, but the commanders in chief did not fix an exact date for the offensive. This started a debate between London and Cairo which continued until May. Churchill, backed by the War Cabinet and the Chiefs of Staff in London, pressed Auchinleck to attack as soon as possible, in order to take the pressure off Malta. Sir Claude, however, did not want to strike until he had the number of tanks he felt he needed for a reasonable chance of success. He reported on 4 March, for example, that Middle East Command had 1,315 tanks; however, only 591 of them were with the units. The rest were under repair or awaiting repair. He agreed with Churchill and Gen. Sir William Dobbie, the governor of Malta, that the island-fortress was valuable but maintained that Egypt and the Suez Canal were infinitely more important and correctly argued that a defeat in the Western Desert would threaten the entire sector.[4] Meanwhile, on top of the loss of western Cyrenaica, the British colony of Singapore fell to the Japanese. This was quickly followed by the Allied collapse in the Netherlands East Indies, the Japanese invasion of Burma, and the "Channel Dash," in which the German battleships *Scharnhorst* and *Gneisenau* and the heavy cruiser *Prinz Eugen* escaped from their bases in France to havens in Norway via the English Channel. These disasters caused a great deal of indignation in the United Kingdom, and public morale was low. A major victory, Churchill knew, would change all of this; therefore, on 8 March 1942, he asked Auchinleck to come home for consultations. The general bluntly refused, stating that he could not leave his awesome responsibilities, even for a few days; besides, he added, his presence in London would not make any difference: it would not speed up the offensive even one day. Churchill—who (perhaps correctly) took Auchinleck's refusal as an attempt to escape pressure—considered removing the general and replacing him with Lord Gort, who had led the British Expeditionary Force during the Dunkirk evacuation, but did not.[5] Instead, he sent Sir Stafford Cripps, the Lord Privy Seal, and Lt. Gen. Archibald E.

Nye,[6] the Vice Chief of the Imperial General Staff, to the Middle East, to impress the War Cabinet's views on Auchinleck. After visiting Cairo and checking out the situation, however, Cripps and Nye sided with Auchinleck—much to the disgust of Churchill, who signaled Nye: "I have heard from the Lord Privy Seal. I do not wonder everything was so pleasant, considering you seem to have accepted everything they said, and all we have got to accept is the probable loss of Malta and the Army standing idle, while the Russians are resisting the German counter-strike desperately, and while the enemy is reinforcing himself in Libya faster than we are. Do not hasten your return."[7]

But Cripps and Nye did hasten home. After their return, they reported the outcome of their discussions to Churchill and the Defense Committee on 21 March, and they basically confirmed Auchinleck's arguments. Far from being intimidated by Churchill, General Nye was especially outspoken, pointing out that there was something London tended to overlook—the need for proper training before going into action in the desert. Not convinced, Sir Winston felt that his emissaries had failed to properly deal with Auchinleck's arguments; now, however, he had little choice but to reluctantly agree to the mid-May date. On 2 April, however, the Middle East C in Cs signaled that they would not be bound even to this timetable. This naturally led to more arguments. Finally, on 6 May, the C in Cs signaled that the latest comparison of tank strengths made it unjustifiable to attack before mid-June, despite the threat to Malta. The Chiefs of Staff in London were inclined to agree to the postponement, but Churchill and the War Cabinet were not. Sir Winston, one of the most persuasive people in history, convinced them that the C in Cs were overestimating the Germans. On 10 May, he signaled Auchinleck that Malta—with its more than 30,000 men and hundreds of guns—would not be allowed to starve and fall without a battle being fought by the entire Eighth Army. He gave Auchinleck two choices: launch an offensive not later than the dark moon phase of June, or resign. Under such pressure, Sir Claude submitted to the prime minister's timetable.[8]

Auchinleck later wrote of Churchill: "He was first class as far as leadership was concerned. Leadership was what was required and he

had the power. People respected him. I respected him. He was a little bit dangerous when he tried to be too technical militarily—he'd been in the army but he wasn't a trained commander." Churchill's main problem and weakness, according to Auchinleck, was impatience.[9]
He was certainly right about that.

Axis strategic planning was much simpler. Rommel planned his own offensive with no help or interference from Berlin, which regarded the Desert War as nothing more than a sideshow. Convinced that the High Command failed to grasp the importance of the North African theater, he flew to Führer Headquarters at Rastenburg and met with Hitler on 16 February. Here he spoke openly of his intentions to destroy the British forces in the Gazala Line–Tobruk sector. Much to the Desert Fox's annoyance, the dictator was indifferent to his plans and refused to give him any more reinforcements, and Field Marshal Wilhelm Keitel, the commander in chief of OKW (*Oberkommando des Wehrmacht*, the High Command of the armed forces) made it clear that he was annoyed by Rommel's untimely visit. Like the Führer, Keitel (a longtime enemy of Rommel's) was preoccupied with the situation in Russia. The Desert Fox left East Prussia in a disgusted and unhappy mood. He took a three-week leave and visited his family at Wiener Neustadt, Austria, where he had commanded the infantry school before the war. While here, he attended a reception held by local Nazi Party officials and—characteristically—gave full vent to his feelings.

It was soon made clear even to Rastenburg, however, that something had to be done about Malta. In late April, Hitler tore himself away from his eastern front planning and flew to Berchtesgaden, his home on the Obersalzberg, a mountain in the Bavarian Alps, where he met with Mussolini, Kesselring, and Gen. Count Ugo Cavallero, who had succeeded Badoglio as chief of the Italian general staff.[10] Cavallero, backed by Mussolini and Kesselring, proposed a joint German-Italian invasion of the island. Hitler—who had a fear of amphibious operations—reluctantly agreed, and preparations were soon being made to launch Operation "Hercules," as the Maltese invasion was code-named. It called for an initial airborne landing by

30,000 German and Italian paratroopers and gliderborne soldiers under the Prince of Piedmont, to be followed by seaborne landings by six Italian divisions (about 100,000 men). Major General Hermann Ramcke, an elite Nazi airborne specialist, was named chief instructor of the Italian Folgore (Thunderbolt) Parachute Division, and ten Luftwaffe air transport groups (500 airplanes) under Col. Conrad Seibt assembled in Sicily for the drops.[11] General Kurt Student, the "father" of the German parachute branch, was the senior German "advisor" at the prince's headquarters.[12] Against this massive attack, the British garrison could muster only 30,000 men, with little hope for reinforcement. Before "Hercules" was unleashed, however, the Führer said that Rommel was to be allowed to try to capture Tobruk. Axis grand strategy in the Mediterranean for 1942 soon evolved into a three-step process: (1) capture Tobruk; (2) next, take Malta; and (3) then Panzer Army Afrika was to invade Egypt.

On 28 April, Field Marshal Kesselring flew to Libya and met with Rommel and several other key personalities in Africa, including Maj. Gen. Alfred Gause, chief of staff of Panzer Army Afrika; Col. Siegfried Westphal, Rommel's operations officer; and Lt. Gen. Otto Hoffman von Waldau of the Luftwaffe, the air commander, Africa (*Fliegerführer Afrika*). Apparently some of Rommel's bitter words after his Rastenburg trip had reached Hitler's ears; in any case, in front of the other generals, the OB South (*Oberfehlshaber*—commander in chief) informed Rommel that he had the Führer's complete confidence and that he and Hitler promised to do everything in their power to fulfil the panzer army's logistical requirements.[13] Later that afternoon, Gen. Ettore Bastico, the Italian governor of Libya and Rommel's nominal superior, decorated the Desert Fox with the Grand Order of the Colonial Star in the presence of the Italian corps commanders.[14] Four days later, on 2 May, Bastico and his chief of staff, Gen. Curio Barbasetti, visited Rommel. They inspected the Italian units, and Bastico expressed his complete approval for Rommel's offensive plans. He also promised to do everything he could to help and to get the Italian forces ready for the attack. As if to underscore his words, four ships docked in Benghazi and Tripoli that day. They off-loaded 272 vehicles, twenty-seven guns, and twenty tanks.[15]

PREPARATIONS AND ORGANIZATION FOR COMBAT

Meanwhile, both the British Eighth Army and Panzer Army Afrika reorganized for the next battle. This was much more difficult for the British, because it involved fundamental changes in their entire outlook on how battles should be fought. British tactical doctrine, which had been developed in the 1920s and 1930s, evolved around the basic idea that heavy "infantry" tanks should assist the infantry in conducting deliberate assaults against the enemy's continuously held front lines, as they had done during World War I; then, once a breakthrough had been achieved, they would commit their pursuit tanks into the enemy's rear areas. This led to the development of two distinctly different categories of British tanks: infantry, or "I," tanks and pursuit, or "cruiser," tanks. More importantly, it contributed to the dangerous idea which developed in the Royal Tank Corps that it was an army within an army—that it was an elite formation that should do battle only with the German panzers. The drawback to this doctrine was the fact that General Rommel also had something to say about how their battles were fought, and he and his subordinates were not about to let the RTC do battle with unsupported German tanks. The Desert Fox and his clear-thinking companions were skilled and well trained in combined-arms tactics. Since their panzers were in no way superior to some of the British tanks, they worked their tanks, antitank guns, artillery, and infantry in harness, so that none was without the protection of the others. They especially liked to use their armor against the infantry and soft-skinned vehicles of their enemies, and their antitank guns against the British tanks. British tanks at this time could not adopt these tactics, as they had only armor-piercing shells. Rommel's panzers had both armor-piercing and high-explosive (HE) ammunition, and they frequently used the latter to pound British trucks and foot soldiers. The British tanks they usually left to their antitank gunners.

Rommel's antitank gunners are perhaps the unsung heroes of the desert war and one of the keys that allowed Rommel to win his victories. These men were skilled, mobile, exceptionally well trained, and of very high morale (like all of the Afrika Korps, which had the comrade-in-arms attitude of the underdog). They had boundless confidence in themselves and their leadership, and their tactics were decidedly superior to those of the Allies. The Germans pushed their antitank guns right up to the front, often in advance of the panzers; in fact, they frequently called themselves *panzerjäger*—"tank hunters." Due to the hot-air layer immediately above the ground, even large guns could not be seen clearly, even at a distance of fifty yards. Everything was distorted and apparently reduced in size, as if one were looking through the wrong end of a pair of binoculars. This enabled the Germans to take liberties they would never have taken in Europe, and they blasted tank after tank. The British, on the other hand, used their AT guns almost exclusively as defensive weapons, mainly in support of the infantry.

The German antitank weapons were also better than the British antitank guns. The standard German antitank gun, the Pak 38, for example, was a long-barreled 50mm gun with a greater range and almost twice the penetration power of the standard British two-pounder (about 40mm), and its armor-piercing shell weighed more than 4.5 pounds—more than twice that of the British shell.[16] Rommel was also reinforced that spring with a number of captured Russian 76mm antitank guns, which fired a fifteen-pound shell and completely outclassed anything the British had, and which could defeat any Allied tank. The British did sometimes use the twenty-five-pounder gun in an antitank role. Even though it was not an antitank gun, it could fire a fifteen-pound armor-piercing shell, which made it very dangerous under certain circumstances; however, it was also very vulnerable to German armor. The British also had six-pound guns (approximately 57mm), which fired a 6.25-pound armor-piercing shell, but they had just begun to arrive in the desert and their crews were, in general, hastily equipped and inadequately trained.

If the German 50mm and 76mm guns were formidable to the Allies, the German 88mm gun was downright intimidating. Originally designed by Krupp in 1916 as an antiballoon gun, the models of the 1940s were considered antiaircraft guns and were still used in that role; they were not as mobile as the 50mm guns, but their range was so great that they did not have to be, and the 88 could fire an extremely dangerous twenty-one-pound armor-piercing shell almost two miles with complete accuracy. At the battle of Sidi Omar in November 1941, for example, a British tank regiment lost forty-eight of its fifty-two tanks, all knocked out by 88s. None of the British tanks even got close enough to open fire on the German guns. The historian of the 9th Queen's Royal Lancers Regiment recalled:

> A direct hit [from an 88] felt as though a gigantic sledge-hammer had hit the tank. The shell made a neat, round hole about four inches in diameter, and then filled the turret with red-hot chunks of flying metal. Such a hit usually meant death. . . . Right up to the end of the war the 88mm remained our most bitter enemy . . .[17]

The German 88 did have a serious weakness: it was designed as an antiaircraft gun, not as an AT gun. It was therefore very vulnerable to enemy artillery, but the Allied commanders (especially their tank commanders) were slow to appreciate this weakness; in fact, the British tank-artillery coordination was no better than the coordination between their tank and antitank units.[18]

The British did have a gun similar to the 88: the 3.7-inch heavy antiaircraft gun. Roughly 94mm, it might have been as effective against the panzers as the 88 was against Allied armor, but the senior British officers would not allow it to be used in an antitank role—much to the disgust of the junior combat officers and to Gen. Sir Frederick Pile, who served as C in C of Anti-Aircraft Command throughout the war. A former tank officer, he repeatedly tried to persuade the War Office and the cabinet to use the 3.7 HAA (heavy antiaircraft) gun in an antitank role, but, for some incomprehensible reason, neither would listen to him.[19]

Meanwhile, Auchinleck struggled against the prevailing mindset of his tank commanders concerning the employment of armor, as did Gen. Sir Maitland "Jumbo" Wilson (later Field Marshal Lord Wilson), commander of the Ninth Army in Palestine and Transjordan, and later British commander in Persia and Iraq.[20] Auchinleck—who was convinced of the necessity of using combined-arms tactics after the winter battles of 1941–42—decided that British armored divisions would be better balanced if they had less armor and more infantry—like the German panzer divisions. In the future, he decided, an armored division would consist basically of one armored brigade group and one motor brigade group. The armored brigade group would have three tank regiments, one motor battalion, and a combined regiment of field artillery/antitank guns. The motor brigade group would have three motorized battalions and a combined field/antitank regiment. In addition, both brigade groups would have light antiaircraft guns, engineers, and the normal administrative and supply units. He hoped in this way to achieve cooperation between British armor, infantry, and artillery. He also reorganized the British infantry division. Each, he ordered, would consist of three infantry brigade groups, which would each have three infantry battalions, a regiment of field artillery/antitank guns, and other units (antiaircraft guns, engineers, etc.).

Smaller units were also reorganized. Field- and horse-artillery regiments (which were now equipped with trucks, not horses) were to contain three batteries of eight twenty-five-pounder guns each and one battery of sixteen antiaircraft guns. A motor battalion would now have three motor companies and one antitank company of sixteen guns, and an infantry battalion was to consist of a headquarters company, three rifle companies, and a support company (with a mortar platoon, a carrier platoon equipped with Bren carriers, and an antitank platoon of eight guns). Auchinleck's reorganization was largely (but not 100 percent) complete when Rommel began his next drive on Tobruk.

Sir Claude hoped his reforms would result in closer cooperation between the various branches of the British Army—especially between the tanks and the other arms. His success, however, was very limited, as we shall see. The predicament he struggled against was not really an organizational problem as much as it was a mindset and attitude problem, and his reform attempts had little impact on the accepted tank doctrine, which dated back to World War I. During the period between the world wars, British military writers Maj. Gen. J. F. C. Fuller and B. H. Liddell Hart theorized and wrote about their concepts of armored warfare. Their ideas—which centered around mobile, hard-hitting combined-arms formations, spearheaded by tanks—were eagerly adopted by German General Staff officer Heinz

Guderian (the "father" of the blitzkrieg) and his colleagues, but the practical development of British tactical doctrine and of the Royal Tank Corps (RTC) lagged far behind the ideas of Fuller and Hart. British tankers came to regard themselves as the successors to the cavalry; in fact, they were officially described as "mechanized cavalry," and they were charged with the tasks of providing covering forces and probing enemy positions to discover his strength and dispositions, just as the cavalry had in the era of Napoleon and before.[21] The members of the RTC even came to regard themselves almost as knights from an even earlier bygone era. And knights fought only against knights; they did not find it necessary to cooperate with peasants. In the 1920s and 1930s, this thinking led to an inflexible "all-tank" concept, which permeated the RTC and was not at all what Fuller and Hart had in mind. One of the leading proponents of this concept was a determined, energetic, and (when it came to the all-tank concept) narrow-minded officer, Maj. Gen. Sir Patrick Hobart, who formed and trained the Mobile Division in 1938 and 1939. This unit later became the 7th Armoured Division, and Hobart definitely stamped it with the imprint of his own ideas and personality.[22]

In summary, there were two major flaws in the British Army's mentality vis-à-vis the use of tanks: (1) obsolete experience drawn from World War I and (2) nostalgia for the cavalry. Analyses of the successful Allied tank battles of 1917–18 led to the conclusion that the only way to use tanks was as escort vehicles for the infantry. Very few Western military thinkers grasped the fact that the tank tactics of World War I had been forced on the commanders by the technological shortcomings of those days, and that new technological developments demanded new tactics. Guderian and his chief of staff, Col. Walter Nehring, understood these facts, but the leaders of the British Army did not.

This rigid military thinking was further distorted by the civilian thinking of the day. The politicians and general public embraced the ideas of disarmament and permanent peace, which many on both sides of the Atlantic actually believed was possible. Military expenditures, naturally, were cut to the bone—far below safe levels. There was no money in the British military budget for experimentation, and very little for research, development, and practical training. In any case, the exhortations of Auchinleck and Wilson were not enough to erase two decades of erroneous thinking. O'Connor's successful offensive against the Italian Tenth Army further reinforced the fallacious British tank concepts; here, the cruisers and light tanks of the 7th Armoured Division (preceded by the armored cars of the 11th Hussars) outflanked and isolated or surrounded the static Italian garrisons, which were then finished off by the infantry—supported by the slow, heavy Matildas of Lt. Col. R. M. Jerram's 7th Royal Tank Regiment.[23] Rommel's early victories did nothing to shake the confidence of the senior British tank officers in the rightness of the all-tank concept. As late as November 1941, a British armored-brigade commander ended his message to his men before they went into battle in this manner: "This will be a tank commanders' battle. No tank commander will go far wrong if he places his gun within killing range of an enemy." Things were no better in the Battle of the Gazala Line than they had been in "Crusader." Even after the battle, Rommel had no idea he had supposedly been fighting a combined-arms force. "The cumulative result [of the "all-tank" concept] was a corpus of confused tactical doctrine which put British armoured formations at a grave disadvantage when called upon to join battle with clear-headed and well-trained opponents," the South African Official History recorded.[24] The "all-tank" theories, as Lord Wilson tartly observed, were finally discredited only by the practical demonstrations of General Rommel.[25] And he canceled them out in blood.

While Auchinleck reorganized his mobile forces and his artillery, the British engineers and conventional infantry built up the Gazala Line, which became one of the technical marvels of the war. The Italians (who were excellent engineers) had built some fortifications in this area prior to 1940, but these were pitiful efforts indeed compared to what the British and their allies accomplished. They constructed a huge series of thick minefields that extended forty miles, from the Mediterranean Sea to Bir Hacheim. Colonel von Mellenthin later said that it was mined ". . . on a scale never yet seen in war."[26] More than 1,000,000 mines were laid. The line included several fortified strongpoints, called "boxes," which were designed to cover the minefields and prevent the Germans and Italians from breaching them. The boxes were usually about two miles in diameter and were defended by a brigade group. (Map 3, p. 37, shows the Gazala Position and the key points behind it.)

Each box had almost every modern defensive device at its disposal, including mines, barbed-wire entanglements, bunkers, listening posts, machine-gun nests, artillery, antitank guns, and infantry tanks. Each box was well provisioned and had an abundance of food, water, ammunition, and supplies of every description, and each box had the potential to hedgehog (i.e., to survive, isolated and completely on its own) for several days. The artillery and infantry patrols were assigned the task of covering the gaps between the boxes.

The British actually hoped to draw Rommel into a static battle of position, the type of warfare for which they were specially trained and in which they excelled. Rommel, however, had no intention of being led into this World War I type of battle, which he knew he had little chance of winning. Instead, he prepared for another fast armored battle of maneuver.

Eighth Army at this time controlled two corps: Lt. Gen. William H. E. "Strafer" Gott's XIII, and Lt. Gen. C. Willoughby H. Norrie's XXX. The XIII Corps was responsible for holding the Gazala Line and Tobruk. It included the 1st South African Division under Maj. Gen. D. H. "Dan" Pienaar, which occupied the northern (coastal) flank of the Gazala Line with the 1st, 2d, and 3d South African Infantry Brigade Groups. Just south of the South Africans lay Maj. Gen. W. H. C. Ramsden's 50th (Northumbrian) Infantry Division, which took over from the battered 4th Indian Division in the second half of February. Built from British North Country Territorials, it included (north to south) the 151st, 69th, and 150th Infantry Brigade Groups and extended as far south as Sidi Muftah. The 32d Army Tank Brigade initially supported the 1st South African Division, while the 1st Army Tank Brigade supported the 50th Northumbrian. Gott's XIII Corps also included the 2d South African Division (Maj. Gen. H. B. Klopper), which included the 6th South African Brigade (responsible for defending the coast between Gazala and Tobruk against Axis amphibious or airborne landings) and the 4th South African and 9th Indian Brigades at Tobruk. Gott's corps also in-

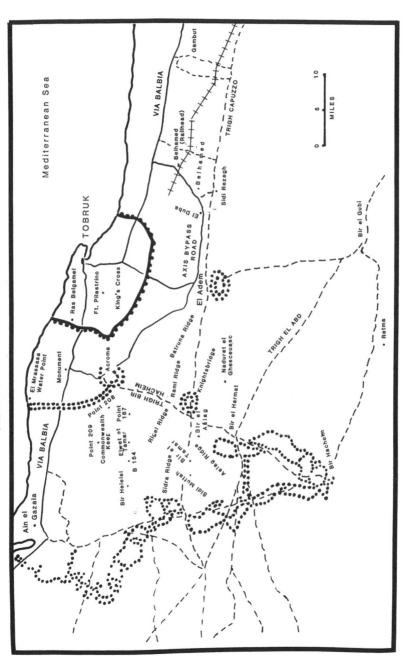

THE GAZALA LINE–TOBRUK BATTLEFIELD

Mediterranean Sea

Gambut

VIA BALBIA

Belhamed
(Railhead)

·Belhamed

TRIGH CAPUZZO

Sidi Rezegh

·El Duba

AXIS BYPASS ROAD

El Adem

TOBRUK

Ras Belgamel

Ft. Pilastrino

King's Cross

Bir el Gubi

·Retma

Batruna Ridge

Raml Ridge

Naduret el Ghesceuasc

Knightsbridge

TRIGH EL ABD

El Mrassasa Water Point

Monument

Acroma

TRIGH BIR HACHEIM

Bir el Aslag

Bir el Harmat

VIA BALBIA

Point 209

Point 208

Commonwealth Keep

Elwet et Tamar

Point 187

Rigel Ridge

·Bir el Tamar

Aslag Ridge

Bir Hacheim

Ain el
·Gazala

Bir Heleisi

B 154

Sidra Ridge

Sidi Muftah

0   5   10
MILES

cluded the 5th Indian Division (the corps reserve), which had one brigade at Gambut and another at Bir el Gubi.

Norrie's XXX Corps controlled the British tank and motor forces, as well as the 1st Free French Brigade.[27] It was responsible for directing the mobile forces of the army and holding the positions of Bir Hacheim, Knightsbridge, El Adem, and El Gubi, which guarded the open southern (desert) flank of the Eighth Army.

The Free French held Bir Hacheim, the southern anchor of the Gazala Line, fifty miles southwest of Tobruk and about thirteen miles south of Sidi Muftah, the southernmost position of the XIII Corps. These thirteen miles were covered by patrols and deep minefields, but not by permanent defenders. The ability of these minefields to stop the Germans and Italians was grossly overrated by the Allied staffs.

The XXX Corps's tank forces included Maj. Gen. Herbert Lumsden's 1st Armoured Division, which consisted of the 2d and 22d Armoured Brigades, and the 201st Guards Brigade, a motorized brigade initially located in the Knightsbridge Box; and Maj. Gen. Frank W. Messervy's 7th Armoured Division, which consisted of the 4th Armoured, 7th Motor, and 3d Indian Motor Brigade Groups. It also controlled the 29th Indian Brigade Group (detached from the 5th Indian Division), which was spread out over the open desert flank, covering the area between Bir Hacheim and Bir el Gubi.

In reserve, the Eighth Army had Maj. Gen. Harold R. "Briggo" Briggs's 5th Indian Division, which controlled the 10th Indian and 2d Free French Brigade Groups. It also had "Dencol," a small column of all arms, including South Africans, Free French, Libyan Arabs, and Middle Eastern Commandos. In addition, several major formations were en route to the Eighth Army, including the 10th Indian Division (20th, 21st, and 25th Indian Brigades) from Iraq and the 11th Indian Infantry Brigade (of the 4th Indian Division) and the 1st Armoured Brigade, both coming from Egypt.[28] Table 1 shows the Order of Battle of the Eighth Army.

Finally, the British had a few special forces set up to defend certain key locations. These included "Stopcol," which was posted on the coastal escarpment, just south of the Via Balbia. Its purpose was to prevent German forces coming from the desert from penetrating

Eighth Army Order of Battle, Gazala Line
26 May 1942

Front Line	Reserves

1st South African Division
  3d South African Brigade Group
  2d South African Brigade Group
  1st South African Brigade Group
	2d South African Division
	  6th South African Brigade
	  4th South African Brigade
	  9th Indian Brigade

50th Infantry Division
  151st Infantry Brigade Group
  69th Infantry Brigade Group
  150th Infantry Brigade Group
	32d Army Tank Brigade
	
	1st Army Tank Brigade

1st Free French Brigade Group	1st Armoured Division
	  2d Armoured Brigade
	  22d Armoured Brigade
	  201st Guards Brigade

	7th Armoured Division
	  4th Armoured Brigade
	  7th Indian Motor Brigade
	  3d Indian Motor Brigade
	  29th Indian Brigade

Table 1

to the coastal road. It controlled the bulk of the 8th Royal Tank Regiment (RTR) (two-thirds of a regiment of Valentine infantry tanks), a company of the 2d Transvaal Scottish Battalion, the 6th South African Field Battery (an artillery unit), and the 6th South African Anti-Tank Battery, as well as signal and engineer troops. Another such unit was "Seacol": a squadron of tanks from the 8th RTR, a company of the 2d South African Police Battalion, a South African field battery, and some armored cars from the 7th South African Reconnaissance Battalion. Its job was to counter German sea landings and, along with the 6th South African Brigade, to keep the Coastal Road open between Gazala and Tobruk.

Well forward of the Allied front lines were the reconnaissance forces, mainly the 4th South African Armoured Car Regiment (4th

SAACR), the King's Dragoon Guards, and the 12th Lancers battalions, all attached to the 7th Armoured Division; the 6th South African Armoured Car Regiment (farther north, under the command of the 50th Division); and the 3d South African Reconnaissance Battalion, under the 1st South African Division. The 4th SAACR maintained a screen seventy miles forward of the main British positions and kept Rommel and his intelligence section largely ignorant of Allied dispositions and of the strength of the Gazala Line.

The British dispositions had two major drawbacks: their desert flank was open, and the distances between the frontline brigade groups sometimes were too great, so that they could not support each other. The gap between the Free French at Bir Hacheim and the 150th Infantry Brigade Group Box was thirteen miles, and it was six miles between the 150th and the 69th Infantry Brigade Group Box to the north.

On 20 May, Auchinleck informed Ritchie in writing that he thought Rommel might try to envelop the southern flank and head for Tobruk; otherwise, he would try to break through the center of the British line on a narrow front, widen the gap, and then drive for Tobruk. He regarded the second course as more likely and more dangerous, and he expected the Germans to feint to the south, to draw the British armor away from the decisive point of the attack. He suggested that Ritchie place both of his armored divisions astride the Trigh Capuzzo, an unimproved road west of El Adem, where they could meet either threat. Ritchie, however, expected the main attack to come around the desert flank, so he stationed the 7th Armoured Division farther south than Auchinleck suggested. Map 4, p. 41, shows the dispositions of the main British forces on the eve of the offensive.

During the period 6 February to 25 May 1942, a lull descended on the North African front, at least insofar as the ground forces were concerned. The lack of fighting at the front was somewhat deceptive, however, because behind the lines both sides were engaged in feverish preparations for the attack. This race for supplies resembled the one that had taken place the year before, with one important difference: this time Malta was neutralized. Even so, the British

DISPOSITIONS OF THE 8th ARMY, MAY 26, 1942

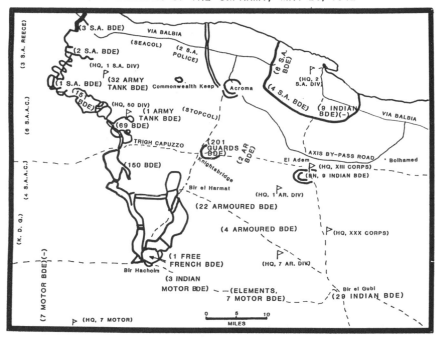

should have won this race (as they did the earlier one), for they had an overall ground force superiority of more than two to one, and the desert was not a secondary front to the Allies. While Hitler funneled reinforcements and resources to the all-consuming Russian front, he and the German High Command regarded the North African theater as little more than a nuisance, and Rommel did not receive a single new division. To the British, on the other hand, North Africa was the only theater of operations where they were in actual combat with the Germans. Churchill and his subordinates—aided by their American allies—rushed supplies and units to Egypt and Libya on a priority basis and spared nothing in preparing the Eighth Army for this battle. The Allies, in fact, outnumbered Rommel in every material category. They badly outnumbered the Germans in tanks, and—perhaps more importantly—the quality of their tanks was generally superior to that of the panzers.

• • •

After the war, General von Mellenthin wrote: "Contrary to the generally accepted view, the German tanks [in World War II] did not have any advantage in quality over their opponents, and in numbers they were always inferior."[29]

Arguably the best tank on the desert battlefield in May 1942 was the Grant, a latecomer from America. It was well protected and heavily armored. It weighed 28.5 tons and mounted both 75mm and 37mm guns, although the 75mm had a limited traverse and, in a hull-down position (the least exposed position), could only use its 37mm. Also, its telescopic sight was very much inferior to the German sights and its cross-country speed (ten mph) was slightly less than that of the PzKw IIIs. Nevertheless, the arrival of the Grant was hailed by the soldiers of the Eighth Army as a major event, because it could destroy a German tank at a range of 1,500 yards, could fire either armor-piercing or high-explosive ammunition, and was superior to any German tank except the PzKw III Special. Rommel had only 19 PzKw III Specials; the British had 167 Grants when the battle began.[30]

The rest of the British tanks were very much inferior to the Grant. Due to the flawed development of British armored doctrine, they fell into two categories: infantry and cruiser tanks. The most effective "I" tank was the Infantry Tank Mark II, the "Matilda." It was heavily armored (up to 78mm—more than three inches), weighed 26.5 tons, and was very slow and underpowered, being propelled by two eighty-seven-horsepower engines. Its maximum speed (i.e., a road speed) was fifteen miles per hour. This was not regarded as a handicap in tanks advancing with the infantry, but it was a major problem in dealing with the fast-moving Afrika Korps.

The Matilda received its name because its predecessor, the Mark I, waddled like a duck and reminded people of Matilda the Duck, a popular cartoon figure of the day. It was, however, a very tough tank. Of the fifty Matildas engaged in the battle of Sidi Baranni, only one was destroyed. It was blown up when a driver opened the visor of his viewing port and an artillery shell went through it at that very moment. One Matilda was hit thirty-eight times and was still fully operational.[31]

The Valentine, another infantry tank, was similar to the Matilda, but had slightly thinner armor (65mm maximum) and weighed only 16 tons. Like the Matilda, it was very slow. Its cross-country speed across the desert was listed as eight mph—two miles per hour faster than the Matilda's. Both were armed with the standard British two-pounder (i.e., 40mm) gun, which was obsolete by 1942 and unable to deal with the later-model German tanks.

The other category of British tank was the cruiser. Its function was similar to that of the old cavalry: avoid major battles and get into the enemy's rear. There it was to deal with soft-skinned vehicles, such as trucks, jeeps, etc. According to British doctrine, it would need little armor (since it was not designed for major tank battles) but would require a considerable amount of speed. This led to the development of the Crusader, which had a maximum speed of twenty-seven mph (twelve mph cross-country), but which had a maximum armored thickness of 49mm—under two inches. It sides were protected by only 25mm of armor—less than one inch. It was also equipped with the inferior two-pounder main battle gun and had a reputation for being mechanically unreliable. (Its bogey wheels were too large and it was likely to throw a track during violent changes of direction.) The best cruiser, of course, was the Grant.

An American tank, the Stuart, was also used as a cruiser, largely because it was the fastest tank in the desert. It could exceed thirty-six mph (fifteen mph cross-country), could outrun any panzer ever built, and was nicknamed the Honey by the Americans because of its mechanical reliability. It was, however, a light tank, with a maximum armored thickness of 44mm, and it only weighed 12.5 tons. Its main battle gun was the 37mm—not a very effective weapon. But perhaps its major weakness was its range. The Stuart had to be refueled after only seventy miles, as opposed to two hundred miles for most of the panzers.

Rommel had five main types of German tanks in May 1942: the Panzer Mark II (PzKw II); the Panzer Mark III, Model H (PzKw IIIh); the Panzer Mark III, Model J (PzKw IIIj, also known as the PzKw III Special); the Panzer Mark IV, Model E (PzKw IVe); and the Panzer Mark IV Model F2 (PzKw IVf2) or PzKw IV Special, which was just making its appearance in North Africa.

The PzKw IIIh was Rommel's workhorse; he had 220 of them. It weighed 23 tons, was armed with a short-barreled 50mm main battle gun, and (like the other three models) had two 7.92mm machine guns. Its maximum armored thickness was 62mm, and it had a road speed of twenty-five mph (eleven mph cross-country). This tank's low-velocity 50mm gun was not much better than the British two-pounder.

The PzKw III Special had similar characteristics, but was armed with a 50mm long-barrel main battle gun, which was similar in effect to the Pak 38 antitank gun and was very deadly. It was generally considered the best tank in Rommel's arsenal, but he had so few of them that they did not have much of an impact on the battle.

The PzKw IV Special was also an excellent tank. It weighed 23 tons, had a maximum armored thickness of 50mm, and had a long-barreled 75mm gun, making it potentially extremely dangerous. Rommel, however, only had four of them in the entire panzer army, and they had no ammunition when the battle began.

The PzKw IVe was handicapped by its very short-barreled, low-velocity 75mm gun. Ineffective against British armor, it was used as a close-support weapon for German infantry. All in all, therefore, the German armor in 1942 was not impressive; the legend of German armored superiority was not based in fact, at least not until 1944, when the Tigers (PzKw Vs) and Panthers (PzKw VIs) made their appearances in strength.

Rommel also had about fifty obsolete PzKw IIs. The J Model was armed only with a 20mm gun, weighed only 10.5 tons, had very little armored protection, and could be penetrated by even the smallest enemy antitank gun. By 1942, it was used as a reconnaissance vehicle or as an infantry support vehicle of limited value.

If the German tanks were mediocre, the Italian tanks (like all Italian equipment) were very poor. The two main types, the M 13/40 and M 14/41, weighed 13.5 and 14.7 tons, respectively. They were armed with a low-velocity 47mm gun, had a maximum armored thickness of 40mm, and had a cross-country speed of eight mph. The Carro Armato M 13/40 also overheated after about thirty minutes of operation. The Italian tanks were called "mobile coffins" and "self-propelled coffins" by the rank and file. In fact, a joke about them made its way through the Afrika Korps:

> Q: Who are the bravest soldiers in the world?
> A: The Italians.
> Q: Why?
> A: Because they go into battle with the equipment that they have.

To Erwin Rommel, however, it was no laughing matter. He commented that his hair stood on end when he saw the equipment with which Mussolini sent his troops into combat. Rommel, however, sympathized with the ordinary Italian soldier, as did most of his "Africans." They knew that the Italian private had to endure an archaic, class-based social system in which merit and talent played little or no part. The Italian military hierarchy, Wolf Heckmann wrote, "made a clear distinction between the gentlemen giving the orders and urging the men on, and a faceless mass of cannon fodder."[32] The officers (who were mostly aristocrats) had every available comfort, including good rations and mobile brothels; the enlisted man had to get by on abysmal rations and whatever else was left, if anything. By 1943, many Italian soldiers did not even have shoes. Small wonder that the average Italian's morale was low and he often did not perform well in battle.

On the other hand, the Italian soldier showed himself open and responsive to positive leadership when someone of senior rank paid a little attention to him. Rommel, for example, spoke only a little Italian and spoke it badly, but at least he tried to speak it, and he liked to join the Italian soldiers for lunch or dinner. He sat on the ground with them, joked with them, and happily ate standard enlisted rations. As a result, he was almost worshipped by the Italian soldiers.[33]

The arrival of the Grant in large numbers led to another reorganization of the British armored brigades. There were obvious advantages to equipping each regiment with only one type of tank, but there were also strong psychological reasons for giving every regiment at least some Grants. As a result, Eighth Army decided that some regiments would have two squadrons of Crusaders and one squadron of Grants, while others would have two squadrons of Grants and one of Stuarts. In the end, the 4th Armoured Brigade had a ratio of one Grant to two Crusaders; the 2d and 22d Armoured Brigades had a ratio of two Grants to one Stuart; the 1st Army Tank Brigade was equipped with two regiments of Matildas; and two regiments of the 32d Army Tank Brigade were equipped with Valentines, while one was supplied with Matildas. In addition, the 1st and 8th Armoured Brigades were not committed to the Gazala battles; rather, they were cannibalized to provide reinforcements and replacements during the campaign. This was a questionable practice, since two well-trained formations were disbanded in order to provide replacements (strangers) for units disorganized and battered in combat. The idea definitely did nothing to maintain unit integrity, an intangible but very important factor in any battle.

General Auchinleck later stated that "numerically the Eighth Army undoubtedly had a considerable superiority" in tanks and a "much larger reserve of tanks to draw on than the enemy."[34] Sources differ on exact numbers, but, even without the defensive advantages of the Gazala Line, the Allies had an overall two-to-one superiority over the Germans. In first-line tank strength, von Mellenthin put the Panzer Army's total at 333 German and 228 Italian, against 900 British tanks.[35] General Playfair's figures are similar. In the British Official History, he placed Allied tank superiority at 849 to 560. His exact figures are shown in Table 2.

Playfair's figures are somewhat misleading if taken strictly at face value, because they do not take into account the quality of armored fighting vehicles involved. The Italian tanks, for example, were nearly useless. If German tanks alone are taken into consideration, Rommel was outnumbered 849 to 282—almost three to one.

In terms of manpower, Panzer Army Afrika was only outnumbered about 100,000 to 90,000, but, again, this figure is deceptive, because Italian morale was low. Many Italians had already lost their faith in the government and their military, and had little taste for the kind of hard fighting that Rommel was planning. The Desert Fox was hampered by a severe shortage of men in key units—especially infantry battalions. For instance, the average infantry company in the 90th Light had only fifty men in mid-May—about half of its normal establishment. Some of the Italian infantry divisions were also below half of their authorized infantry strengths.

The Allies also maintained a considerable numerical superiority in other critical areas besides tank strength. They dominated ten to one in armored cars, eight to five in artillery, and six to five and one-half in aircraft.[36] The RAF outnumbered the combined German-Italian air forces 604 to 542 in airplanes,[37] but the margin becomes much greater if the poor quality of Italian equipment is taken into account. On the other hand, however, 120 of the German fighters were Messerschmitt 109Fs, which were much superior to the Hurricanes and Kittyhawks of the Desert Air Force. (The best Allied fighter, the Spitfire, had not yet made its appearance in the desert.)

Opposing Tank Strength
May 1942

Allies			Axis	
Cruisers			Main Battle Tanks	
Grants	167		PzKw IIIs	223
Crusaders	257		PzKw III Specials	19
Stuarts	149		PzKw IVs	36
Infantry Tanks	277*		PzKw IV Specials	4
Total:	**850**		**Total:**	**282**
			Obsolete Tanks	
			PzKw IIs	50
			Italian Tanks	228
Grand Total:	**850**		**Grand Total:**	**560**

Table 2

*Included 110 Matildas and 167 Valentines.
Source: Maj. Gen. I. S. O. Playfair, *History of the Second World War, The Mediterranean and Middle East*, Volume III, p. 220.

In addition, the German airmen were much better trained in close-support operations at this stage of the war; on balance, therefore, the Luftwaffe enjoyed at least air parity in the desert and was capable of establishing local air superiority under certain conditions.

Many historians of the Desert War have not properly appreciated the importance of artillery in the various campaigns. (This—alas—includes Mitcham in his earlier writings.) But artillery fire was responsible for the greatest number of casualties on both sides in the Western Desert. The rocky desert ground absorbed little of the force of exploding shells, so deadly shrapnel and equally lethal pieces of rock flew in all directions. Unfortunately, the desert environment proved to be a double-edged sword for the gunners. When they fired their guns they threw up clouds of dust; it was therefore impossible to conceal their locations, and they were very vulnerable to counter-battery fire.

Once again, due to their utilization of combined-arms tactics, the Germans made better use of their artillery than did the Allies. In addition, their artillery was easier to control, since much of it was centralized under *Artillerie-Kommandeur 104* (the 104th Artillery Command)—the Panzer Army artillery.[38] Although the results of its barrages are not always as easy to assess as, say, that of an attack by a panzer regiment, the artillery was nevertheless a major (and often decisive) factor in many of Rommel's victories.

The lull in the desert fighting applied only to ground forces; active fighting continued in the air, although on a somewhat reduced scale. During this period, Air Vice-Marshal Arthur Coningham, the commander of the Desert Air Force, put many of his units through intense training programs, and the air-fighting standards of the RAF fighter pilots were increased considerably. New tactics were developed for dealing with the Me-109s, and training for daylight bombers was intensified, especially for the Boston bomber squadrons. In addition, the Desert Air Force equipped every single-engine fighter to carry one or more bombs.

None of these improvements, however, could make up for the loss of the air bases in western Cyrenaica. General of Fliers Bruno Loerzer's II Air Corps in Sicily and Air Command Afrika, now under Lt.

Gen. Otto Hoffmann von Waldau (who replaced the less capable Lt. Gen. Stefan Froehlich in March), were able to bomb Malta to the point it lost its offensive capability.[39] During the fifteen-week lull in the ground war, the Wellington bombers based on Malta could only fly about sixty sorties against Tripoli. The only Allied bomber that could reach Tripoli from Egypt was the Liberator, and it was May before it arrived in significant numbers. As a result, Rommel was able to build up his supplies fairly rapidly.

Benghazi was Rommel's closest port to the front. Quite a few Wellingtons attacked it during the lull (a total of 741 sorties from February to May—an average of 8 per day), and there were also night attacks by Bostons and day attacks by long-range Kittyhawks. To counter this threat, German and Italian ships entered the harbor at dawn and unloaded during daylight hours. RAF photographs gave the Desert Air Force the impression that the port of Benghazi had been badly damaged, but these proved to be misleading. The capacity of the port actually rose steadily during the lull. Meanwhile, the Luftwaffe under Hoffmann von Waldau launched major attacks against Tobruk, the British desert railroad, the RAF airfields (especially Gambut and Fuka), and the forward troop areas. Neither side, however, was able to gain a decisive advantage over the other or to significantly delay the supply buildup of the enemy ground forces.

While the Luftwaffe and RAF struggled unsuccessfully for the control of the air, command changes took place on both sides.

Auchinleck had fewer changes to make, but he had the most difficult decision: whether or not to sack his army commander.

General Sir Neil M. Ritchie—Britain's youngest general at age forty-four—was a very tall, physically impressive man who was an excellent staff officer, and who was rich and politically well connected. Born in British Guiana on 20 July 1897, the son of a sugar planter, he grew up in Malaysia (where his father took up rubber growing after a disease ruined his sugar plantation), and in England, where he attended preparatory schools. He entered Sandhurst in the summer of 1914, but his schooling was cut short by the outbreak of World War I. He was commissioned second lieutenant in the famous Black Watch Regiment in December 1914, and was sent to France six months later. Wounded in the battle of Loos, he was posted to the 2d Battalion in Mesopotamia after he recovered, became battalion adjutant, and took part in the capture of Baghdad in 1917. He also participated in the campaign in Palestine in 1918.

Ritchie remained adjutant of the 2d Black Watch until 1923 (for a time Wavell was his commanding officer), did a tour of duty in the War Office, and returned to the 2d (then in Scotland) as a company commander in 1926. He attended Staff College (1928–30), went to India, and later toured the Pacific and North America. He met his future wife on a blind date in New York. As a major, Ritchie was given command of a company in the 2d Black Watch in the Sudan in 1936, before transferring to the King's Own, a Lancashire regiment, in 1937, in order to command a battalion. He took his command to Jerusalem in 1938, and served as Brigadier General Staff to Gen. Alan Brooke, the commander of II Corps, in Flanders (1939–40), and Brooke—who soon became Chief of the Imperial General Staff—became his devoted friend. After Dunkirk, Ritchie had become Brigadier General Staff to Sir Claude Auchinleck, who was leader of Southern Command in England in 1940. Sir Claude was also very much impressed with the robust and vigorous staff officer, who was both intelligent and thorough.

Neil Ritchie was promoted to major general and was given the task of reforming the 51st Highland Division, which Rommel and the 7th Panzer Division had smashed at Saint-Valéry. He was soon transferred, however, this time to Cairo, where he was named Deputy Chief of the General Staff, Middle East Command, under his old CO, Wavell, and later under Auchinleck.[40] When "the Auk" sacked Alan Cunningham as commander of the Eighth Army on 25 November 1941, during the middle of Operation "Crusader," he named Ritchie to succeed him.

Initially, Auchinleck looked at Ritchie's appointment as temporary. Cunningham had obviously lost control of the battle, as well as of his nerves, and, with a major action in progress, there was no time to fly in a replacement from England. Ritchie was junior to both corps commanders, Norrie of the XXX and A. R. Godwin-Austen of the XIII, but both were heavily engaged against Rommel, and Auchinleck did not want to pull them out of their important positions at a critical time in the battle; in addition, Godwin-Austen had little experience in handling armored formations, and Norrie's performance to date had not been impressive. Finally, Auchinleck did not want Sir Maitland Wilson (the commander of the Ninth Army in Palestine and Transjordan) to command the Eighth Army, because he felt Wilson was too slow, and it would take too long to fly another army commander from England to Libya. Besides, at that moment, what the Eighth Army needed was a tenacious commander of supreme self-confidence, and Ritchie was that; however, Auchinleck intended to select a permanent commander after the battle.[41] Ritchie lacked too many qualifications to be kept at this post. A career staff officer, he lacked command experience and had not held a command position above the battalion level. Besides, just four years before he had been only a major.

In his defense, it must be emphatically pointed out that Sir Neil Ritchie recognized many of his own deficiencies and opposed his own selection as commander of the Eighth Army. Like Churchill, Ritchie thought Auchinleck should assume command of the army himself. Auchinleck, in fact, had to force the appointment on him.

Sir Claude came with Ritchie to Maddalena (Eighth Army Headquarters) and had acted as de facto army commander during the second half of Operation "Crusader," while Ritchie essentially acted as his deputy. On 11 December 1941, however, after Rommel abandoned the siege of Tobruk and retreated, Churchill held a press conference and announced Ritchie's appointment as commander of the Eighth Army as if it were a permanent one. Now Auchinleck could not replace him without affecting the morale of the general public; it, after all, believed that Ritchie had led the Eighth Army to victory over the Desert Fox. Besides, Auchinleck rationalized, he had been satisfied with Ritchie's performance in "Crusader." Perhaps it would be best to leave him in command . . .

"Auchinleck's judgments of professional ability were too often coloured by his personal liking for the person concerned," historian Corelli Barnett wrote later. "His warm-heartedness and his sense of loyalty as a man sometimes betrayed him as a general."[42]

Sir Frank Messervy later called Ritchie "a very fine figure of a man, brave and confident, and decisive in his speech. But one did not always feel that he was quite so confident and decisive in his mind. I would assess him as an absolutely honest, downright soldier who was put into a position which at the time was beyond his capacity. Ritchie was an optimist—always a little too optimistic."[43]

General A. R. Godwin-Austen, the XIII Corps commander, would certainly have agreed with this assessment. "It seemed quite impossible to persuade Eighth Army HQ there was any danger from Rommel," he recalled. "I informed them that I had had a man sent out specially to check on German tank reinforcements and he had reported seeing at least forty [of the] newest Mark IV panzers, with heavier armour-plating and higher velocity guns. Yet Army HQ literally laughed in my face." General Ritchie told him: "I can take Tripoli any time I like and what is more I could do it with one battalion!"[44]

How badly wrong Ritchie was, and how mistaken Auchinleck was for leaving him in command, became obvious during Rommel's second Cyrenaican campaign (January–February 1942), when the Desert Fox routed the forward elements of the Eighth Army and smashed the 1st Armoured and 4th Indian Divisions. Ritchie's leadership was cautious, slow, and indecisive, and he certainly proved that he was no match for the fast-moving Rommel in a mobile battle. Instead of relieving Ritchie, however, Auchinleck sacked his own chief of staff, Sir Arthur Smith (whom he had inherited from Wavell), and his director of military intelligence, Brigadier John Shearer. Smith was succeeded by Gen. T. S. Corbett, who had commanded IV Corps in Iraq. Colonel (later Major General) Francis de Guingand succeeded Shearer.[45]

After the Benghazi debacle, Godwin-Austen was so dissatisfied with Ritchie's leadership that he asked Auchinleck to relieve him of his command.[46] The C in C did so, and, as Barnett wrote, ". . . Eighth Army lost an able, strong general and a much-loved man."[47]

W. H. E. Gott, a desert veteran and former commander of the 7th Armoured Division, replaced Godwin-Austen as commander of the XIII Corps on 6 February, and, at the end of the month, Sir Frank Messervy, the former commander of the 4th Indian Division, was appointed to succeed Maj. Gen. J. C. "Jock" Campbell (who had been killed when his armored car turned over near Halfaya Pass) as CG of 7th Armoured. Neither appointment was a fortunate one.[48]

Major General Sir Frank Messervy was a "front line" officer known for his daring and fearlessness. He was described as "tall, athletic looking, with a facial expression that clearly showed his strong sense of purpose . . ."[49] He also had a strong sense of religious faith, which helped sustain his legendary courage. But Sir Frank was under a dark cloud throughout the spring and summer of 1942. An old Indian Army soldier, he had served in the cavalry in World War I, fighting on the Somme and in Palestine, Syria, and Kurdistan. As a young man at Eton, he had been noted for his escapades; however, after 1927, when he married Patricia Courtney, the daughter of Wadegrave Courtney, a regular army colonel, he settled down and was most happy with married and domestic life. When the war began, Colonel Messervy had a nine-year-old daughter and two sons, aged five and two. He was, like many fathers, most delighted with his little girl.

After helping to raise and train the 5th Indian Division, Messervy was sent to Africa, where he commanded the ad hoc "Gazelle Force" (about 1,000 men) in the Sudan and Eritrea with considerable distinction. In 1940 he was promoted to brigadier and given command of the 9th Indian Brigade (5th Indian Division) and, at the end of April, was promoted to major general and named commander of the 4th Indian Division, which he led in Operation "Crusader."

Meanwhile Rosemary Messervy, the young daughter of the general, fell backward through some French windows at school and seriously injured her spine, breaking one vertebra and displacing several others. Her father was very worried that his little girl might be crippled for life.

On 26 February 1942, the day Jock Campbell had his fatal accident, Sir Frank was in an airplane, en route to India, where he was scheduled to take charge of the 1st Indian Armoured Division. Even though he was instructed to return to North Africa as quickly as possible, Messervy flew on to Calcutta, on the other side of the subcontinent, where his daughter was hospitalized. The sight of her lying helpless, stretched out in a hospital bed with wires and weights all about, was almost more than her combat-hardened father could stand. He left India in great distress. To add to his worries, the Japanese were advancing on India from the east and were expected to bomb Calcutta at any time.[50] The commander of the "Desert Rats" had a great many things on his mind in May 1942—perhaps too many. His heart was definitely facing east—not west—during the critical days when Erwin Rommel battered the Gazala Line.

William Henry Ewart Gott, the new leader of the XIII, was a better man than he was a corps commander. He was born at Scarborough on 13 August 1897, into a family of vicars. Educated at Harrow and the Royal Military College at Sandhurst, he was gazetted into the King's Royal Rifle Corps (KRRC) in 1915, at the age of eighteen. In July 1917, while fighting in France, he was wounded and captured. Released at the end of World War I, he spent much of the interwar years in India and Egypt, where he commanded the 1st Battalion, KRRC.

Six feet two inches tall, "Strafer" Gott had an impressive military bearing and was noted for his "searching blue eyes." Gyles Isham also recalled that he had a "marked, because unsought, capacity to gain the confidence of the troops . . ."[51] He had served as chief of operations (GSO I) of the 7th Armoured under Hobart and commanded the division's Support Group (including the artillery and motorized infantry battalions) in the early 1940s. He very skillfully directed the British withdrawal against Graziani and distinguished himself at Sidi Barrani and in the first Cyrenaican campaign. When the Eighth Army was formed in the summer of 1941, Gott was given command of the 7th Armoured, which he led in the winter battles of 1941–42, without any great laurels; nevertheless he was named commander of the XIII Corps when Godwin-Austen quit in disgust in February.

Not only was Ritchie hesitant in dealing with Rommel; he found himself surrounded by more experienced corps commanders. Gott, "a man of immense prestige," had been fighting in the desert since the days of the Western Desert Force, and Norrie was actually senior to Ritchie. Norrie's "knowledge of armour, lately acquired though it was, far outstripped Ritchie's," Correlli Barnett wrote later. "His too was a strong personality: urbane, cool, easy, he wore his ability, as a gentleman should, slightly carelessly." Surrounded by people like Gott and Messervy, Norrie and Auchinleck, it is not surprising that one brigadier noticed "an air of uncertainty about his [Ritchie's] face."[52]

After the British retreat halted at Gazala, Auchinleck had serious second thoughts about Ritchie and considered relieving him of his command. He summoned an old friend, Brigadier Eric "Chink" Dorman-Smith, Ritchie's successor as deputy chief of staff, and ordered him to visit Eighth Army, ostensibly to monitor staff techniques.[53] His real job, however, was to conduct a fact-finding mission and to sound out the divisional commanders, in order to find out their opinions of Ritchie's leadership. Dorman-Smith, whom Roger Parkinson described as "forceful, outspoken and quick-witted,"[54] was no friend of Ritchie's. He returned to Cairo on 16 February, and, despite the fact that it was a cold and depressing day, Auchinleck invited him for a picnic on the shores of Lake Fayoum, so they could talk privately. Dorman-Smith pulled no punches: he said that the generals were dissatisfied with Ritchie's leadership, that his approach to command was vague and amateurish, and that slang terms, such as "Jock-cols" and "swanning," now had great tactical significance with Eighth Army Headquarters.[55] In conclusion, he said, Ritchie was "not sufficiently quick-witted or imaginative enough" to command the army, and recommended that he be replaced.

Auchinleck was shaken by Dorman-Smith's report, but replied: "I have already sacked one army commander. To sack another within three months would have effects on morale."[56]

If Sir Claude Auchinleck had had a talent for making good appointments, and had he not let his personal feelings get in the way of his military judgment, he would today be listed among the great military commanders of World War II. But in ignoring the advice that he himself had solicited, he had sown the seeds for a major military disaster.

Rommel also had several changes to make. During the "Crusader" battles of November and December 1941, he had lost all three of his highly talented German division commanders: Maj. Gen. Baron Johann von Ravenstein, commander of the 21st Panzer, had been captured when his staff car blundered into New Zealand positions on 29 November; Maj. Gen. Walter Neumann-Silkow, the much-loved commander of the 15th Panzer, had been mortally wounded by artillery fire on 6 December and died three days later; and Maj. Gen.

Max Suemmermann, the commander of the 90th Light, had been killed on 10 December, in a rearguard action near Mamali, during the retreat from Cyrenaica. Finally, Ludwig Cruewell, who had led the Afrika Korps so well during "Crusader," was named deputy commander of Panzer Army Afrika, so the DAK needed a new commander as well.[57]

The new Afrika Korps leader was one of the best tank commanders of all time: Lt. Gen. Walter Nehring. He had worked very closely with Heinz Guderian, the "father" of the blitzkrieg, during the formative years of the panzer arm, and had been Guderian's chief of staff in Poland and France. After that he led the 18th Panzer Division with considerable success on the Russian front, before assuming command of the Afrika Korps on 9 March.[58]

Major General Gustav von Vaerst, the former commander of the 2d Rifle Brigade, was given command of the 15th Panzer Division. A highly capable panzer grenadier officer, he would be wounded twice, promoted twice, and given command of the Fifth Panzer Army within the next ten months.[59]

Major General Karl Boettcher, leader of the 104th Artillery Command (the Panzer Army Afrika's artillery), had taken over the 21st Panzer Division when Ravenstein was reported missing in action, but his health was not good. He went into Führer Reserve on 19 February 1942, and was replaced by an old friend of Rommel's: Georg von Bismarck.[60] A thirty-two-year veteran of the German Army, Bismarck had assumed command of the 7th Cavalry Regiment prior to the war. This unit was converted into a rifle regiment during the winter of 1939–40 and was assigned to the 7th Panzer Division, which Rommel led with such glory in France in 1940. Later Bismarck led the 20th Rifle Brigade (10 December 1940–17 December 1941), before Rommel arranged to have him transferred to North Africa. He arrived on 5 January 1942, and took command of the 21st Panzer on 11 February.[61]

The commander of the 90th Light was Maj. Gen. Richard Veith, a Bavarian who arrived in time to direct the division in the reconquest of Cyrenaica. His record was not as distinguished as those of Nehring, Vaerst, or von Bismarck, nor did he distinguish himself in Africa.[62] On 10 April 1942, he was relieved of his command and was replaced by Maj. Gen. Ulrich Kleemann.[63]

Leadership of the Panzer Army artillery (the 104th Artillery Command) was given to Col. Fritz Krause, who had previously commanded the 36th Artillery Regiment on the Russian front. An artilleryman since he entered the service in 1913 and an excellent commander, Krause would be in charge of the German artillery in Africa almost until the end of the war in North Africa.[64]

IN THE DESERT

Meanwhile, Panzer Army Afrika camped in the open desert between Derna and Gazala. The troops, who called themselves "Afrikaner" (native inhabitants of the African continent, or "Africans"), usually pitched their tents two at a time, one over the other, with a small space between them, giving them some insulation from the heat. When the ground was not too hard, the tent tops were erected above pits dug in the sand. This gave them cover from enemy fire and made them invulnerable to anything except a direct hit. Where the ground was too hard to dig, the tents were strung alongside vehicles, or were surrounded by low mounds of rock called "sangars." The troops liked to camp near sangars, because they provided cover from air attacks; otherwise, trenches had to be dug. The tents were always well dispersed because clusters attracted enemy fire. After some time sleeping in the desert—with its impressive nighttime silence—the men found they did not like sleeping in buildings or barracks. Sleeping under the stars was more relaxing. Nights on the desert were cool, and a gentle breeze normally blew in from the sea. The men stripped off their uniforms and felt "blessed relief" from the hot desert sun. "The atmosphere" on the desert, Antony Brett-James recalled, "was one of intimacy and friendliness. Life had a new sense of simplicity, and was nomadic, primitive. Men found a new sense of values. . . . Life had been reduced to the essentials. . . . Most vital was the mere process of existence."[65]

Around the camps were scattered the usual objects, including jerry-cans (the ones with white crosses on the side were used only to carry water), wooden and metal ammunition boxes, which served as tables and chairs, and the chimneys of the mobile field kitchens (called "Goulash cannons" by the troops). In the smaller camps, food was brought in, using insulated containers from the central kitchen, or was cooked or warmed up over small fires. The most popular method was to pour sand into a tin can, pour gasoline onto the sand, and light it.

The Germans were masters in the art of camouflage. Camelthorn bushes were very abundant in the desert and were used to break up the silhouettes of vehicles. The rocks and brush gave a mottled pattern to the landscape which absorbed the tents covered with camelthorn. Wadis also made popular camps but were dangerous on the rare occasions on which it rained.

The colors of the desert are brown, yellow, and gray. Skillful use of these colors in painted patterns and/or in camouflage nets enabled both the Germans and the British to hide themselves and their vehicles, or at least to make it difficult for the enemy to find them.

Cleaning anything was difficult in the desert because everything had to be transported from Europe. Because of the limited shipping space available and the constraints imposed by the enemy, Rommel demanded fuel, weapons, and ammunition. Everything else—including needles, soap, and clothes—had a strictly secondary priority and was almost always in short supply. The troops cleaned their cotton uniforms by washing them in gasoline or in sea water and rubbing them clean with dry sand. Mostly, however, the troops on both sides simply grew accustomed to being dirty. Antony Brett-James of the 5th Indian Division recalled:

> All vehicles could be seen moving from afar because of the trail of dust that billowed up behind or to one side. . . . You might wear sand goggles, but your face was coated with sand, that caked itself into a beige mask, clinging to the sweat of your countenance, collecting in the corners of your eyes. Hands and arms, necks and knees, became coated with this same sand, which penetrated under your shirt, and caught in your throat, and made your eyes smart. Your hair became matted and bistre. Along your limbs the trickling sweat would cleave little rivulets through the sandy coating.[66]

One of the worst aspects of the desert, of course, was the heat. During the day it gradually became unbearable. "Everyone sought out a little patch of shade," Maj. Baron Hans von Luck, the commander of the 3d Panzer Reconnaissance Battalion, recalled. "Some men really did fry eggs on the overheated armored plating of the tanks. It was no fairy tale; I have done it myself."[67]

The diet of the German soldiers was bad, but not as bad as that of the Italians. The standard diet consisted of processed cheese in tube containers, tinned sardines, Italian military-issue tinned sausage meat (called "AM"), German *Dauerbrot* (moist and wholesome bread made from "black" rye or wheat and wrapped in foil), occasional fresh wholemeal bread, onions, dehydrated vegetables (legumes), oatmeal gruel, and hard, dry Italian army biscuits. AM was a dietary staple among the Axis forces and received its name from the "AM" (*Amministrazione Militare*, or Military Administration) stamped on the side. The Germans called it *Alter Mann* (Old Man), but the less charitable Italian soldiers nicknamed it *Arabo Morte* (Dead Arab). Sweets and food from the Fatherland (ham, beer, potato salad, etc.) were rare, and, whenever possible, the soldiers traded with local Arabs for eggs, chickens, tomatoes, dates, and other commodities.

Naturally, captured food (especially corned beef, white bread, and tinned fruits) was considered a highly valued delicacy. "Only when we captured British depots did the Afrika Korps eat well," F. W. von Mellenthin told the American Lt. Col. Verner R. Carlson after the war. "The bully beef, so despised by British soldiers, became *haute cuisine* for the Desert Fox and his troops," Carlson wrote later. "Some even packaged it and sent it home to their relatives in Germany!"[68]

The staple drink of the Afrika Korps was purified water, which was so filled with chemical agents that it tasted like chemical soup. Often it was consumed as reconstituted lemon "juice" or as ersatz coffee, which the troops called "nigger sweat." They also tasted of chemicals. Naturally, dysentery was widespread in Panzer Army Afrika.

Encouraged by Hitler, the Wehrmacht provided a great many vitamins as dietary supplements, although naturally their quality was not on a par with Nutrilite or Double-X, the highest-quality supplements of the 1990s. When they first captured carton after carton of German vitamin pills in November and December 1941, the British intelligence officers were amazed, and the Allied press reported that the Germans were using drugs to create Aryan supermen with great physical strength.[69]

As if boredom and bad rations were not enough, life in the desert was made miserable by sand fleas and flies. Baron von Luck remembered:

> One even got used to the cold nights. We didn't take off our tropical coats, and thick, nonregulation scarves, until well into the morning when the heat had slowly worked through them. This was the thermos principle, which we had learned from the Bedouins [Arab nomads]. But the millions of flies were a real torment. Only when one got deeper into the desert did their numbers diminish.[70]

Wolf Heckmann reported that flies "covered every slice of bread and butter like a black layer the moment it was prepared, and often had to be swallowed along with the food, no matter how hard you shooed them away . . . "[71] Scorpions and sand vipers were also occasional problems.

There was very little entertainment in the desert, and the Afrika Korps enjoyed few creature comforts. Propaganda Kompanie Afrika was the only organized effort to entertain the troops in the field. Members of the company sang songs, did popular light operas, played magic tricks, and showed a selection of popular movies. There were no women in the unit.

Most of the troops in the field played soccer, tug-of-war, etc. Reading and playing skat, a card game, were prevalent pastimes, and *Die Oase*, the army's field newspaper, was very popular and was read from cover to cover. The soldiers liked to gamble with the little money they had. Also, radio reception in the desert was good, and a number of European stations could be picked up on the shortwave from early evening to early night.

Even in the rear area there were few comforts or recreational facilities. There were canteens and bars in Tripoli and Benghazi, and a rear-area club in Derna and one or two other locations. There was also one rear-area Wehrmacht brothel at 4 Via Tassoni, Tripoli, but most of the "Africans" never saw it. I have seen photos of the "ladies" employed there; they were obviously recruited for their willingness and not for their beauty. Incidentally, they were Italians. The only

German women in the desert war were 200 or so nurses, most of them working in the large rear-area hospital at Derna. Their skills would be sorely needed in the days ahead.

ROMMEL'S PLAN

For his next drive, Rommel planned to divide Panzer Army Afrika into two parts: a pinning force under General Cruewell and a strike force under his personal command. Group Cruewell consisted of the X and XXI Italian Infantry Corps and Col. Erwin Menny's German 15th Rifle Brigade, which included the 200th and 361st Grenadier Regiments of the 90th Light Division. While Cruewell occupied the Eighth Army's front, Rommel himself would lead the main strike force, which would outflank the Gazala Line to the south. Next he would turn north, cut the Coastal Road, and trap and destroy the Allied forces in the Gazala Line. Then he would turn east again and drive on Tobruk, whose capture had obsessed him for more than a year. The main strike force would consist of Gen. Enea Navarini's Italian XX Motorized Corps (Trieste Motorized and Ariete Armored Divisions) on the left, Nehring's Afrika Korps (21st and 15th Panzer Divisions) in the center, and 90th Light Division on the right. The Italian motorized corps had the task of taking care of the British minefields north of Bir Hacheim. Nehring's job was to defeat and disperse the British armored and mobile reserves, and to cut the Coastal Road (i.e., to fight the main battle). The 90th Light (minus two grenadier regiments, but reinforced with the 3d and 33d Panzer Reconnaissance Battalions from the Afrika Korps) was to cover Nehring's right flank. The 90th also included Special Unit 288 (*Sonderverband 288*), a regimental-sized command which was "heavy" with antitank guns.[72] Table 3 shows Panzer Army Afrika's Order of Battle on 26 May 1942.

To cooperate with the main thrust, Rommel created Group Hecker. Led by Col. Hans Hecker, the Panzer Army engineer, it was to conduct an amphibious assault behind the Gazala Line as Nehring approached the Coastal Road from the rear. Hecker's job was to sever the Coastal Road between Gazala and Tobruk, thus isolating the

Axis Order of Battle, Gazala Line
26 May 1942

Pinning Force: General Cruewell   **Striking Force:** Colonel General Rommel

15th Rifle Brigade (1)
  200th Grenadier Regiment
  361st Grenadier Regiment

XXI Italian Infantry Corps
  Sabratha Infantry Division
  Trento Infantry Division

X Italian Infantry Corps
  Brescia Infantry Division
  Pavia Infantry Division

Afrika Korps: General Nehring
  21st Panzer Division
  5th Panzer Regiment
  104th Panzer Grenadier Regiment
  155th Panzer Artillery Regiment
  200th Panzer Engineer Battalion

  15th Panzer Division
  8th Panzer Regiment
  115th Panzer Grenadier Regiment
  33d Panzer Artillery Regiment
  3d Panzer Engineer Battalion

  90th Light Division
  155th Panzer Grenadier Regiment
  288th Special Purposes Unit
  190th Motorized Artillery Regiment
  3d Panzer Recon Battalion (2)
  33d Panzer Recon Battalion (3)
  580th Reconnaissance Battalion
  900th Motorized Engineer Battalion

XX Italian Motorized Corps
  Trieste Motorized Division
  Ariete Armored Division

(1) Detached from 90th Light Division
(2) Detached from 21st Panzer Division
(3) Detached from 15th Panzer Division

Table 3

British forces in the Gazala Line. His forces included a battalion of Italian marines, German engineers, a detachment of German support weapons (including twelve field guns), and three captured British tanks.

Rommel's plan relied on speed and boldness. He wanted to create the impression that a heavy attack was coming between the sea and the Trigh Capuzzo, so Group Cruewell was to close in on the

Gazala Line on the afternoon of 26 May, while British positions were pounded by artillery fire and Luftwaffe bombing and dive-bombing attacks. This demonstration was to continue until after dawn. Meanwhile, Rommel himself would lead the mobile force in the main sweep to the south. They were to overrun Bir Hacheim that night. The next morning, the panzer divisions would turn north toward Acroma and get into the rear of the British XIII Corps. The 90th Light was to advance farther east and create havoc in the El Adem-Belhamed sector. After Nehring defeated the British mobile reserves, the 1st South African and 50th Divisions were to be attacked from the east and west, while Group Hecker cut their communications with Tobruk from the sea. The capture of Tobruk would follow. Four days was considered enough time to complete the entire operation. In the initial advance, the Afrika Korps was to be followed by supply columns carrying four days' rations of food and water, three days' supply of ammunition, and enough fuel to cover 300 miles. The water ration amounted to only three quarts per man per day, plus four quarts per truck and eight quarts for each panzer.[73]

At the last minute, Rommel got some more information about British dispositions and learned that there were British mobile forces northeast of Bir Hacheim. He then modified his plans and ordered Ariete to capture Bir Hacheim, while the DAK and 90th Light made a wide sweep around it. He issued his final orders on 25 May.

The major flaws in Rommel's plan were that he had only the vaguest idea of British dispositions, and he badly underestimated their strength. Allied aerial parity, commendable radio security, excellent camouflage techniques, and the armored car superiority of the South Africans prevented Rommel's intelligence network from gathering a realistic picture of the situation facing them. When the Germans struck, they did not know of the existence of the Grant tank or of the extent or depth of the minefields. They thought the belts ended near the Trigh el Abd, near the center of the Gazala Line, when in fact they extended many miles to the south. They did not know that the 22d Armoured and 32d Army Tank Brigades were close behind the Gazala Line; they failed to discover the existence of the Sidi Muftah Box, which was held by the 150th Infantry Brigade Group, or the Knightsbridge Box, which was held by the 201st

Guards Brigade; nor did they learn that the 29th Indian Brigade was at Bir el Gubi, nor that the 3d Indian Motor Brigade was southeast of Bir Hacheim. In all, they either missed entirely or failed to correctly identify two armored and three infantry brigade groups, plus the extent and depth of the minefields, and the major change in the technological sphere (the Grant). Rommel's intelligence chief later admitted: "Perhaps fortunately, we underestimated British strength, for had we known the full facts even Rommel might have balked at an attack on such a greatly superior enemy."[74]

CHAPTER III: The Desert Fox Strikes First

ROMMEL'S INITIAL VICTORIES

The Axis offensive began at 2:00 P.M. on 26 May. Group Cruewell launched the initial (diversionary) assault at this unusual hour, spearheaded by the 361st Grenadier Regiment of the 90th Light Division. This unit was one of the most unique to fight in the North African War because its men were veterans of the French foreign legion; they were an ill-disciplined lot but were excellent warriors. Rommel liked them but always ordered his driver to lock up the spare tires anytime they neared the 361st. This day, the 361st and its sister regiment, the 200th Grenadier, had the task of convincing the British that the main attack had come in the north, and it was liberally supported by artillery, dive-bombers, and dust units—trucks with airplane engines mounted on their rear beds, designed to throw up huge clouds of sand, in order to create the illusion that panzer and motorized infantry columns were deploying. The main body of the Afrika Korps also maneuvered as if it intended to strike along the Trigh Capuzzo, and Heinkel 111 and Junkers 88 bombers blasted the Tobruk and El Adem airfields. By nightfall, the British command believed that the main blow would fall at dawn the next day against the center of their line, just as Auchinleck had predicted.

It was 10:30 P.M. before Rommel issued the code word "Venezia," and the strike force of Panzer Army Afrika began the long swing to the south. "It was a fantastic sight, a remarkable convoy, as diverse as that of a circus on the move," Erwan Bergot wrote later. First came the light reconnaissance vehicles and motorcycles, followed by the tanks, intermixed with 88mm antiaircraft guns; in the center were the command and signal vehicles, which bristled with aerials and antennas; next came the field guns, and, at the end, the fuel tankers and ammo trucks.[1]

Rommel advanced in three columns: Gen. Enea Navarini's XX Italian Motorized Corps on the left, the Afrika Korps in the center, and the 90th Light on the right. Off to their left, they could see Bir Hacheim, burning brightly. To help them navigate, the Luftwaffe had bombed it with incendiaries. The night march in the moonlight excited the Desert Fox as much as his men. "I was tense and keyed-up," Rommel recalled, "impatiently waiting the coming of day."[2]

At 5:00 A.M., Colonel Prestissimone's 132nd Regiment of the Ariete Division turned off to the left and attacked Bir Hacheim ("Dog's Well"), the southern anchor of the Gazala Line, which was guarded by the 1st Free French Brigade. Neither Rommel nor the Italians expected much of a fight from these "rebels"—which included Jews and French foreign legionnaires, but they were in for a surprise. Colonel Prestissimone advanced boldly, but soon had three tanks shot out from under him. Before he could find a fourth, he was captured by a group of legionnaires. In all, Ariete lost thirty-two tanks that morning, without making any sort of impression on the defenses.[3]

Despite the fact that Rommel's men traveled with their lights off and maintained radio silence, the scouts from the South Africans' armored-car units reported that the German columns were wheeling around Bir Hacheim before midnight. These brave and independent men, operating well forward of their own lines, like cavalry scouts from a previous century, maintained contact throughout the night and kept the 7th Armoured Division and the XXX Corps Headquarters informed of the movement of Rommel's main body. Generals Messervy and Norrie, however, did not grasp the full significance of their dispatches, because no one expected the Desert Fox would make such an important move at night. Only Lt. Col. Michael Carver, a staff officer with XXX Corps, seemed worried, despite the assurances of Lt. Col. Harold F. "Pete" Pyman, the chief of operations of the 7th Armoured Division, that the movement was a feint. "I had become increasingly convinced during the night that these movements represented the main threat," Carver wrote later, and was disturbed by Pyman's apparent complacency, suggesting that the armoured cars at night could only rely on what they heard and were likely to exaggerate numbers. I warned Pyman that I was going to wake Norrie up again. (I had done so at 0215 hours [2:15 A.M.]) and get him to ring Messervy. I tried to persuade Norrie to ring Lumsden also to ensure that one of his brigades would be ready to move to support 7th Armoured Division at first light, but, after he talked to Messervy, who took the same line as Pyman had with me, he said he would not do so, as the movement reported could be the feint everyone had predicted.[4]

Precious hours slipped by, but no important decisions were made on the Allied side. The British generals had decided to wait until dawn, when the armored car reconnaissance reports and those of "Y," the army radio intercept service, could be confirmed by the RAF.[5] By daybreak, however, the Desert Fox had already traveled fifty-five miles, had rounded the Gazala Line, and had turned north; he achieved a considerable measure of surprise when he surfaced in the British rear with 10,000 vehicles.[6]

The first victim was the 3d Indian Motor Brigade south of Bir Hacheim. Many of its men were eating breakfast when the storm broke. At 6:30 A.M., its commander, Brigadier A. A. E. Filose, signaled that it was being attacked by "a whole bloody German armoured division." It was, in fact, being attacked by the Ariete—the best of the Italian divisions—plus a few elements of the 21st Panzer Division. The 3d Indian, which included the 2d Royal Lancers, the 11th Prince Albert Victor's Own Cavalry, and the 18th King Edward's Own Cavalry regiments, supported by the 2d Field Regiment (Indian artillery), was quickly overwhelmed and dispersed, losing eleven officers and more than two hundred men killed, many more wounded, and some thirty officers and a thousand men captured in the process, along with much of its equipment. (About half of the artillery regiment escaped.) Among the POWs was Sir Walter Cowan, a seventy-one-year-old British admiral who had retired in 1931 and who had accompanied the 18th Cavalry Regiment as a volunteer. He had just finished emptying his revolver into a PzKw III and was in the process of reloading when the tank commander jumped out and took him prisoner.[7] Colonel Fowler, the regimental commander, was also captured.[8] His regiment, like the rest of the brigade, was so badly battered that it had to be sent back to the frontier to reform.[9]

The next victim was the British 7th Motor Brigade, which was commanded by Brigadier J. M. L. Renton. Like the 3d Indian, the 7th Motor was not ready. Most of its men were relaxing or drinking tea when, according to Renton, "some gunner started banging away like mad. Thinking it was trigger-happiness, I was about to have it stopped, when we saw something moving in the desert away to the south, about four miles off. It was the whole of Rommel's command in full cry straight for us."[10]

Even though he had a direct telephone line to 7th Armoured Division's Headquarters, Renton did not know the Afrika Korps was thirty miles from where it was supposed to be until he actually saw it advancing on his position. He desperately tried to assemble his battalions and man the Retma Box, but the job was only half finished and his columns were strung out over twenty miles of desert southwest of Bir Hacheim when the 90th Light Division struck at 8:30 A.M. The 7th Motor Brigade could not offer effective resistance, and the Germans soon broke through, but Renton managed to extricate his troops and withdraw before the brigade could be completely smashed. The prearranged rallying point for the 7th Motor was Bir el Gubi, east of the Retma Box, but when the brigadier arrived there, he discovered that 7th Armoured Division HQ had given half of the garrison permission to go to Tobruk—for a swim! There were not enough men left to fire all of the guns.[11] Meanwhile, the Afrika Korps continued its advance to the north.

Unaccountably, Brigadier G. W. Richards's 4th Armoured was the third Allied brigade to be surprised on the morning of 26 May.

The 4th Armoured had an advantage which seldom presented itself in war. General Ritchie had posted it just north of Bir Hacheim because he had correctly guessed that Rommel would come this way. The 4th thus had the opportunity to pick its own battlefield. The section of ground it chose was called "Blenheim," in memory of a great victory the British Army had won over the French and Bavarians in

Germany in 1704. Here the brigade had the luxury of surveying the terrain, digging trenches, foxholes, and gun emplacements, registering its artillery and tank guns on key positions with ranging shots, selecting and marking the low ground individual tanks would occupy so that they could fight in hull-down positions, and so on. The ground was not permanently manned, however, and for a good reason. If the Luftwaffe reconnaissance pilots figured out what the brigade was up to, the German ground forces would avoid the area like the plague. The brigade, therefore, bivouacked about six miles north of Blenheim. It planned to occupy Blenheim well in advance of Rommel's panzers.

The 4th Armoured was alerted during the evening of 25 May, and all nonessential vehicles were sent to the rear, but nothing happened that night. By 7:30 A.M., the HQ, 7th Armoured Division, knew that the enemy was present in unknown strength about twenty-five miles southwest of Bir Hacheim, that the 7th Motor was withdrawing on the Retma Box, and that the 3d Indian Motor was under attack. Therefore, at 8:45 A.M., General Messervy ordered the 4th Armoured to take up its prearranged battle positions southeast of the 3d Indian. He had waited too long.

That morning, Maj. John Hackett was commanding a squadron of Stuarts in the 8th Hussars Regiment. Since the other two squadrons of the regiment were equipped with Grants, his unit naturally moved out first and led the way toward Blenheim. He had barely started out, however, when he received a radio report that the Germans may have already advanced past Blenheim. Hackett uttered a profanity and, a moment later, topped a small hill. Below him he saw a huge dust cloud and both the panzer regiments of the Afrika Korps, spearheaded by the 8th Panzer, advancing in an arrowhead formation. It was 9:07 A.M.

Hackett signaled that he was engaging and was ordered to hold off the enemy until the Grants could warm up their engines and get into battle formation. It was already too late, however; Hackett's tank was quickly knocked out, along with several other Stuarts, and the rest were pushed back. Meanwhile, Lt. Col. Willi Teege's tank battalion of the 8th Panzer Regiment (15th Panzer Division) slammed into the flank of the Hussars and most of the regiment's Grants were destroyed before they could even move.[12] The 8th Hussars was destroyed as a fighting unit.

The brigade's other major unit, 3d Royal Tank Regiment (RTR), at least had time to defend itself, although its reaction was definitely hasty. "We were expecting to attack, there was no question of us being attacked," L. Sgt. Frank Shepherd, the commander of one of the 3d RTR's Grant tanks, recalled. "No one took much notice of the Very lights [German signal flares] that night because Jerry was always putting them up . . . We had a brew-up [i.e., made tea] . . . The next thing was an alarm. We were ordered forward and as we topped the ridge directly ahead saw a sight that took our breath away—drawn up on the desert before us, their squat black shapes stretching right away to the horizon it seemed, was the whole Afrika Korps."[13] The 3d Royal Tank Regiment nevertheless waded in and gave Rommel his first nasty surprise of the campaign. For the first time, he met the Grant in combat and found its 75mm gun vastly superior to the 50mm gun of the PzKw III. To complicate matters even further for Colonel Teege, the 33d Panzer Artillery Regiment had not been able to keep up with the advance. The 3d RTR inflicted heavy casualties on his battalion, but Col. Gerhard Mueller of 21st Panzer Division led his 5th Panzer Regiment directly into the fray, and the fighting became desperate all along the line.[14] Erwin Rommel dashed forward with Generals Nehring and von Vaerst and assumed personal command of the battle. The Grants took a heavy toll on the panzers, and several German crews were wiped out by direct hits from their powerful main battle guns, but German leadership was the decisive factor in this battle. By employing superior tank tactics, adapted to the terrain, and by using their antitank guns, the Afrika Korps was finally able to break the back of the 4th Armoured Brigade. The 3d RTR, which had lost sixteen Grants, and the remnants of the 8th Hussars could not prevent the Germans from overrunning the brigade's administrative echelon, and soon the remnants of the 4th Armoured were falling back in the direction of El Adem, pursued by the 90th Light Division. Map 5, p. 71, shows the first phase of the Battle of the Gazala Line.

Sergeant Shepherd's tank was hit ten times and was knocked out of action when a solid shot wedged in the turret ring. He was ordered to the rear, to find a tank delivery squadron that could replace his Grant. He had to go all the way to Capuzzo on the Libyan-Egyptian frontier before he found one. Shepherd later described the British rear in one word: "chaos."[15]

Before long, Major Hackett (who had scrambled into another tank) only had seven "Honeys" left. Like most of the other squadron commanders, he had given up running zigzag attack patterns (aimed to throw off the German gunners) because they consumed too

THE GAZALA LINE, PHASE 1

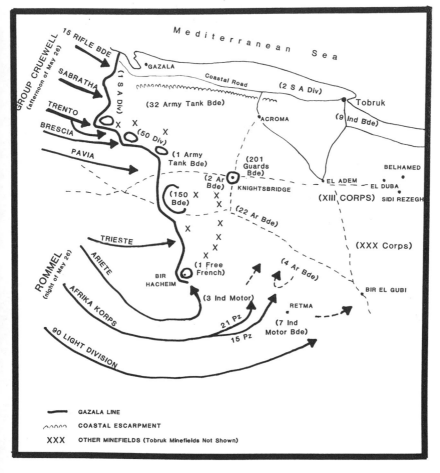

GAZALA LINE

COASTAL ESCARPMENT

XXX OTHER MINEFIELDS (Tobruk Minefields Not Shown)

much gasoline, and was now trying to hold up the Afrika Korps's advance as long as possible, using the best available cover behind ridge lines and low hills. His situation was becoming desperate, however, because his low-range Stuarts were running out of fuel. Suddenly, to the north, he spotted a large number of tents. He made for the compound, which turned out to be a major headquarters, complete with supply and fuel depots, and asked for fuel. He was met by a suspicious, well-dressed staff officer who demanded to see his identity papers. The officer did not believe the tattered and grimy Hackett (who had been burned when his tank was blown up) when he told him that the Germans were right behind him, and seemed to think that he might be some kind of Axis spy. Then, suddenly, a pair of light PzKw IIs appeared over the top of a nearby ridge and fired, but were quickly driven away by the Honeys. (The obsolete Panzer Mark II, with its 20mm main battle gun, was the only German tank in the desert that was inferior to the Stuart.) This little demonstration convinced the staff officer; dozens of four-gallon tin canisters appeared like magic and were poured into the empty tanks of the Stuarts.[16] Soon, however, Hackett was forced to leave, because he knew that, if the PzKw IIs were there, the heavier Panzer Mark IIIs and IVs could not be far behind.

Shortly after 10:00 A.M., the depot was seized by the Afrika Korps, and the command post (CP) of the 7th Armoured Division disappeared. Even after the 4th Armoured Brigade had been attacked, General Messervy and his staff had failed to appreciate how rapidly the Germans were advancing, and the headquarters of the 7th Armoured Division was overrun by German armored cars. Messervy himself tried to escape in his armored command vehicle, but a German armored car spotted it and fired several 30mm shells into its side; then another attacked it from the front and fired several shells into the engine. The burning ACV rolled to a stop and Messervy, Pyman, Major Richardson, the G-2 (chief intelligence officer), and Captain Read of the operations staff all bailed out, along with three enlisted men.

Messervy hurriedly tore off his badges of rank, just before an armored car pulled up to the fugitives. A German officer jumped out, pointed a machine pistol at them, and snapped: "Get up! You are prisoners."[17] A few minutes later, a German officer approached General Messervy.

"Aren't you a bit old for a private?" he asked.

"You're right," he declared, indignantly. "It's a bloody disgrace they've called me up at my age!"

Captain Read had been wounded during the unsuccessful escape attempt, so "Private" Messervy carried him to a German ambulance and learned firsthand how the German troops fraternized with their prisoners and gave them water, oranges, and chocolates. An English-speaking German medical officer dressed Read's wounds and told Messervy that he thanked God he would soon be going home. He would be thirty-three years old in a few weeks and no one over thirty-three served in the Afrika Korps. Next, Messervy and his comrades were herded into a German truck. Fortunately for them, a British forward observer had noticed this concentration of German vehicles, and a twenty-five-pounder battery opened fire on it. DAK trucks dispersed in all directions, and, in the confusion, Messervy and his colleagues jumped out of the moving vehicle, scrambled down a wadi, and later hid under an artillery tarpaulin. Here they remained—despite the suffocating heat—until nightfall. They then walked throughout the night and reached British lines at about 4:00 A.M. on 28 May.[18] They were still miles from their brigades, however, and the HQ of the 7th Armoured Division had temporarily ceased to exist.

The German bag was almost even greater. As Messervy's CP was being overrun, General Norrie, the corps commander, approached it in his staff car from the north. He would have been captured as well, had not Major Hackett intercepted him and prevented him from proceeding. The disaster was big enough as it was.

At the same time, a dozen miles farther north, the 1st Armoured Division lay idle in its camp near the Trigh Capuzzo, while the 4th Armoured Brigade was being smashed. As was usual for this stage of the war, the Allies had failed to concentrate; had the 1st and 7th Armoured Divisions acted in concert, as the 15th and 21st Panzer Divisions had, they might easily have turned back Rommel's main attack. This piecemeal effort by the British was to be repeated throughout this battle and would cost the Eighth Army the lives or freedom of many of its best men.

Meanwhile, General Norrie ordered the 1st Armoured Division to prepare to move south and give battle. These orders were passed on to the 22d Armoured Brigade, which was about twelve miles north of the place where the Afrika Korps had smashed the 4th Armoured. The 2d Armoured, between Knightsbridge and El Adem, also prepared to move south. Norrie was himself temporarily out of action, however. He was spotted and pursued by one of the recon battalions of the 90th Light Division, and he and his staff were forced to take refuge in the El Adem Box, which already sheltered General Gott and the HQ, XIII Corps. Control of the battle on the Allied side now devolved upon the more capable General Lumsden, the commander of the 1st Armoured Division, and the entire complexion of the fighting soon changed, for Lumsden was a man who did not believe in letting Rommel crush his units individually, one at a time.

ROMMEL FALLS INTO A TRAP

The vanguards of the Afrika Korps ran into the 22d Armoured Brigade as it advanced south, toward Bir el Harmat. The fighting was heavy and confused. The Royal Gloucestershire Hussars lost thirty tanks, but German losses were also high. In the end, the British were forced to retreat, but this time in reasonably good order, toward Knightsbridge. Lumsden ordered the 22d Armoured to reform for a second attack to the southeast, while the 2d Armoured Brigade struck the German right flank from the east.

It was not yet noon, but Panzer Army Afrika had already scattered or smashed two British armored brigades and two motor brigades, had turned back a third armored brigade, had overrun the headquarters of the 7th Armoured Division, and had forced the HQ, XXX Corps, to flee across the desert. Rommel believed that he had won the battle and jubilantly ordered Nehring to press on to the north, toward the Trigh Capuzzo and Acroma. This was a serious mistake on his part, for he had badly underestimated the strength of the Allied armor. By sending the Afrika Korps off at pursuit speed, he strung its columns out all over the desert. Rommel assumed this drive would force the British to defend the area south of the Coastal Road with their remaining tanks, where Nehring would destroy them; instead, Lumsden refused to fall into the trap. He held back his armor, avoided another frontal confrontation with the Afrika Korps, and allowed Nehring's spearheads to pass west of Knightsbridge. Now it was the Germans who were advancing into a trap.

The tide of battle began to turn early that afternoon, when the 2d Armoured Brigade struck the Afrika Korps in the flank. At 2:15 P.M., the DAK reported that it was under attack from the east, north, and northeast, and complained that the Italians (i.e., the Italian XX Motorized Corps) were lagging behind (which they were; the Ariete only reached Bir el Harmat at nightfall, and the Trieste Motorized Division was lost in the minefields north of Bir Hacheim). But the troubles of the Afrika Korps were about to become much, much worse. About 2:30 P.M., the 22d Armoured Brigade joined the battle, and the British 1st Army Tank Brigade (whose presence German military intelligence had not detected) attacked from the 50th Infantry Division boxes toward Bir el Aslag, into Nehring's rear, and cut off the DAK from its supply units. The 3d Battalion, 104th Panzer Grenadier Regiment (21st Panzer Division), took the main blow of the British army tank brigade and suffered so many casualties that it had to be dissolved. At the same time, the 115th Panzer Grenadier Regiment of the 15th Panzer Division lost one-third of its men killed, wounded, or captured, and Colonel Roske, the regimental commander, was taken prisoner.[19] "Our antitank gunners exacted a heavy toll," Colonel von Mellenthin recalled, but "the British tanks forced their way up to the very muzzles of the guns and wiped out our crews."[20] In the process, the German AT gunners knocked out eighteen of the monstrous Matilda infantry tanks of the 44th Royal Tank Regiment alone. By now, however, the Afrika Korps was virtually surrounded and fighting for its life. It was under attack from the east (i.e., on the right flank) by the 2d Armoured, from the northwest by the 22d Armoured, and from the west by the 1st Army Tank Brigade, which had also cut into its rear.

Rommel himself was with the 90th Light Division in the El Adem sector when Lumsden struck. At once he decided to rejoin the Afrika Korps but was attacked by British tanks and could not reach the main battlefield. The entire area between Maabus er Rigel, El Adem, and

Bir el Harmat was now a mass of confusion, as the British attacks broke down, lost unit cohesiveness, and deteriorated into a series of small unit actions. In one of these, the 9th Queens Royal Lancers Regiment (with one Crusader squadron, a Grant squadron, and a mixed Stuart/Crusader squadron), "practically wiped out" the 2d Battalion, 155th Panzer Grenadier Regiment of the 90th Light Division, to quote Captain Hubner of the 15th Panzer.[21] Most of the German supply and fuel columns fled to the southwest, while tank elements of the DAK tried to continue to push northward to Acroma, in accordance with orders. "If we had not got excellent leadership and a first-rate corps of officers, things would look black indeed," Captain Hubner recorded in his diary.[22]

The crisis of the battle occurred at 4:00 P.M., when British tanks struck the left flank of the 15th Panzer Division. The panzer grenadier battalion covering von Vaerst's flank was quickly overrun, and the whole division was in danger of being wiped out.

General Nehring reacted immediately. "A flak front!" he roared at Col. Alwin Wolz, the commander of the 135th Motorized Flak Regiment. "Wolz, you've got to build up a flak front to act as a flank defense with all available guns!" Sixteen of the deadly 88mm antiaircraft guns were quickly rolled into position, and the regiment formed a line a mile and a half long, with overlapping fields of fire. The British tankers, having dealt with the grenadiers, attacked this final defensive position just as Wolz completed it. They soon discovered, however, that not even the Grant could withstand the jolt of the 88s, which opened up on them at a range of 1,200 yards.[23] Soon twenty-four Grants were burning and the survivors withdrew out of range. But the British were not through with Wolz's line. Deviating from standard practice, they bombarded it with their heavy artillery and knocked out several guns, wiping out the crews in the process.[24] Fortunately for the Germans, nature intervened before they could mount another attack. A ghibli covered everything with dust, ending the fighting for the day. Among those seriously wounded in this battle was General von Vaerst, the promising Hessian commander of the 15th Panzer Division. He would not be able to return to active duty until August, and was temporarily replaced by Col. Eduard Crasemann, the commander of the 33d Panzer Artillery Regiment.[25]

As night fell on 27 May, the DAK dug in along the line from Rigel Ridge to Bir Lefa, while the British tanks disengaged and fell back toward the Knightsbridge Box and the 150th Infantry Brigade Group Box at Got el Ualeb. Meanwhile, the Ariete Division laagered with the German supply echelons and fuel tanker trucks near Bir el Harmat. Uncoordinated as they were, the British attacks had caused heavy losses on both sides and had forced Nehring to turn back to meet them, just when it looked as if he were going to succeed in reaching the Coastal Road, cutting off the XIII Corps from the rest of the Eighth Army. Rommel now realized that he had badly underestimated British strength and was "very worried indeed."[26] The bulk of his striking force was isolated between the Gazala minefields and El Adem, was very short of supplies, and was nearly surrounded. The DAK had lost more than a third of its tanks, and the 21st Panzer Division was down to twenty-nine "runners," although the repair crews and maintenance units worked through the night and had fourteen others operational by noon the following day. Even more seriously, Nehring's fuel and ammunition were almost exhausted. To the south, the situation was hardly any better. The Trieste division was still missing, stuck in the minefields north of Bir Hacheim, Ariete had failed to take Bir Hacheim (losing a sizable number of tanks in the process), and, with the Free French launching raids into Ariete's rear, the strike force's communications with the rest of Panzer Army Afrika (i.e., Group Cruewell) were tenuous at best.

By midnight, it was apparent that the worst German intelligence omission had been its failure to locate the 150th Brigade Box, situated a few miles west-southwest of the Afrika Korps's nighttime camp. The 150th had prevented the Pavia and Trieste divisions from breaching the Gazala Line minefields and supplying the trapped panzer forces. Despite the seriousness of the situation, Rommel (communicating by radio) nevertheless ordered Nehring to advance the next day, even though he could only do so with the 21st Panzer, because the 15th Panzer was out of fuel.

General von Bismarck led the 21st Panzer Division out of its laager on the morning of 28 May and scattered "Stopcol" south of Elwet et Tamar, destroying nine tanks from the 8th Royal Tank Regiment and a South African twenty-five-pound gun in the process. That afternoon, he captured Commonwealth Keep and reached the coastal escarpment, and the panzers opened fire on "Seacol" and the Headquarters of the 2d South African Police Battalion. The German tanks, however, could not negotiate the escarpment and thus could not cut the Coastal Road, so their advance was stopped and no serious damage was done. Most of the division then returned to the area north of Rigel Ridge, but Bismarck left a strong battle group (*Kampfgruppe*) in the Commonwealth Keep area, under the command of the 39th Anti-Tank Battalion.

The date 28 May 1942 should have seen the annihilation of the Afrika Korps, but it did not. This fact is attributable less to the brilliance of Rommel and the Germans than to the ham-fisted way the British armored commanders fought the battle that day. General Lumsden intended for the 2d and 22d Armoured Brigades to attack Bismarck's advance in the flank, in order to destroy the 21st Panzer Division. Instead, the 22d Armoured Brigade remained behind, inactive all day, watching the 15th Panzer at the Maabus er Rigel Ridge, obviously without realizing how vulnerable the immobilized division was. Instead of attacking the 21st Panzer, the 2d Armoured struck the Ariete Division, which had decided to move north from Bir el Harmat, in order to join the Afrika Korps. While the 2d Armoured advanced from the east, the bulk of the 1st Army Tank Brigade launched several attacks against the Italian division from the northwest, but its attempts to coordinate its efforts with those of the 2d Armoured failed, and the British never succeeded in delivering a concentrated blow. Despite the inferiority of its tanks, Ariete—always the best of the Italian divisions—met fury with fury and turned back every attack. The battle ended only slightly in favor of the British. During this action the 10th Hussars (of the 2d Armoured) became separated from the rest of the brigade, blundered into a nest of Afrika Korps antitank guns, and lost all but three of its Crusader tanks.[27]

Meanwhile, to the east, the 90th Light was in the process of retreating from El Adem when it was attacked by the 4th Armoured Brigade, which had rallied and reorganized. The attack caused considerable alarm (the partially reequipped British brigade struck with more than one hundred tanks), but the 90th Light, as usual, was saved by its antitank gunners, who held the British at bay. It then fell back to the southwest and managed to hedgehog near Naduret el Ghesceuasc. The 4th Armoured failed to press its attacks and returned to its camp on Batruna Ridge. Artillery fire, skirmishing, and firefights between hostile patrols, however, continued throughout the night.

The confusion of the battle is perhaps best illustrated by an exploit of Maj. C. C. Lomax, the commander of the Headquarters Squadron of the 9th Queen's Royal Lancers. Leading a column of supply trucks and trying to find the 201st Guards Brigade Box at Knightsbridge, he veered too far north and got lost in the darkness. Suddenly he spotted a low trip wire, which denoted the boundary of a minefield. His driver hit the brakes and they stopped a few feet from the wire. Two sentries approached and identified themselves as Guardsmen. Lomax asked if this was the Knightsbridge Box, and they replied that it was.

"How very fortunate!" the major exclaimed. "Another few yards and we would all have been in the minefield."

"On the contrary, sir," one of the sentries replied, "another few yards and you will be out of it."

He and his whole convoy (which was following in his tracks) had passed through the entire minefield without hitting a single mine![28]

Not everyone was as lucky as Major Lomax. Nearby, the colonel of another British armored regiment was trying—without success—to direct his supply echelon through the darkness to his tank squadrons by using the radio. His transmission was interrupted by a German artillery salvo, which flew over his head and exploded a mile or so behind him, leaving the telltale orange glow of one or more burning vehicles.

"Now, then," the colonel resumed, "where are you in relation to that bright light?"

"I *am* that bright light!" came the miserable reply.[29]

And where was the Desert Fox all this time? He was on the run shortly after dawn on 28 May, when his command post was attacked and dispersed near Bir el Harmat. Later in the day, when he learned that the 15th Panzer Division was almost out of ammunition, he became even more anxious to make contact with the Afrika Korps. With a small escort, he made his way to a position ten miles north of Bir el Harmat, where "the typical panorama of a desert battle was spread out before our eyes. Black clouds rose to the sky, lending a weird and sombre charm to the landscape."[30] He was not able to get through, but he thought he saw a route through which he could push a supply column. When he returned to his battle headquarters, no doubt to pick up a supply convoy, he found that his staff had again been scattered by British armor. Map 6, p. 81, shows the situation at midnight on 28 May.

By the end of the day, General Ritchie was still satisfied with the way the battle was progressing. British armor (which had lost 150 tanks) had been battered but not defeated, Rommel's striking force was scattered over a wide area, his HQ had been dispersed, and the German supply situation was serious. The Eighth Army, however, had not pressed its advantages. In addition, an event had occurred, the significance of which neither Rommel nor the British had yet grasped. The Italian Pavia and Trieste Divisions cut two small gaps in the minefields near the Trigh Capuzzo and the Trigh el Abd, in places not continually covered by British fire. These gaps—ten miles apart and on either side of the 150th Brigade Box—were still hard to use and were very dangerous, due to British artillery—but they held the promise of relief for the trapped "Africans."

Rommel decided to take some of the pressure off his main striking force by getting the Italians to open another major battle far to the northwest. During the night of 28–29 May, he ordered General Cruewell to "break through the minefield from the west to disengage the rear." Cruewell promptly alerted the Italian Sabratha Infantry Division and went to the headquarters of the 104th Artillery Command (Arko 104), to plan a supporting bombardment with Major General Krause, the Panzer Army Artillery commander. Then, after commenting that he did not like to fly in tiny airplanes, he jumped in the back seat of a Fieseler Storch reconnaissance aircraft and flew back to the front, but the flares that were supposed to mark friendly lines were never fired—the officer who was supposed to shoot them off was called to the telephone only a moment before Cruewell's airplane appeared. The general suddenly found himself over British

SITUATION AT NIGHTFALL, MAY 28, 1942

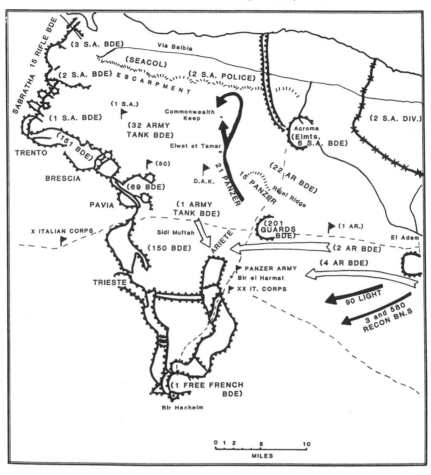

lines at an altitude of only 500 feet. Enemy machine-gun fire riddled the light plane, the engine was destroyed, and the pilot slumped over dead. From the back seat, Cruewell was unable to reach the controls and was helpless. Miraculously, as if guided by the hand of God, the airplane landed itself. Rommel's second-in-command emerged without so much as bursting a pimple. He was, however, promptly captured by members of the British 150th Infantry Brigade, who treated him as an honored guest, fried him a huge steak, and sent him on to GHQ in Cairo. The German Army had lost one of its best men. Without him, the attack of the Sabratha Division could be expected to come to nothing, which is exactly what happened. Sabratha struck the 1st South African Division's positions north of Alem Hamza at dawn, but the attack immediately collapsed under the heavy fire of the Cape Town Highlanders and the 2d Transvaal Scottish battalions. Four hundred Italians surrendered, including thirteen officers.[31]

When Col. Siegfried Westphal, the Panzer Army operations officer, learned that General Cruewell was missing, he became concerned that certain nervous Italian generals would take charge, since Rommel was pinned down behind enemy lines. Westphal was afraid that they might order a retreat, leaving the strike force in the lurch. Fortunately, Field Marshal Albert Kesselring, the OB South, commander in chief of the Second Air Fleet and Rommel's nominal superior, happened to be visiting Panzer Army Headquarters when the news arrived that Cruewell was missing. Westphal—not a man who was afraid to take things upon himself—asked the Luftwaffe marshal to assume command of Group Cruewell. Kesselring was reluctant to take this unusual step, but Westphal finally convinced him to do so. It was an unselfish act almost unprecedented in military annals—a field marshal had subordinated himself to a more junior general.

Meanwhile, at daybreak, Erwin Rommel personally led the supply echelons of the panzer divisions through the gap he had spotted the day before, and resupplied his tank forces. "The battered Axis forces reacted at once to his leadership," the South African Official History recorded.[32] He had retained his composure in the face of disaster and, by his personal efforts, had resupplied the stranded Afrika Korps, and partially restored contact between the scattered forces of his army. Shortly after he arrived in the Afrika Korps's laager, however, he seemed to hesitate, as if he were not sure what to do next. General Gause and Col. Fritz Bayerlein, the chief of staff of the Afrika Korps, suggested that they fight their way back to the west and then announce that the entire operation had been just a major raid, which had gone according to plan.

They had hit a nerve. Rommel suddenly became the Desert Fox again. He chewed the officers out, partially for advising him to retreat, but mainly for suggesting that he resort to subterfuge. He alone would make decisions of this nature, he declared, and, as far as he was concerned, there were no roads leading back. Suddenly he again acted as if he knew exactly what to do. "The man grew immensely in stature in proportion with his task," General Westphal said after the war. "Events chip away at every man," Wolf Heckmann commented later. "What remains under these influences depends on the material he is made of."[33] Rommel now demonstrated that he was made of some pretty determined stuff. He received reports from south of Rigel Ridge that the British 2d Armoured Brigade was moving west from Knightsbridge, in an obvious attempt to cut off Ariete from the DAK. Rommel decided to prevent this and provoked another major battle in the process. At 8:00 A.M., the 2d Armoured spotted thirty-five German tanks, evenly spaced along a small ridge, about thirty yards apart. It was the 15th Panzer Division, now partially refueled. General Lumsden arrived at this moment and ordered the 2d to attack them head-on from the west. The 9th Queen's Lancers spearheaded the attack with its Grants, followed by the Queen's Bays and the 10th Hussars. They soon discovered that many of the panzers were inoperable derelicts that had been towed into position to give the British an erroneous impression of their strength; to their dismay, however, the Lancers discovered that there were several 88mm guns behind the tanks, and they were not derelicts. One by one the Grants were knocked out. Lieutenant Colonel J. Ronald Macdonell, the Lancers' commander, ordered his cruisers to put down a smoke screen and, under this artificial cover, pulled back what was left of his regiment to its starting line. He had only twenty tanks left.[34]

After the 2d Armoured Brigade had been checked to the west, the 21st Panzer attacked it from the north. Ariete then joined the battle from the south, and the British brigade was under fire from three sides. Two regiments of Brigadier Carr's 22d Armoured Brigade were diverted from a planned attack against Bir el Harmat to help the 2d Armoured, and suffered heavy losses in the confused fighting. Lumsden himself narrowly escaped death when a Stuka dive-bombed him, and his aide was killed.

By 3:00 P.M., the 9th Lancers were again in position and preparing to attack the ridge, which was still held by the 15th Panzer. It was planned that the British artillery would open up at 3:20 P.M. and cover the area with smoke. According to the script, Macdonell's Grants, Stuarts, and few surviving cruisers would take advantage of the smoke screen and push forward rapidly, so that they could deal with the panzers and 88s at close range. Unfortunately, British tank/artillery coordination was again poor, and the guns opened up ten minutes before the tanks were ready. By the time the tanks advanced to the ridge line, the smoke screen had dissipated, the air was "as clear as a bell," and the gunners were out of smoke shells. The Lancers were smashed. Colonel Macdonell's tank was hit but he managed to "change mounts," although he could not make an impression on the German line. Seeing that the attack was foiled, the commander of the 2d Armoured Brigade ordered the 9th Lancers to withdraw. Out of the forty-five tanks the Lancers had on 26 May only ten were still operational. Still the battle continued. "The area of desert on which we had been fighting for the past three days was an incredible sight," Capt. Joan Bright recalled.

> Every yard of it was criss-crossed with tracks and pockmarked with shell-holes, while everywhere lay piles of enemy [shell] cases. Slit trenches and gun pits had been dug all over the place and round the circumference lay the wreckage of our own and enemy tanks, burnt-out armoured cars and the skeletons of lorries and trucks. Every puff of wind raised a white, powdery dust.
> There had been no time for shaving or proper washing, and everyone was tired out through lack of sleep and nervous strain. We looked like a lot of ragged tramps, with sweat-stained shirts and bloodshot eyes.[35]

By 4:00 P.M., the 10th Hussars Regiment had only three "runners" (i.e., operational tanks) left, and the 9th Lancers had lost half its remaining tanks, its medical supply three-ton truck had been blown away by a Stuka, and its senior medical officer had been seriously wounded by a German shell. It had suffered so many casualties that it had to ask the Queen's Bays' medical officer to take care of it. The next day, the 9th was ordered to give its remaining Grants and their crews to the Bays and to withdraw to the rear. Like several other British armored regiments, it was operationally bankrupt.

The battle was ended at 5:00 P.M., when a major sandstorm struck the area. "Tanks and lorries huddled together like sheep," B. G. Simpkins wrote later, and "men cowered behind their vehicles panting for breath while the scorching wind swept round them."[36]

The British would have done better that day had General Lumsden's plan not misfired. The XXX Corps placed the 4th Armoured Brigade under his command at noon, but its commander missed connections with Lumsden due to a sandstorm. It was late afternoon before Lumsden was finally able to order the brigade south, toward the main battlefield, but it did not reach it due to sandstorms. Instead it clashed with the 90th Light near Bir el Harmat and lost five Grants and three Stuarts to the ubiquitous German antitank gunners.

Meanwhile, to the north, Brigadier Willison's 32d Army Tank Brigade tried to retake Commonwealth Keep, but without combined-arms support—even though the 1st South African Infantry Division was nearby. The defenders (the 39th Anti-Tank Battalion) knocked out seven infantry tanks before the British retreated. The Germans abandoned the position that night, however, when Rommel ordered a general retreat.

By now, even the Desert Fox was forced to admit that his original plan had failed. He canceled the seaborne landing of Group Hecker and decided to fall back to the southwest, against the line of British minefields, which he intended to breach. Through these gaps he would be able to restore contact with his base and the rest of his army. This plan, noted historian Correlli Barnett wrote later, "illustrated the originality of his genius."[37] The British assumed Rommel would try to break out of the trap to the east and, for the next several days, based their dispositions accordingly. Rommel, however, intended to break out to the west. Once again, he was going to try to do what the enemy least expected him to do.

On the British side, there was a general feeling of satisfaction. Rommel's strike force was still pinned against the minefields, and it was estimated that it would consume the last of its supplies the next day. (Throughout the battle, the British consistently overestimated the value of unguarded minefields and minefields covered only by patrols.) General Ritchie—who was still at his headquarters in Gambut, east of Tobruk—thought he had a chance of shelling the German armor to pieces, while his own tank and motor brigades sought out and destroyed the supply columns to the south. "Rommel on the run!" he signaled HQ, Middle East Command.

General Auchinleck was also swept up in the general optimism and euphoria of the moment. "Bravo, Eighth Army!" he signaled back. "Give him the coup de grâce." He even suggested a possible advance to the west, with light mobile forces driving as far as Mechili and Benghazi.

The Battle of the Gazala Line was not yet over, however. Rommel, as General Playfair wrote later, "was far from beaten, and the perils of the situation seem to have been matched by his confidence and determination."[38] He had already made his plans. First, he would withdraw the entire striking force to an area soon to be famous as "the Cauldron," where it would be protected by Sidra and Dahar el Aslag Ridges, as well as by a British minefield running north from Bir Hacheim to the Aslag Ridge. (This minefield was part of the second line of defense of the main Gazala Line minefield.) Second, he would eliminate Bir Hacheim and destroy the 1st Free French Brigade. Third, he would resume his interrupted drive to the north, cut the Coastal Road, and isolate and capture the Allied divisions in the Gazala Line. Finally, he would capture Tobruk. Bloody but unbowed, he was going to let nothing distract him or deter him from reaching his objective.

THE DESTRUCTION OF THE 150TH INFANTRY BRIGADE

By the evening of 28 May, Brigadier C. W. Haydon, the commander of the British 150th Infantry Brigade Group, was sure that his command—which stretched from the Trigh Capuzzo to the Trigh el Abd—was threatened with attack and possible annihilation from the east. He therefore drew in his southernmost battalion (which had been holding up the Trieste Division) and prepared for an all-around defense of his main defensive position, the Got el Ualeb Box, near Sidi Muftah.

Haydon's command consisted of the 4th Battalion, East Yorkshires Regiment; the 4th and 5th Battalions, the Green Howards; D Company of the 2d Battalion, Cheshire Regiment (a machine-gun unit); 72d Field Regiment, Royal Artillery; 25th/26th Medium Battery, 7th Medium Regiment, Royal Artillery; 259th Norfolk Yeomanry Battery, RA (an antitank unit); 81st/25th Light Anti-Aircraft Battery, Royal Artillery; and the 232d Field Company, Royal Engineers. On the morning of 29 May, he was reinforced with the Tactical Headquarters of the 1st Army Tank Brigade and the 44th Royal Tank Regiment, as well as a squadron of the 42d RTR—thirty infantry tanks in all. The brigade group, however, was still defending a front of more than five miles, and it would soon be facing much of the German Afrika Korps.

During the night of 29–30 May, Rommel's forces established themselves in "the Cauldron." Bismarck's 21st Panzer Division dug in on Sidra Ridge on the northern face of the Cauldron, while Ariete faced east on Aslag Ridge. Strong elements of the 90th Light, which now joined the rest of the striking force, faced west, toward Got el Ualeb, while the 15th Panzer covered the positions to the south. Early on the morning of 30 May, strong detachments of the DAK, including Mueller's 5th Panzer Regiment, were sent to open a supply route west of Sidi Muftah. The operation was called off, however, after the 5th Panzer was ambushed and lost eleven tanks almost immediately. The Germans now realized, for the first time, that the ground between the Trigh Capuzzo and the Trigh el Abd was very well fortified and held by strong forces, including "I" tanks.

That afternoon, Rommel traveled through a narrow gap in the minefield to the Headquarters of the X Italian Corps, where he met with Kesselring and Maj. Nicolaus von Below of the Luftwaffe, the Führer's personal adjutant. Here he learned that his lines of communication to Group Cruewell were still not secure. The two gaps that the Italians had cut in the minefields were under fire from the Got el Ualeb Box, which was defended by the 150th Brigade and the 44th Royal Tank Regiment. Rommel must have been astonished. "We never knew that it was there," Col. Fritz Bayerlein, then chief of staff of the Afrika Korps, recalled.[39] Now it had to be eliminated.

The German-Italian failure to identify the 150th Brigade Box earlier had placed the Afrika Korps in a do-or-die situation. "Got el Ualeb must fall," Rommel ordered curtly. "The 150th Brigade must be evicted."[40] With his initial probes turned back, the battle began in earnest on 31 May.

The British also knew what was happening, and the RAF concentrated its efforts against enemy trucks and tankers trying to drive through the gaps in the minefield on 30 May. (The narrow gaps, which were dubbed Peter and Paul, were about ten miles apart, north and south of the 150th Brigade Box, respectively.)[41] The Luftwaffe, of course, responded by flying interdiction missions, and there were several dogfights over the Gazala Line. The Desert Air Force lost a dozen airplanes in these battles, but a raid by Boston bombers inflicted considerable losses on the supply convoys forming up west of the gaps.

Ritchie's attempt to administer the coup de grâce went astray on 30 May. Rommel expected a major effort to destroy the Afrika Korps in the Cauldron via a concerted attack from all available British armored forces, but nothing of the kind happened. The commanders of the 2d and 22d Armoured Brigades noticed the Axis withdrawal into the Cauldron and decided to attack, but their tanks ran into heavy fire and suffered several losses, mostly inflicted by the Ariete Division; then they ran out of ammunition and were forced to retire behind a smoke screen. In their defense, it must be noted that both brigades were now at about one-third of their original tank strength and were pretty much spent.

On the German side, the bulk of the fighting was done by Maj. Curt Ehle's 3d Battalion of the 115th Panzer Grenadier Regiment, 15th Panzer Division. (This unit was the former 15th Motorcycle Battalion, but the German motorcycles—which had proven so useful in Europe—were mechanically unsuited to the desert, so the battalion had been incorporated into the infantry.) Major Ehle was standing by General Nehring when a British fighter-bomber suddenly came out of the sun. Everybody "hit the dirt," but one shell ripped through Ehle's right hand, cutting an artery. The major got up, saluted Nehring, and tried to report himself wounded in the regulation manner, but the commander of the Afrika Korps jumped back in surprise and horror. The major's blood was spurting into his face.

Curt Ehle was given first aid and evacuated back to the hospital at Derna, where he woke up in the mortuary. The medics had thought he was dead.[42]

Lieutenant Colonel Westphal was also wounded that day, but, unlike Ehle, he had only himself to blame. He had gone forward with Rommel, who was conducting a reconnaissance of the Got el Ualeb Box, to make sure that the Stukas were attacking it correctly. En route, Rommel and Westphal had a disagreement, during which Rommel made a sharp remark. They were observing the situation from the soft-skinned part of their armored recon vehicle when they came under British artillery and mortar fire. Rommel dove for cover in the armored part of the car and shouted for Westphal to do the same. The colonel, however, was still sulking and did not obey. Suddenly there was an explosion beside the vehicles; Westphal flew through the air and landed on the desert floor with a huge piece of shrapnel in his upper thigh. The recon vehicle immediately took off; fortunately for Westphal, he was picked up by a Kübelwagen (the German equivalent of a jeep) and was taken to panzer army headquarters, from which he was evacuated back to Derna. Like Ehle, he would soon be on his way back to Europe.[43]

Meanwhile, a regiment from the 4th Armoured Brigade attacked toward Bir el Harmat, but without success. The rest of the brigade went south toward Bir Hacheim, securing more than thirty abandoned British tanks and capturing sixty Axis supply vehicles and two hundred Germans in the process. This haul was not insignificant, but it hardly justified the use of an armored brigade at a time when Rommel was throwing everything he could get his hands on at the 150th Infantry Brigade. The British Official History described this entire operation as "a wild goose chase."[44]

At 8:45 P.M., the British 201st Guards Brigade (which was being misused in a static role, guarding the Knightsbridge Box) sent a reinforced infantry column (with artillery and antitank guns) west along the Trigh Capuzzo, to shell one of the gaps by which Rommel's forces were receiving supplies. It was ambushed by the Afrika Korps. It lost 157 men missing, as well as five twenty-five-pounders and seven six-pounder antitank guns captured or knocked out; only a handful of its men ever returned.

On 31 May, Rommel struck the 150th Brigade with all available forces, including the Trieste and 90th Light Divisions and elements of the Afrika Korps. It was to no avail. The Germans recalled with admiration the stubborn and gallant defense put up by the 150th Infantry. Meanwhile, RAF fighters and fighter-bombers continued to attack German vehicles and supply columns, and Air Command Afrika met them with its Messerschmitts, while the Stuka dive-bombers blasted Gob el Ualeb. By the end of the day, the British had lost sixteen airplanes, mostly to German fighters. The Luftwaffe lost three fighters and two dive-bombers. No significant amounts of supplies were able to reach the Afrika Korps, but RAF losses were prohibitively high. Air Vice-Marshal Coningham signaled Air Marshal Tedder for replacements, pointing out that some British squadrons were now down to seven or eight operational aircraft.[45]

Despite their exhaustion, the greatly superior numbers of Rommel's forces began to tell on the stubborn defenders of Got el Ualeb. By the end of the day, Brigadier Haydon had been forced to commit his last reserves, and only eight of his thirty Matildas were still operational. As night fell, however, the Afrika Korps was also on its last legs. If supplies could not reach it by the next day, it would be finished. Only the superb conditioning and esprit de corps of the individual soldier had kept it going this far.

During the night of 31 May–1 June, Major Archer-Shee of the 10th Hussars was in the Cauldron, an unwilling guest of the Afrika Korps. He had been captured early in the battle, when the 3d Motor Brigade was overrun, and now he was parched with thirst. At this point he found himself in a makeshift POW compound, ringed by 88mm guns, on the edge of the minefields. He had had no water for some time. When he learned that Rommel's headquarters was nearby, he worked up his courage and demanded to see him. To his surprise, he was soon ushered into the presence of the Desert Fox. In broken German, he informed the C in C of Panzer Army Afrika that, if he could not provide his prisoners with food and water, he had no right to keep them. They should be fed and watered or returned to Allied lines immediately, he said.

Rommel listened sympathetically to the Hussar and then, to Archer-Shee's surprise, said: "You are getting exactly the same ration of water as the Afrika Korps and myself: half a cup. But I quite agree that we cannot go on like this. If we don't get a convoy through tonight I shall have to ask General Ritchie for terms. You can take a letter to him for me . . ."[46]

The Afrika Korps was that close to capitulation. But Rommel did receive enough supplies that night to keep fighting one more day. Meanwhile, about 600 prisoners from the 3d Indian Motor Brigade had been held for forty-eight hours without food or water. Since they still could not feed them or give them drink, the Germans released the enlisted men, who soon reached friendly lines at Bir Hacheim. The Free French gave them food and water, and they were eventually returned to their regiments, which were reorganizing on the Egyptian border. Another 200 men from the 3d Indian Motor had been freed earlier when a British raiding party discovered their provisional POW compound.[47]

On 1 June, the battered 150th Brigade was subjected to heavy dive-bombing attacks and was at last running low on ammunition. For yet another day it received no help from the Eighth Army, and, for the first time, there was no air support from the RAF, which had lost one-fifth of its 250 operational fighters and was now forced to conserve its strength. Rommel, on the other hand, had strengthened his attacking forces with more artillery and with elements of the 21st Panzer Division. The Afrika Korps signaled: "Positions have to be taken in hand-to-hand fight for each individual bunker."[48] But the bunkers were beginning to fall, and the 150th was under heavy attack from all sides. Rommel threw in his last available reserves. The first attack of the 5th Panzer Regiment was repulsed, and a dozen more panzers were knocked out. Rommel's personal escort, the Kiehl Combat Group (a battalion-sized force sometimes called the *Kampfstaffel*) was also checked, and, following another heavy Stuka attack, General von Bismarck sent in the 104th Panzer Grenadier Regiment. It made surprisingly rapid progress. Rommel, who was right up at the front with his men, realized that the British resistance was at last faltering. "The enemy's weakening!" he cried in a Swabian accent, into which he always lapsed when he was excited. Turning to Captain Reissmann, the commander of the assault spearhead, he ordered: "Wave a white flag and he'll surrender!" Reissmann did not believe him but naturally obeyed the command. To his astonishment, the British dropped their weapons and walked out of their positions, their hands raised.[49]

Not all of the British positions fell as easily as this one, but fall they all did. A platoon from the Green Howards was the last to be overwhelmed. Brigadier Haydon—who had led his command with what Ronald Lewin called "conspicuous skill and gallantry" in both France and North Africa—was among the dead.[50] The British had lost the 150th Infantry Brigade Group and the 44th Royal Tank Regiment, as well as 3,000 prisoners, 101 tanks and armored cars captured or destroyed, 124 guns of all kinds, and large quantities of supplies and equipment of every description (except ammunition). The Afrika Korps had been saved. But it had been a close-run thing. Indeed, some of the Allies had already claimed their victory. On 2 June, Radio Moscow announced that Colonel General Rommel had been captured. Apparently they had confused him with General Cruewell, who was conducting himself in typical Afrika Korps fashion as a prisoner of war. Taken to Shepheard's, the famous hotel in Cairo, Cruewell glanced at his luxurious accommodations and observed that they would make excellent headquarters for Rommel. Adolf Hitler was so pleased by the remark that he had the story broadcast around the world.

The victory at Got el Ualeb was not without its costs, however. Among others, Rommel's chief of staff, Maj. Gen. Alfred Gause, was a casualty. Following the Desert Fox, he had gotten too close to the front and was nearly hit by a British tank shell. The force of the blast hurled him backward through the air and bounced him off a panzer, leaving him with a severe brain concussion. He would not be fit for duty again until December. This came right on top of the losses of Generals Cruewell and von Vaerst, and Colonel Westphal. But Rommel's philosophy was that no one was indispensable. He abolished Cruewell's position, named Bayerlein acting chief of staff of the Panzer Army, and replaced Westphal with Col. Friedrich Wilhelm von Mellenthin.[51] At the same time, Maj. Baron Hans von Luck, the commander of Rommel's favorite unit, the 3d Panzer Reconnaissance Battalion, was forced to step down. He had been severely wounded (shrapnel in the groin) on 27 May, but, with typical Afrika Korps tenor, had continued to command his battalion from a jeep, with the help of morphine injections. Now, however, the battalion medical officer sent him to the casualty clearing station at Derna, which soon put him on a hospital ship bound for Italy. The major was close to tears because of his disappointment and rage when he handed his command over to Captain Everth.[52]

Located about forty miles to the rear—too far from the action— the Headquarters, Eighth Army, and the XXX Corps HQ realized the situation the 150th Brigade was in, but too late to help it. They only began to move to save the brigade on 1 June, and even then the effort did not amount to much. The 1st South African Division was asked to send an ammunition train to Got el Ualeb. A convoy was quickly organized, and a group of brave men volunteered and rushed to the south, but they disappeared and were never heard from again. That same day, the 10th Indian Brigade Group was ordered to make a night attack against Aslag Ridge, but it could not concentrate rapidly enough, so General Messervy called off the operation. It was already too late anyway. The 150th Brigade Group had ceased to exist. "[The] 150th Brigade was down and out before Ritchie realized it," Sir Frank recalled.[53]

Despite his thin margin of victory, his heavy losses, and the serious personnel losses in the higher echelons, Rommel had broken the encirclement and fought his way out of the trap into which he had plunged himself. In addition, the capture of Got el Ualeb instantly became a major asset. A serious breach now existed in the Gazala Line. At this point, an ordinary commander might have been content to pull his battered strike force out of the Cauldron, retreat to the west, and proudly brag about how he escaped a deadly trap in the face of vastly superior enemy forces. Rommel never even considered this course of action. He turned south, toward Bir Hacheim, the southern anchor of the Gazala Line, where he had already decided to fight his next battle.

Unbelievably enough, the mood of optimism still reigned at Eighth Army HQ. "I am distressed over the loss of 150th Brigade after so gallant a fight," Ritchie signaled Cairo, "but still consider the situation favourable to us and getting better daily."[54]

The Eighth Army commander, General Messervy recalled, "was rather stupidly optimistic in remarks and demeanour, but uncertain beneath it all." He now held another series of committee meetings, in which various counterattack plans were considered and disposed of, usually on logistical grounds. The idea of a drive along the coast by the 1st South African Division was discussed, an advance by Briggs's 5th Indian Division around Bir Hacheim against Rommel's line of communications was talked about, and the concept of a frontal attack against the Cauldron was debated at length.[55] Rommel, however, acted first.

He did not believe in committee meetings.

CHAPTER IV: The Cauldron and Bir Hacheim

THE BATTLE OF THE CAULDRON

Field Marshal Albert Kesselring, OB South, commander in chief of the Second Air Fleet, and the nominal superior of General Rommel, was an unhappy man during the first week of June 1942. Although beyond a doubt a competent military leader, as he was to prove in the Italian campaigns of 1943–1945, his service had been in the artillery and in General Staff or aviation positions. Polished, sophisticated, well schooled, well connected, and highly cultured, he had nothing in his background or education to prepare him for Erwin Rommel, the tough, blunt, hard-charging, and sometimes embarrassingly outspoken commander of Panzer Army Afrika. Rommel's method of leadership shocked and appalled the urbane Kesselring, who was accustomed to visiting a headquarters and finding the commander there. Rommel, on the other hand, felt it was his job to fight the battle; he had staff officers to handle visiting Italian and air force generals.

Kesselring knew that speaking to Rommel would have no effect—his words (like orders the Desert Fox did not like) would be ignored. Instead, the field marshal decided to try to influence the panzer general's behavior through two of his more trusted General Staff officers, Alfred Gause and Siegfried Westphal. As an indirect result of Rommel's method of leadership, he found them sharing a room in the seaside hospital at Derna, along with Curt Ehle, the wounded battalion commander.

"My dear Gause," Kesselring began, ". . . things can't go on like this. Rommel must not cruise about at the front line. He's no longer a divisional or corps commander. As an army commander it must be possible to reach him. You must make him see this."

If Kesselring expected agreement from these two fellow General Staff officers, he was disappointed. "Herr Feldmarschall," Gause replied, "the colonel general can't be restrained. He simply drives off, and then the wireless truck can't keep up with him or gets shot up. . . . But how could he lead here in Africa from the rear? This is the type of warfare where everything has to be decided from the front."

As Kesselring considered this statement, Westphal added: "Herr Feldmarschall, it's impossible to pin Rommel down. In order to make grave decisions he has to have a picture of the terrain."

The conservative and orthodox Bavarian remained unconvinced. "One day it might have disastrous consequences, gentlemen," he said, gravely.[1]

Major Ehle took no part in this discussion, which he watched with remarkable detachment. He had recently been visited by some of his officers, who had presented him with bottles of champagne. Thus fortified, he was not at all bothered by the visit from the field marshal—or by anything else.[2]

It was a good thing Albert Kesselring could not see through space, for, at the front, Erwin Rommel was off and running again.

"Get into the car, Bayerlein," Col. Gen. Erwin Rommel snapped. "I'm going to Bir Hacheim."

Thus was Col. Fritz Bayerlein inducted into his new job as acting chief of staff of Panzer Army Afrika.[3] Both the move and the statement were typical of Bayerlein's new boss. There was no warmth in the announcement, no friendship, no false platitudes, none of the usual amenities, and the customary "congratulations on your promotion" had been dispensed with entirely. The two men had been friends since the 1920s, when they served together in Dresden at the infantry school, but those days were long forgotten. Bayerlein was now just another subordinate who was expected to perform at the highest level of loyalty and efficiency; if he did not, he would be sent back to Germany "on his camel." (In the early days of the Afrika Korps, Rommel had sacked several General Staff officers, two regimental commanders, a division commander, and his own chief of staff—among others—for being disloyal and/or inefficient.)

Rommel did not expect serious resistance from the 1st Free French Brigade at Bir Hacheim. Apparently he had succumbed to the propaganda image of the Free French soldiers as "rebels" and "adventurers"—certainly not first-rate soldiers. The Italian failure to subdue them he put down to the ineptitude or lack of offensive spirit on the part of the latter-day Romans. (This view was incorrect in the extreme; witnesses later recalled that the ground around Bir Hacheim was littered with the wrecks of Italian tanks.) In any case, he initially sent only the 90th Light and Trieste Motorized Divisions to deal with them. He covered their rear from intervention by the British armor by continuing to hold the Cauldron with the Afrika Korps and the Ariete Division.

Despite his decision to use his main panzer forces in a basically defensive role, the Desert Fox was anything but passive. On 2 June, he sent the 21st Panzer Division in a sortie to the north, where it attacked Elwet et Tamar and drove "Stopcol" to Acroma in disorder. The 4th Armoured Brigade tried to intervene, and one of its regiments was mauled. When Bismarck's division returned, it had destroyed nineteen Grants, eight field guns, and two self-propelled artillery pieces, without loss to itself.

Meanwhile, on 2 June, 90th Light and Trieste began to invest Bir Hacheim. General Pierre Koenig, the commander of the 1st Free French Brigade, rejected the usual surrender demand, but the Axis did not launch a ground attack; they had decided to soften the position via aerial bombardment instead. Air activity was limited on 2 June due to sandstorms, but the next day saw several dogfights over Bir Hacheim. Stuka dive-bombers with their screaming sirens launched numerous attacks on the French box, while RAF fighter-bombers strafed and bombed the soft-skinned vehicles of 90th Light and Trieste, and fighters from both sides tried to intervene against the activities of the other. In addition, the antiaircraft defenses of Bir Hacheim were very good. During the first two days of aerial fighting, the Luftwaffe lost thirteen airplanes (ten of them Stukas, as well as a Ju-88 bomber and two Me-109 fighters), the RAF lost thirteen aircraft, and the Italians lost three. Nine of the Stukas were shot down by a single South African fighter squadron, despite the fact that they were escorted by Lt. Hans Joachim "Jochen" Marseilles, the leading ace of the North African war. The South African pilots, however, had to pay a high price for their success. Marseilles shot down six of them in eleven minutes, despite the fact that his 20mm cannon jammed after firing only ten rounds, and he fought the rest of the battle with only his machine guns.[4]

Kesselring, predictably, was angry over his air fleet's losses and flew to the front, where he gave the Desert Fox a rare dressing down. "We can't go on like this, Rommel!" he shouted. "Attack the bloody nest with all available ground troops. Abandon these economical combat tactics!"[5]

Instead of yelling back (as was his custom), Rommel responded by launching a ground attack, led by Colonel Wolz, the commander of the 135th Motorized Flak Regiment. Wolz and his 88s had saved the Afrika Korps a few days before, but his ad hoc combat group (which consisted of a reconnaissance battalion and some AT guns) made no impression on Bir Hacheim. The 90th Light and Trieste did little better, although they did tighten the noose around the French fortress somewhat.

With Bir Hacheim invested, Rommel returned to the Cauldron, where he and Nehring waited for the British armored onslaught, "which," Colonel von Mellenthin recalled, "to us seemed to be very long in coming."[6]

Mellenthin was right: the British were inexcusably slow in reacting to their favorable situation, which was growing less favorable with every passing day. The Afrika Korps used the lull to recover and repair some of its damaged armor. By 2 June, its strength stood at 130 serviceable battle tanks, compared to the 282 with which it started the battle.[7] The British, on the other hand, had about 400 tanks left (a clear three-to-one superiority), but they did nothing.

General Auchinleck wanted Ritchie to attack west toward Bir Temrad with the 1st South African Division, against the Italians and the 15th Rifle Brigade. Ritchie discussed the possibility (dubbed Operation "Limerick"), but finally gave up the idea due to the strong objections of Gen. Dan Pienaar, the commander of the 1st South African. In addition, Ritchie and both of his corps commanders were afraid that they might not be able to hold off German armor while such an advance was being made. In the end, on the evening of 3 June (after Auchinleck sent him a message warning him that he was losing the initiative), Ritchie signaled Cairo and informed the C in C that he had decided to crush the German forces in the Cauldron. General Gott, the commander of the XIII Corps, refused to assume responsibility for the new operation, so Ritchie turned it over to Messervy and Maj. Gen. H. R. Briggs, the commanders of the 7th Armoured and 5th Indian Divisions, respectively. General Norrie, who should have been placed in charge of the entire operation, was bypassed altogether.

On 4 June, as the lull continued for the third day, Rommel decided to regain some more of his tank strength by carrying out a panzer-salvaging operation in the Bir el Harmat area the next day. Accordingly, elements of the 15th Panzer Division opened up several gaps in the minefields southwest of Bir el Harmat. This turned out to be a tremendous piece of luck for the Germans and a terrible misfortune for the British, as we shall see.

The British plan to annihilate the Cauldron was named Operation "Aberdeen." It called for the Allied infantry to drive a wedge through the enemy's front line and antitank screen in the dark; then, at first light, the British armor would be committed. Specifically, the 10th Indian Brigade (Brigadier Charles H. Boucher), supported by the 4th Royal Tank Regiment, would advance west under the cover of darkness, pass around the northern end of the inner minefield running from Bir el Harmat to Bir Hacheim (this minefield would protect its left flank), and breach the Axis position on Dahar el Aslag Ridge, which was held by the Ariete Division. At dawn, the 22d Armoured Brigade (now operating under the 7th Armoured Division and replacing the battered 4th Armoured Brigade) would pass through the breach, advance westward, and seize Sidi Muftah. The 9th Indian Brigade would follow the 22d Armoured and consolidate the captured ground by building fortified localities or "boxes" in the vicinity of Aslag Ridge and Bir et Tamar. Command of the operation would alternate between the 7th Armoured and 5th Indian Divisions, depending upon which formation was chiefly engaged. Brigadier

John C. O. Marriott's 201st Guards Brigade in the Knightsbridge Box was kept in reserve. Gott's XIII Corps was to launch a secondary attack against Sidra Ridge with the 32d Army Tank Brigade (and the attached 7th Green Howards), a mile or two north of the Trigh Capuzzo. Later, according to the plan, this brigade would exploit the success gained in the Cauldron by advancing on Tmimi; however, there was no cooperation between the British XIII and XXX Corps. A joint 7th Armoured/5th Indian tactical headquarters was set up near Bir el Harmat.

At the last moment, the 1st Duke of Cornwall's Light Infantry (DCLI), the vanguard of the 10th Indian Division, arrived in Tobruk on 3 June. The battalion—which had traveled 1,500 miles in two weeks—was rushed to the southern end of the Allied line, to guard the left flank at Bir el Harmat. General Briggs felt that more forces were needed on the left and asked that the 157th Field Regiment, Royal Artillery, be attached to it, since it had neither armor nor artillery, but General Messervy assured him that the flank was adequately manned. Apparently he thought the minefields alone would be strong enough to discourage the Germans. Map 7, p. 101, shows the situation in the Cauldron sector at dawn on 5 June.

The basic British idea—to attack the Cauldron—was a good one, but it was long overdue. The execution of the maneuver, however, turned out to be extremely poor; in fact, one participant likened it to sticking your arm into a wasps' nest. In addition, British command arrangements can best be described as weird, because they violated every possible interpretation of the military principle of unity of command. The XIII Corps was to command the attack on Sidra Ridge, and Aslag Ridge was the responsibility of the XXX Corps, while responsibility for the main breakthrough was to rotate between the 7th Armoured and 5th Indian Divisions. And all of this was to be done at night, over unfamiliar terrain! Since Roman times, there have been those who have held to the adage that it is better to have one poor commander in charge of an operation than two good ones. While I would not go so far as to say that, I would point out that it is a generally accepted principle of war that one person—and only one person—should be in charge of every operation, and he should have full authority and responsibility for that operation. Perhaps Brigadier

THE CAULDRON, DAWN, JUNE 5, 1942

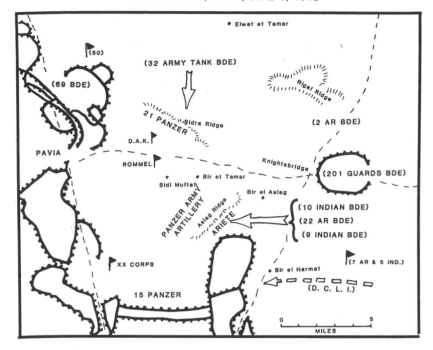

W. G. F. Jackson put it better when he wrote: "There has to be a unifying force to steer all the many strong-willed men in an agreed direction. That force is the commander's will, but it cannot make any impact without a policy and plan which all can understand."[8]

Allied tactical intelligence was also uncharacteristically bad. The Ariete Division "false fronted" the British, who failed to see through the deception; as a result, they thought that the Italians' main defensive line was half a mile closer to them than it actually was. In addition, intelligence placed both the 21st and 15th Panzer Divisions in the vicinity of Sidi Muftah, near the northern face of the Cauldron. The 21st Panzer was defending this sector, but the 15th was five or six miles farther south.

At 2:50 A.M., the British history recorded, "the night exploded with the shock of heavy guns. The earth rocked . . ."[9] Four regiments of

Royal Artillery, supporting the 5th Indian Division, opened up a concentrated bombardment, mainly with their excellent twenty-five-pounder guns—field howitzers of 88mm caliber, which were respectfully called "Ratschbum" (Crash-Bang) by the men of the DAK.[10] This barrage tipped off Rommel and his men that a major attack was coming; unfortunately, that is about all it accomplished. Because Ariete's positions were farther west than the Allies thought, the bombardment fell short on empty desert and did no damage.

Prior to dawn, Boucher's 10th Indian Brigade pushed forward toward Peter, the northern gap in the minefields, and captured all its initial objectives with deceptive ease. But when the 2d Battalion, West Yorkshire Regiment of the 9th Indian Brigade, and a squadron of the 4th RTR passed through the 10th Indian to exploit the breach, they were halted 1,200 yards farther on. It was daylight before the Allies realized their mistake. Ariete, always the best of the Italian divisions, put up a fierce resistance, in spite of its horrendous equipment, and inflicted heavy losses on the Indians. The Allied generals countered by committing the 22d Armoured Brigade (156 tanks—Grants, Stuarts, and Crusaders) to the battle, and finally managed to shove Ariete off the ridge, but the Italians retreated in good order, fighting all the way. The 22d Armoured pushed forward between two and three miles when the Italians fell into line with the guns of Panzer Army Artillery, which promptly brought the Allied advance to a halt. At a range of only 1,000 yards, Colonel Krause's massed German and Italian cannons, howitzers, and antitank guns blasted Lt. Col. Douglas Thorburn's 2d Highland Light Infantry (HLI) to bits.[11] Brigadier Carr's 22d Armoured was also in trouble. Near Bir el Scerab, just north of the 2d HLI, it ran into a nest of antitank guns, which were covering the 21st Panzer Division north of Sidi Muftah. After suffering heavy casualties and losing sixty tanks (mainly to the 88s), the brigade—which had no infantry, artillery, or antitank gun support—withdrew a few hundred yards behind the 2d Highland Light, which was holding the ridge at Bir et Tamar.

Meanwhile, to the south, the 22d Armoured's shift to the north and subsequent withdrawal dangerously exposed Colonel Langram's 2d West Yorkshires.

"It must have been about now that the German armour (15th Panzer Division) counterattacked," Captain Wiberg of the West

Yorkshires recalled. "They had, of course, been waiting to do this, and completely overran our two forward companies and more or less wiped them out. All nine officers were killed except one, who was taken prisoner."[12]

Colonel Krause's guns continued to blast the 2d Highland Light Infantry, while the 22d Armoured Brigade, a few hundred yards to the rear, did not lift a finger to help them. Colonel Thorburn appealed to Brigadier Boucher for armored support; the brigadier urgently recommended that the request be approved and passed it on to General Briggs, who also backed up the call for assistance. The 22d Armoured, however, did not move. "Resolution did not mark the handling of our armour at the crisis of the battle," the historian of the 5th Indian Division noted with both irony and understatement.[13]

Meanwhile, under a hail of Axis gunfire, one company of the 2d HLI was reduced to a strength of twelve men.[14]

About noon, the Germans and Italians counterattacked the 2d Highland Light in strength, spearheaded by forty tanks from the 8th Panzer Regiment. Judging that his brigade had nothing to do with this action, Brigadier Carr, the commander of the 22d Armoured (which could easily have intervened) did nothing to help as the panzers systematically smashed the helpless infantry battalion. Once again, the Allies violated the principles of combined-arms operations. Frantically, Colonel Thorburn rushed to the armoured brigade and almost begged them to help his battalion. He was standing on top of a tank, pleading with a squadron commander, when he was hit in the head by a piece of shrapnel. He was carried away by his own men, and his wound was dressed; then he resumed command long enough to order the remnants of the battalion to abandon the ridge of Bir et Tamar and to retire behind the Gurkhas. He was then driven back to the rear for medical attention. Major Kindersley took charge of the survivors and took them back to the Trigh Bir Hacheim, to lick their wounds. In the meantime, Colonel Langram also brought the 2d West Yorkshires off the battlefield, despite the fact that the 15th Panzer Division had destroyed almost all of his trucks. The battalion had lost 180 killed. All six of its two-pounder antitank guns had been destroyed and most of its other equipment was lost.[15] Clearly, the Allied attack in the center was over.

"There appears to have been a complete misunderstanding between the 22d Armoured Brigade and Nine Brigade as to the capa-
bilities and tasks of the two brigades," Brigadier Fletcher remarked
shortly after the battle.

> The 22d Armoured Brigade appears to have thought that a
> battalion could establish itself in a box in the Desert in a mat-
> ter of half an hour . . .
> I consider that infantry who have to operate with tanks
> should be trained with them. . . . In the Desert infantry require
> forty-eight hours in which to establish a box which can stand
> by itself against an enemy tank attack . . . Lack of mutual un-
> derstanding and common doctrines extended beyond the fail-
> ure of the tanks and infantry to understand each other.[16]

To the north, the British XIII Corps threw Brigadier Willison's 32d
Army Tank Brigade into an attack against the 21st Panzer Division
on Sidra Ridge. The Panzer Army operations officer, Colonel von
Mellenthin, later described it as "one of the most ridiculous attacks
of the campaign."[17] General Gott apparently did not attach too
much importance to this attack, because the British tankers were
supported by only a dozen field guns and a small infantry battalion—
both hopelessly inadequate. Rommel, on the other hand, considered
the ridge so important that he guarded it with the entire 21st Panzer
Division. The XIII Corps artillery remained silent as the 32d Tank
advanced in broad daylight across open terrain—a perfect target for
the Germans. As they approached the ridge, the veterans of the Siege
of Tobruk were shelled by the 155th Panzer Artillery Regiment, and,
as they came still closer, they were blasted by the grenadiers, antitank gunners, and panzers. Lieutenant Colonel H. R. B. "Fairey"
Foote, the commander of the 7th RTR, had two tanks shot out from
under him and was wounded in the neck, but continued to direct
his regiment on foot, using hand signals. The battle was, in many
ways, typical of the entire Eighth Army at this stage of its development—incredible courage, neutralized by inferior tactical doctrine
and the absence of any hint of combined-arms fighting. The army
tank brigade was cut to ribbons. Finally, the tanks of the 5th Panzer

Regiment, closely supported by the antitank guns, caught the brigade in the flank and pushed it back—into a minefield. The 32d Army Tank Brigade lost fifty of its seventy Matilda and Valentine tanks and practically ceased to exist. Brigadier Willison escaped the slaughter and pulled the remnants of his command back to Tobruk, where he began the process of hastily rebuilding it.

While the 32d Army Tank was being annihilated, the 2d Armoured Brigade Group (one tank regiment, one motor battalion, and one regiment of Royal Horse Artillery) arrived at a point seven miles south of Knightsbridge. Here it was placed under the command of the 7th Armoured Division and received a number of conflicting orders that cancelled each other out.[18] It was still far from the battlefield when the fighting reached its climax.

By early afternoon, the 9th Indian, 10th Indian, and 22d Armoured Brigades were extended along Aslag Ridge, in a line running northward from the tip of the loop minefield toward Bir et Tamar. The minefield itself was apparently still considered sufficient protection for the left flank, because the 1st Duke of Cornwall's Light Infantry had still not been reinforced. Earlier in the day, General Briggs had ordered the 4th Field Regiment (Lieutenant Colonel Truscott) to support the DCLI, but later these guns were summoned by General Messervy to support the tanks of his 7th Armoured Division. Still later, Briggs asked Messervy to attach the 157th Field Regiment to the Duke of Cornwall's, but was turned down again.[19] At this point, about 5:00 P.M., the Desert Fox judged that the British offensive had shot its bolt in both the north and the center, and it was time to launch some attacks of his own. Unlike the pitiful efforts of the morning, however, these were controlled by the will of a determined commander who did not believe in half measures, and they were devastating. Rommel ordered a general advance with all available forces.

"It had taken Eighth Army four days to think up Aberdeen," Barnett wrote later. "It took Rommel half a day to plan and launch a counter-stroke against [it]."[20] General von Bismarck started the offensive by driving through the gap caused by the destruction of the 32d Army Tank Brigade; then he drove to the southeast in an effort to double the British right (northern) flank back on its center. Almost simultaneously, Ariete attacked to the east and elements of the 15th Panzer Division, led by Colonel Crasemann and accompanied by General Rommel himself, emerged from the minefields to the south. The failure of the British reconnaissance units to discover the gaps in the Bir el Harmat minefield, or to properly protect their left flank, now became apparent with disastrous clarity. Without tanks or artillery, the 1st Duke of Cornwall's Light Infantry did not stand a chance and was quickly overrun. As Crasemann turned north (to double the British left flank back on the center), he was joined by Kampfgruppe Wolz, which was coming up from Bir Hacheim for the decisive attack. Crasemann barreled almost unopposed into the Allied rear, overrunning or scattering the headquarters of the 7th Armoured Division, the 5th Indian Division, and the 9th and 10th Indian Brigades about 7:00 P.M. Messervy and Briggs managed to escape at the last moment, but Brigadier Boucher was up at the front, visiting his troops, when the storm broke. On their way back, Boucher's party ran into German and Italian troop columns and the brigadier became separated from his escort and signal trucks. Alone except for three Baluchis (Indians), the commander (who was in a troop carrier) tried to find his way through German lines, but his vehicle suffered a direct hit, which killed one of the Baluchis. The general and his two companions slept the night in a derelict three-ton truck, but the following morning found themselves on foot in no-man's-land; soon they heard the sound of a battle between the German 90th Light Division and the 4/10th Baluchi. They set out for friendly lines but were soon under machine-gun fire from a patrol from the 90th Light. Running and ducking, Boucher spotted a German artillery battery and realized that there were German guns all around. (This was almost certainly the 190th Motorized Artillery Regiment.) He would have to hide out first if he wanted to escape. He found a slit trench, covered the two Indians with sand, and used twigs of scrub to provide an air passage; he then covered himself in the same manner.

A few minutes later, another German battery arrived. As the battle continued, the RAF attacked the German guns, and a German gunner dove into the slit trench. After the British airplanes flew away, the gunner saw one of Boucher's boots showing out of a nearby mound of sand. He decided to take it and its partner off the supposed corpse; imagine his surprise when he pulled out a living British brigadier instead! When they saw what had happened, the two Indians surrendered as well.[21]

Back at the front, meanwhile, Allied command and communications were completely broken. Two battalions of Brigadier B. C. Fletcher's 9th Indian Brigade and the survivors of the 2d West Yorkshires infantry battalion hastily tried to check Crasemann and Wolz and were quickly overrun. Meanwhile, the Luftwaffe launched a major attack on the Knightsbridge Box, inflicting heavy losses on the 201st Guards Brigade and temporarily neutralizing the last of the British reserves, except the 2d Armoured, which was still paralyzed seven miles to the south.

Rommel was executing the classic double envelopment. Although it was not nearly on the scale of Stalingrad, it was at least of the same effectiveness. Without central command, the Allied units were left to fend for themselves. Captain Wiberg of the West Yorkshires observed, "All manner of transport from other units, including, I am sad to say, perfectly good anti-tank guns, appeared, entirely unorganized, moving eastward as though they were on a gold rush."[22] Colonel A. H. Napier, the chief engineer officer of the 5th Indian Division, recalled "a disorderly stream of miscellaneous trucks and lorries, going away from the enemy, with a tendency to hurry and apparently motivated by fear. . . . The troops who had set out that morning . . . were now being smashed and decimated and split and driven in flight, overrun and captured, pursued and harried, shelled and dive-bombed, encircled and crushed by armored forces."[23] The 22d Armoured Brigade, now under attack from elements of the 15th Panzer Division, was in no condition to restore the situation. A large part of it managed to withdraw before Rommel could complete his encirclement and spent the night east of the Trigh Bir Hacheim, having lost about half of its tanks. Meanwhile, Rommel's trap closed. The 9th and 10th Indian Brigades, the Support Group of the 22d Armoured Brigade (including the 107th Regiment, Royal Horse Artillery), and the 4th, 28th, and 157th Field Regiments, Royal Artillery, among others, were encircled in the Cauldron.

Following the loss of his headquarters, General Briggs, the commander of the 5th Indian Division, fled to the El Adem Box, where he began to reorganize the remnants of his command. His cocommander, General Messervy, reestablished the headquarters of the 7th Armoured Division in the Knightsbridge Box, where he at least had one more or less intact brigade. Even at this late moment, a determined and coordinated counterattack by the remaining British motorized and tank units might have at least rescued their encircled strike force from the Cauldron, but no such attempt was made. Apparently the Allied generals were stunned by the sudden reversal of their fortunes. "The British system of command was too complicated to deal with the unexpected, and was no match for the strong personal control of the enemy Commander," the British Official History recorded.[24]

Rommel, meanwhile, was up at the front with his troops, personally leading the way. He was, as Gen. (then Major) Sir John Hackett wrote, "bold, imaginative, and brave, with a tactical sense at times approaching genius. His method of command was forceful, direct, and personal. If he wanted something done, he was there to get it done and he was harsh on those he thought had failed him. There was no better commander of armored troops in a fluid battle on either side in this theater of war and no one was more willingly followed by troops. They understood him as thoroughly as he understood them. He led, as all good leaders do, from the inside."[25]

When day broke on 6 June 1942, the twelfth day of the battle, the Afrika Korps was concentrated against the trapped remnants of the Aberdeen forces, which were holding out along a line from Dahar el Aslag Ridge to Bir el Aslag. While the 15th Panzer Division barred the British escape route to the east, the Panzer Army artillery blasted the Cauldron with every available gun, and the 21st Panzer and Ariete systematically crushed one battalion after another. First the 4/10th Baluchi Regiment was overrun, followed that afternoon by the Gurkhas, the 3/9th Jat Regiment, the 50th Reconnaissance Regiment, and all of the artillery. The gunners of the South Notts Hussars Regiment (Lt. Col. Bill Seeley) fought to the bitter end. Its men were almost exclusively from Nottingham, and they were armed with

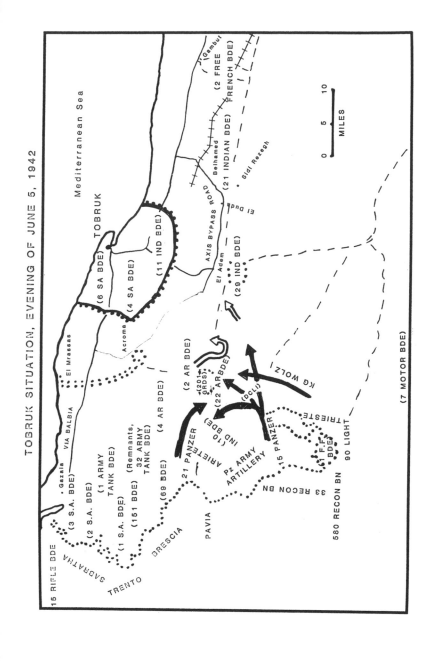

TOBRUK SITUATION, EVENING OF JUNE 5, 1942

twenty-five-pounders. They also had a battery of two-pounder anti-tank guns, on loan from the Northumberland Hussars. Along with the Northumberland Fusiliers and Lieutenant Colonel de Graz's Reconnaissance Regiment, they had started the battle supporting the 22d Armoured Brigade, but were now attached to the 10th Indian Brigade Group.

"Never for a moment did the shelling stop," a survivor recalled. Casualties mounted, and "vehicles were burning everywhere. The enemy, with their guns just out of sight, could direct their fire with great accuracy on the mass of men and vehicles in the Cauldron below . . . and presently a large column, many miles long [it was the 90th Light Division] appeared from the south behind [us] . . . thus sealing the fate of the luckless brigade . . ."[26]

Meanwhile, the 21st Panzer Division attacked from the north. Captain Riepold, a company commander in the 5th Panzer Regiment, particularly distinguished himself leading the tank attacks on the northern face of the pocket—so much so that General Nehring (who accompanied the panzers in a Kübelwagen) recommended him for the Knight's Cross. (Riepold did receive the decoration, but posthumously—he was killed in action on 16 June.)[27]

When the German tanks finally struck, the men of the Recce regiment tried to destroy them at close quarters, but were machine-gunned by the infantry or by supporting panzers. Soon only one intact antitank gun remained, but its crew was gone—either killed or missing. Colonel de Graz—whose vehicle was on fire—ran over to it but was shot and killed before he could fire it. Soon the entire 10th Indian Brigade was overrun—nearly every vehicle was ablaze, and a thick black veil of smoke covered the sky. Even so, the South Notts. Hussars formed a perimeter and continued to hold out, their guns pointed in all directions. Then the panzers closed in on them from all sides, their main battle guns and machine guns blazing. Colonel Seeley's tank was knocked out and caught on fire. The wounded colonel and his adjutant were dragged away from the burning wreck, but both died later in a German field hospital. Of the more than 5,000 men in the 10th Indian Brigade Group, only one officer escaped. Six months later he returned to the Cauldron and found the battlefield untouched. The gunners of the South Notts. Hussars were still at their posts. They had fought to the last man.[28]

That evening, Nehring reported the capture of 3,100 men, ninety-six guns, and thirty-seven antitank guns. Apparently he did not bother to count the dead. The 22d Armoured Brigade Support Group had been destroyed, as well as four regiments of artillery and the 10th Indian Brigade Group; two battalions of the 9th Indian Brigade had been annihilated; and the 21st Indian Brigade had lost a battalion, as well as all of its antitank guns.[29] Among the prisoners was Brigadier Desmond Young of the Indian division. Rommel had captured the man who would later become his foremost biographer.

Meanwhile, disorganization was spreading in the Eighth Army. During the day the 4th Armoured Brigade, which was reorganizing near Commonwealth Keep after its heavy losses four days before, was returned to Messervy's command, giving him control of all three British armored brigades. But all three were badly battered, especially the 22d Armoured, which was placed in reserve northeast of the Knightsbridge Box. The 2d Armoured did make an attempt to reach the Cauldron, but clashed with elements of the 21st Panzer Division at Sidra Ridge and was not able to advance further. The 4th Armoured was meant to go into action between Bir el Aslag and Bir el Harmat—far south of the Cauldron—but did not reach the area until late afternoon, by which time it was all over in the pocket. The 4th did pick up a British major—the only survivor of the Support Group of the 22d Armoured.

The Germans claimed to have destroyed or captured 115 tanks and armored cars in the Cauldron. These figures are about right: the number of British cruiser tanks dropped from 300 on the night of 4 June to 132 on the morning of 7 June. Of this battle, Rommel commented:

As I expected, the British High Command did not throw strong elements of two divisions in the Gazala Line into the battle in order to form a second *Schwerpunkt* [main concentration] in front of the 21st Panzer Division, nor was any unit of the 2nd

South African Division thrown into the battle. At such a critical moment all available forces should have been brought into the action. What is the advantage of enjoying an overall superiority if you allow your enemy to smash your formations one after the other; your enemy who manages in single actions to concentrate superior forces at the decisive point?[30]

And what was the rest of the Eighth Army doing while its armored division and the 5th Indian were being smashed?

On 6 June, General Ritchie fell back on the idea of an advance westward from the Gazala Line—a course of action General Auchinleck had advocated for some time. He relayed his orders to General Gott, who picked the strike force: one brigade group of the 1st South African Division. General Pienaar was only given a few hours to organize the attack, which was to be launched without armor or air support.

Gott and Pienaar were very different commanders and very different people. Pienaar had distinguished himself in Abyssinia and was a skillful and shrewd tactician, but he was also a pessimist by nature, he possessed the Afrikaners' distrust of authority, and he liked to consider every angle of a situation before taking action. "Strafer" Gott was a much more optimistic sort. They met twice on 6 June. Nothing is known about these meetings, but Pienaar made it clear that he did not care for this hastily thrown together attack.

Pienaar's plan called for one company from each of his three brigades to advance between 4:45 A.M. and 5:30 A.M. on 7 June, along a fifteen-mile front to a depth of two to six miles; then a special raiding force (including two infantry companies and nine armored cars) was to strike into the enemy's line of communications.

The attacking forces ran into the Italian Sabratha and Trento Divisions, and the German 15th Rifle Brigade, and went nowhere. The South Africans lost 280 men—150 of them missing. Gott later bitterly complained that Pienaar could have broken through and turned the Axis northern flank, but under the circumstances this is extremely doubtful. Even Gott's own operations order called for a "raid," not a breakthrough.[31] Pienaar was never given time to launch a prepared attack.

• • •

While Rommel continued to destroy or maul their units one by one, indecision and command paralysis continued to dominate British higher commands. About this time, General Messervy met Brigadier Renton somewhere in the desert.

"What is the main idea in the battle now?" Renton asked.

"I wish I knew—the only real order is to fight Germans wherever you see them," the commander of the Desert Rats replied.[32]

Meanwhile, during the first week of June, the bulk of Maj. Gen. T. W. Rees's 10th Indian Division arrived in the zone of operations. Brigadier J. J. Purvis's 21st Brigade (minus the 1st Duke of Cornwall's Light Infantry) was sent to guard the vital RAF base at Gambut; Brigadier MacGregor's 20th Brigade moved up to occupy the three boxes covering the Trigh Capuzzo and the road from El Adem; and Brigadier R. G. Mountain's 25th Brigade was sent to guard the Sollum Pass.[33] The British were clearly planning a defense in depth in the Tobruk sector and were concerned that Rommel might try to cut their supply routes to Egypt or launch a raid against Gambut, to rob them of their air support. For the moment, however, the Desert Fox was not focusing on Tobruk. He was preparing to turn south, to settle the score with the garrison at Bir Hacheim, once and for all.

THE FALL OF BIR HACHEIM

Erwin Rommel realized that he would not have complete freedom of maneuver as long as the 1st Free French Brigade at Bir Hacheim held out in his rear. Even though he had been partially diverted by the Battle of the Cauldron, he had sent strong forces to capture it; however, despite several attacks, Bir Hacheim still showed no signs of yielding. "That accursed Bir Hacheim!" Rommel swore again and again.[34] Twice he had predicted its fall was imminent, and twice he had been proven wrong. And still it defied his every effort to take it.

Bir Hacheim was defended by Gen. Pierre Koenig, whose 1st Free French Brigade had 3,600 men, twenty-six field guns, sixty-two anti-tank guns, forty-four mortars, and an antiaircraft battalion, as well as a battalion of Jews. From 2 June to 9 June, it was subjected to 1,300 aerial attacks. However, the minefields were incredibly thick, and the French defenders put up a furious resistance and turned back the 90th Light and the Italian Trieste Motorized Divisions again and again. Two platoons of the 288th Special Purpose Unit (90th Light Division) could manage to gain only 800 meters in eight days, at a cost of two-thirds of their men killed or wounded.[35] The Stukas kept attacking, however, despite growing friction between Kesselring and Rommel over the issue of close air support. The Desert Air Force intercepted seven raids and shot down twenty-three dive-bombers, but still the air strikes continued, and the German fighters were far from idle. From the beginning of the battle until 10 June, the RAF reported the loss of seventy-six airplanes, against an estimated fifty-eight for the Axis.

During the night of 6–7 June, the 90th Light finally cleared several lanes in the minefield. The next morning it launched an all-out attack, closely supported by Kampfgruppe Wolz, coming back down from the Cauldron. Once again, however, it was turned back by the French and Jewish defenders.

On 8 June, Rommel demanded that Bir Hacheim be captured that very night. To accomplish this, he brought up reinforcements in the form of Group Hecker. This force, which included large elements of the 33d Panzer Engineer, 200th Panzer Engineer, and 900th Motorized Engineer Battalions, had been earmarked to launch an amphibious assault behind the Gazala Line but had been freed when Rommel abandoned the idea. He ordered Colonel Hecker, the Panzer Army engineer officer, to breach the minefield so that the 90th Light could reach and destroy the French and Jewish bunkers. The night attack was supported by strong Luftwaffe forces, including forty-five Stukas, ten Me-110s, and three Ju-88s, escorted by fifty-four Me-109 fighters, as well as by two infantry *Kampfgruppe* and the 190th Motorized Artillery Regiment. Hecker made good progress and pushed to within 500 yards of the main French positions, taking most of the Jewish battalion prisoner in the process.

The next day, OKW sent Rommel an order concerning the "numerous German political refugees" (i.e., Jews) who were fighting on the side of the Free French. The order read: "The Führer has ordered that they are to be terminated with extreme prejudice. They are to be liquidated mercilessly in combat. Where they are not, they are to be shot afterwards, immediately and forthwith, on the orders of the nearest German officer, insofar as they are not temporarily reprieved for the extraction of intelligence. The communications of this order in writing is forbidden. Commanders are to be given oral briefing."[36]

Not one member of Rommel's army remembers hearing this order, and no copy was found in his files after the war. Like other orders that displeased him, it simply disappeared. Apparently, as was the case before and since, he burned his copy of the order and never mentioned it to anyone. It was a dead issue. The Jews were treated humanely by their captors and then were turned over to the Italians, who treated them like all other prisoners of war.

On 9 June, Hecker renewed his attack, but it bogged down again. The colonel himself was wounded when his command vehicle ran over a mine.

Rommel was furious. "This accursed Bir Hacheim has taken a sufficient toll!" he shouted. "I'm going to leave it. We'll attack Tobruk." For more than a year, Tobruk had never been far from his mind.

Colonel Hecker objected, however. "Herr Colonel General, give me a battalion of German infantry to continue the attack. Now that we have already taken several strongpoints, I am convinced that we can bring the battle to a victorious conclusion."

With an effort, Rommel regained control of his temper. After a brief conference with Colonel Bayerlcin, he ordered Group Baade (the bulk of Lt. Col. Ernst-Guenther Baade's 115th Panzer Grenadier Regiment of the 15th Panzer Division) down from the Cauldron area.[37] Baade—a highly capable officer despite his eccentricities (he occasionally went into battle dressed in a Scottish kilt and carrying a broadsword)—led his regiment into the attack against Koenig's Free French Brigade with his usual skill. Well supported by the Stukas, he stormed Point 186, the high ground north of Bir Hacheim, overlooking the main French positions.

Although Renton's battered 7th Motor Brigade had been running convoys of supplies, ammunition, and water to the garrison at night, and taking out wounded, the loss of Point 186 made Bir Hacheim untenable in the long run. The British XXX Corps tried to take some of the pressure off the garrison on 9 June by sending columns from the 7th Motor, 29th Indian Infantry Brigade, and 4th Armoured Divisions to distract Rommel, and they did force him to divert part of the 90th Light to deal with them, but he continued to tighten his grip on the fortress. The next day, forty Stukas and twenty Ju-88 bombers dropped some 130 tons of bombs on Bir Hacheim. This time, the RAF could not break through the fighter screen. Meanwhile, on the ground, the grenadiers of the 90th Light Division (attacking without tank support) broke into the main defensive perimeter, and Rommel signaled OKW that Bir Hacheim would finally fall the next day. For some time, Field Marshal Kesselring had been pressuring Rommel to bring down stronger forces (including panzer battalions) to speed up the capture of the fortress, but, with the British armor bruised but still intact, the Desert Fox wanted to save his tanks for fighting in more open terrain; he did not want to waste them in the minefields around Bir Hacheim.[38] Events were to prove him right.

That evening, Pierre Koenig signaled Ritchie: "Am at the end of my tether. The enemy is outside my HQ." The Eighth Army commander knew that the end had come; he ordered the French general to break out that night.[39]

Early on the morning of 11 June, the German wireless intercept unit picked up the news that the garrison was about to break out. The 1st Free French were attacked as they worked their way through a narrow gap, but, even so, more than half the brigade managed to escape, although it lost twenty-four guns and many of its motorized vehicles. Out of an original garrison of 3,600, about 2,300 or so made their way back to friendly lines, including 200 wounded. General Koenig was among those who got away. Ironically, he would become the military governor of the French Occupation Zone in Germany after the war.

Bir Hacheim finally fell to the 90th Light Division the following morning. The unit took 1,000 prisoners, many of whom were wounded; it also captured twenty-four guns and "hundreds" of motorized vehicles.[40] The "Africans" treated the new POWs with the greatest respect; they had earned everyone's admiration during their courageous fight against overwhelming odds.

Frau Lucie Rommel as a young girl. This photo was taken around 1911, about the time she met Erwin Rommel, the future "Desert Fox." (Courtesy Col. Dr. Edmond D. Marino)

Lieutenant Erwin Rommel and an unidentified fellow officer during World War I. This photograph was taken in 1916 or 1917, after Rommel had been awarded both grades of the Iron Cross but before he won his Pour le Merite. (Courtesy Col. Dr. Edmond D. Marino)

Rommel looking toward the desert. The goggles on his hat are captured British goggles, which he considered superior to the German model. (Courtesy of Tom Smith)

A member of one of the reconnaissance battalions, returning from a mission. German motorcycles generally performed poorly on the desert, and most of them were discarded in 1941. (Courtesy of Tom Smith)

A British Valentine tank. Although generally considered far inferior to most German tanks, this one has been captured by the Afrika Korps and incorporated into the panzer army. (Courtesy of Tom Smith)

A knocked out Panzer Mark IV, being inspected by a British officer. (U.S. Army Military History Institute)

American "Stuart" or "Honey" tanks, which were used extensively by the British during the Gazala Line battles. Although an excellent light tank (it was so mechanically reliable that it was nicknamed "Honey"), it was frequently used as a main battle tank—a role for which it was ill-suited. (U.S. Military History Institute)

Rommel congratulates General of Panzer Troops Ludwig Cruewell on his birthday in March, 1942. Cruewell was captured by the British a few weeks later. The general behind Rommel is Walter Nehring, the commander of the Afrika Korps. (U.S. National Archives)

Major General Georg von Bismarck (left), the commander of the 21st Panzer Division, confers with Ludwig Cruewell, early 1942. (U.S. National Archives)

A German convoy moving down the Coastal Road. The Via Balbia was virtually the only paved road in the entire theater of operations. (U.S. Army Military History Institute)

A German panzer regiment pauses in the desert. (U.S. National Archives)

A German gun firing on the Allies. The artillery inflicted more casualties on both sides in the Desert War than did any other branch. (U.S. National Archives)

Captain Marseille, the leading ace of the Desert War, posing next to an airplane he shot down. Marseille downed 150 British airplanes, more than anyone else in history. He was killed when his airplane malfunctioned over El Alamein in September, 1942. He was 24 years old. (U.S. National Archives)

Rommel conferring with Italian generals in the desert. Although his relationship with the Italian soldiers was quite good, Rommel did not get along well with most senior Italian officers. (Courtesy of Tom Smith)

Italian troops camping in an oasis. (U.S. National Archives)

Admiral Alan B. Cunningham, the commander of the British Mediterranean Fleet. "ABC" stated categorically that the Royal Navy could not supply Tobruk through a second siege. (U.S. National Archives)

British prisoners-of-war, under guard in the desert. (Photo courtesy Tom Smith)

Italian soldiers receiving their pay. (Courtesy of Tom Smith)

British and South African troops march off to the prisoner-of-war camps, 1942. These soldiers were captured near Ain el Gazala, when the Gazala Line was abandoned. (U.S. Army Military Institute)

A Panzer Mark III. (U.S. National Archives)

Rommel's communications vehicle. It is stuck in the soft sand and German soldiers are digging it out. Rommel's command vehicle is seen in the background (U.S. National Archives)

Italian troops digging trenches in the desert, 1941 or 1942. (U.S. National Archives)

Pierre Koenig, commander of the 1st Free French Brigade at Bir Hacheim. After the war, General Koenig commanded the French army in occupied Germany. (U.S. Army Military History Institute)

Luftwaffe Field Marshal Albert Kesselring, demonstrating why his troops nicknamed him "Smiling Al." The commander-in-chief of OB South, Kesselring was Rommel's nominal superior during the Desert War. (U.S. Army Military History Institute)

Rommel's command vehicle, a captured British "Mammoth." It is draped with a Nazi flag so Luftwaffe pilots could identify it as German and not bomb it. (Courtesy of Tom Smith)

A Panzer Mark III. The PzKw was Rommel's "workhouse" and the main battle tank of the Afrika Korps. This tank, a J Model(PzKw IIIj), has a long-barrelled 50mm main battle gun. (U.S. Army Military History Institute)

The German-Italian cemetary near Tobruk. (Courtesy of Tom Smith)

An Italian artillery position in the desert. (Courtesy Tom Smith)

A staff vehicle belonging to the 90th Light Division. (Courtesy of Tom Smith)

A typical desert road or "trigh." (Courtesy of Tom Smith)

A heavy Italian gun. (Courtesy of Tom Smith)

A British armored car, knocked out when the Germans took Benghazi, 1941. (Courtesy of Tom Smith)

CHAPTER V: Knightsbridge and the Drive to the Coastal Road

As of 11 June 1942, more than two weeks after he launched his offensive, Erwin Rommel still had not won the battle, and the road to Tobruk remained blocked, even though the main Allied defensive position had been broken. During the respite provided by the battle of Bir Hacheim, the British Eighth Army had restored its left flank, which now faced generally to the south, instead of west. The key points of this new sector included (west to east) the 69th Infantry Brigade Group Box in the Gazala Line; the Knightsbridge Box, a roughly square fortified locality two miles long on each side and still held by the 201st Guards Brigade; and the El Adem Box, defended by the 29th Indian Brigade Group. The British left flank was anchored on the Tobruk perimeter, which had been extended to the southwest to include Carrier Hill, the highest point of Ras el Medawar, which is part of the Acroma Ridge. It was held by the 2d South African Division.

Several important secondary positions lay between the Gazala Line and the Knightsbridge Box, including B.154 (called "William's Post") and Elwet et Tamar ("Best Post"), which were held by elements of the 1st South African Division; and Point 187, which the 1st Worcesters took over from the 69th Brigade on 10 June. All were well dug in and protected by minefields. Linking these positions to Knightsbridge was Rigel Ridge, which was held by the Scots Guards from the 201st Guards Brigade. This battalion had been reinforced with South African artillery and antitank guns.

Behind this main defensive line were Commonwealth Keep and Acroma Keep, the last defensive positions before the escarpment and the sea. Each was defended by a reinforced company of the 2d Transvaal Scottish.[1]

Despite the fact that it had lost four brigades since 26 May, the Eighth Army still had enough infantry to amply man the new southern flank. More importantly, it had enough armor to support it. In the desert, no defensive line, no matter how strong, is secure unless it has adequate armor to back it up. This the British still possessed. As of 11 June, Ritchie reportedly controlled 330 operational tanks, including 250 cruisers and eighty "I" tanks. These figures do not quite add up when compared to a detailed report made the following day, however. On 12 June, the 2d Armoured Brigade reported a strength of forty-five tanks (seventeen Grants, twenty-five Crusaders, and three Stuarts). The 4th Armoured had ninety-five operational tanks (thirty-nine Grants and fifty-six Stuarts), while the 22d Armoured had thirty-four Crusaders, twenty-seven Grants, and five Stuarts. This adds up to 206 tanks in the three armored brigades of the Eighth Army: eighty-three Grants, sixty-four Stuarts, and fifty-nine Crusaders. In addition, the rebuilt 32d Army Tank Brigade had sixty-three infantry tanks, and the 7th Motor Brigade had a Stuart squadron (sixteen tanks). The strength of the 1st Army Tank Brigade was not reported,[2] but the unit almost certainly had fifty tanks—probably more. These figures suggest that Eighth Army had roughly 340 tanks (twenty more than had been reported the day before), but only 222 cruisers (twenty-eight fewer than originally reported). In either case, however, the Allied forces still significantly outnumbered Panzer Army Afrika in armor.

As of 11 June, the two divisions of the Afrika Korps had a combined strength of eighty-three PzKw IIIs, twenty-seven PzKw III Specials, eight PzKw IVs, and six PzKw IV Specials—a total of one hundred twenty-four panzers. Rommel also had twenty-five obsolete PzKw IIs, about sixty of the hopelessly outclassed Italian tanks in the Ariete Division, and an unknown number of captured British tanks. In all, he was outnumbered almost three to one in armor, if the obsolete and captured tanks are excluded.

Panzer Army Afrika's strength was also low in other important categories. As of 7 June, the DAK had only 40 percent of its authorized manpower, while the strength of the panzer grenadier regiments varied between 34 percent and 50 percent of establishment. On 10 June, the 115th Panzer Grenadier Regiment (the only motorized infantry regiment in the 15th Panzer Division) had a total strength of 667 men, or 35 percent of its authorized number, and it had already dissolved one of its three battalions. The 90th Light Division had only 1,000 men, but this figure excludes the detached 15th Rifle Brigade, which had somewhere between 2,000 and 3,000 men. Only in artillery were the Axis forces well off. The German artillery regiments had 90 percent of their authorized gun strength, and this figure would soon exceed 100 percent, thanks to captured Allied guns. The Eighth Army, on the other hand, had already lost seven artillery regiments.[3]

The British armored units were not as well off as the above figures suggest, however. They had already lost more than half the Grants with which they had entered the battle, and their commanders at all levels were having many problems with their tank units and replacement tanks. Armored units had been shot up, broken up, and combined, disrupting unit integrity; units that once functioned as a team now had to work with many people who were strangers. As a result, the teamwork was no longer there. In addition, the tanks sent to replace damaged or destroyed vehicles often had missing wireless equipment and other problems. Their guns were frequently rusted or encased in grease, and there were many "running in" problems with the engines. In addition, the British use of combined-arms techniques—while better than it had been in the "Crusader" battles of late 1941—varied from not particularly good to nonexistent. The more progressive units were learning, but they still had a long way to go before they caught up with the Germans. In addition, as we have seen and will see again, there were still many British tank commanders who continued to adhere to the "all tank" concept (Chapter II) and had not embraced the tactical doctrine of combined-arms fighting at all. Erwin Rommel had been battling them for more than two weeks and still had no idea that he was supposed to be fighting against a combined-arms force.

By 11 June, Ritchie had disposed both of his armored divisions in the Knightsbridge area, with the 1st Armoured to the north and the

7th Armoured to the south, while the rebuilt 32d Army Tank Brigade lay immediately behind the Tamar position. (The 1st Armoured now consisted of the 22d Armoured and 1st Army Tank Brigades, while Messervy's 7th Armoured controlled the 2d and 4th Armoured Brigades.) That day, despite his relatively enormous losses, Rommel boldly ordered the 15th Panzer, 90th Light, and Trieste Motorized Divisions to advance northeast toward El Adem, while the 21st Panzer demonstrated against the British lines just north of the Cauldron. "As always, Rommel was feeling the communications of the flank-conscious British," Barnett wrote later. "Rommel in attack never worried about his own flanks: a punch protects itself."[4] His plan was a repetition of his original attack on the Gazala Line: hold the enemy on the left, outflank him on the right, knock out his anchor position, and then destroy him. Map 9, p. 121, shows the situation at nightfall on 11 June.

Rommel's movements were not very far advanced by nightfall, when the 90th Light hedgehogged seven miles southeast of El Adem and the 15th Panzer on its left spent the night near Naduret el Ghesceuasc; General Norrie, however, thought he saw an opportunity "to go in and smash him."[5] General Messervy, on the other hand, believed that, in the event of an Axis advance on El Adem, the only effective strategy would be to get away from Knightsbridge and break out to the southeast, into the open desert around Bir el Gubi. Norrie (who wished to profit from Rommel's dispersal) wanted the 2d and 4th Armoured Brigades to advance south and then east, to attack the 15th Panzer Division, while the 1st Armoured Division remained on the defensive north of Knightsbridge. Brigadier Richards, the commander of the 4th Armoured Brigade, doubted the wisdom of this plan because it split the Allied armor, and he said so—via radio dispatch. This transmission was either made in the clear or in a compromised code (probably the latter); in any case it was picked up by Captain Seebohn's Wireless Intercept Service, which promptly informed Rommel of the British plans. The Desert Fox immediately set a trap of his own. He ordered Colonel Crasemann's 15th Panzer to remain on the defensive until the British attacked; then it was to counterattack. Meanwhile, Bismarck's 21st Panzer was to elude the 1st Armoured Division and strike into the British rear, trapping the

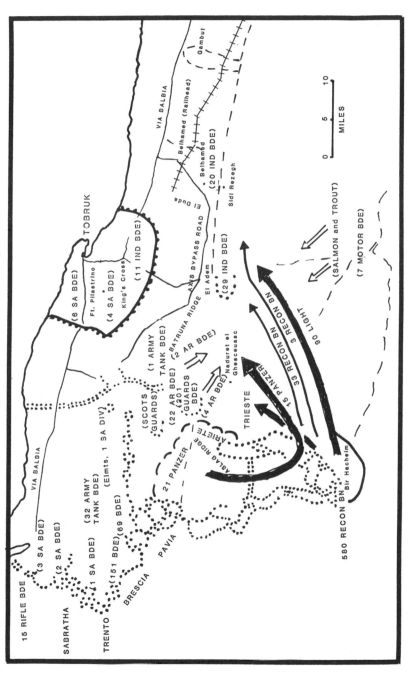

SITUATION, EVENING OF JUNE 11, 1942

7th Armoured Division between the two veteran Afrika Korps divisions south of the Knightsbridge Box. With any luck, 7th Armoured would be encircled and destroyed. This is essentially what happened, although the battle did not develop exactly as Rommel envisioned it, because General Messervy also disagreed with Norrie's plan, on the grounds that it divided British armor. He decided to discuss the matter with his corps commander, but, after leaving his headquarters, was surprised by a reconnaissance patrol from the 90th Light Division and was forced to hide in a dried-up water hole to avoid capture. He was missing for some time, and his division—which was still under orders to prepare to break out into the open desert—was leaderless for most of the day.[6]

Because Messervy was missing, the British did not attack on the morning of 12 June as the Germans expected, so Walter Nehring ordered the 15th Panzer Division to strike the 2d and 4th Armoured Brigades east and west of Point 169. It did so, but showed a distinct lack of its usual spirit and initiative, in spite of Nehring's exhortations. Troop exhaustion was setting in on the Afrika Korps. This fatigue was exacerbated by the fact that, when a soldier is fighting in open desert, it is almost impossible for him not to feel that he personally is being observed by the enemy. During a lull after several days of combat, the troops experienced a feeling of profound relief, followed by a deep exhaustion which could only be mastered by sleep. The men often slept in the most uncomfortable positions, and, since it was not possible for them to get adequate rest, they were becoming sluggish and were reacting more slowly. Even so, the antitank gunners demonstrated their usual cunning and boldness. It was a very hazy day—perfect weather for antitank work, and Rommel's gunners took full advantage of it. Using the haze and dust, they pushed their guns forward by hand and knocked out tank after tank—a performance they repeated again and again on 12 June.

With the 2d and 4th Armoured pinned down by Nehring, Rommel ordered the 21st Panzer to attack them in the rear. "It was a typical Rommel pincer, nipping his enemy as they were redeploying," Ronald Lewin wrote later.[7] The timing was perfect. At noon, while the two British armored brigades were still awaiting orders, suddenly, the panzers plowed into their rear, supported on the right by the Trieste Motorized Division. This attack began the battle which Correlli Barnett called the greatest defeat in the history of British armor.[8] The 4th Armoured Brigade took the main blow and was badly damaged; the 2d Armoured also suffered heavy casualties.

Meanwhile, General Norrie still intended for the 2d and 4th Armoured Brigades to attack and destroy the 15th Panzer Division, so, with Messervy still missing, he placed General Lumsden in charge of the entire operation. By the time he took over, however, the 2d and 4th Armoured Brigades were virtually surrounded. As soon as it became apparent what was happening, General Lumsden ordered his division to counterattack from the north, but the 22d Armoured Brigade suffered heavy casualties when a squadron of the 4th Hussars was pinned down by a battle group of tanks and armored cars from Trieste, and was then taken in the rear by tanks from the 21st Panzers. It was quickly smashed, and the 22d Armoured was not able to rescue its trapped comrades.

Trapped between two fires southeast of Knightsbridge, the 2d and 4th Armoured Brigades took a tremendous pounding until 3:30 P.M., when they at last began to give way. By 4:00 P.M., the 15th Panzer was pursuing the 4th Armoured, which was driven headlong down the escarpment northeast of Knightsbridge; it had to abandon all of the tanks that it had in tow, which was a great many.

By nightfall, the battle of the Gazala Line had finally been decided. "The desert was strewn with the wrecks of Grants, Crusaders and Stuarts . . ." Agar-Hamilton wrote later.[9] Some of these tanks were not too badly damaged, but their losses were nevertheless irrevocable, since Eighth Army had been driven from the battlefield. By the morning of 13 June, the 4th Armoured Brigade had a total strength of 15 tanks, and the 2d and 22d Armoured Brigades combined had a total strength of 50 tanks, while the 32d Army Tank Brigade had only 30 tanks left—a total loss of 185 cruisers and 50 infantry tanks. In addition, German tanks had broken through the main defensive line and cut the Axis Bypass Road south of Tobruk, forcing all British transport to pass through Tobruk, and, from the escarpment, their observation posts could see as far as the fortress's perimeter.

Despite their losses, the mood at Eighth Army's headquarters was tranquil. Auchinleck visited the HQ that day and reported to London that the armored battle had been inconclusive, although Panzer Army Afrika was now relatively stronger and Ritchie was concerned that the Germans might be able to strike north and reach Acroma, thus cutting off the divisions in the Gazala Line. (This was just what Rommel intended to do.) Auchinleck, who recognized that the German troops were nearing exhaustion, but who was not aware of how many tanks his army had lost on 12 June, ordered Eighth Army to continue the battle along the Gazala to El Adem line. He told Ritchie that the remaining British armor should be concentrated and should fight under the artillery support of the infantry positions. The 7th Motor Brigade (still under XXX Corps) was to attack to the north, into the rear of the German forces between El Adem and Knightsbridge, and the 10th Indian Division was to strike the 90th Light east of El Adem. That same morning, now that it was too late, General Ritchie placed General Gott—the old warhorse of the Eighth Army—in charge of the entire battle in the Gazala-Knightsbridge area, and instructed him to hold the essential positions of Acroma, Tamar, Knightsbridge, and El Adem.

On the other side of the line, Rommel planned for the 15th Panzer Division to move west along the Hagiag er Raml, while the 21st Panzer advanced east along the Maabus er Rigel (Rigel Ridge), thus cutting off the Knightsbridge Box. During the morning, the 2d and 22d Armoured Brigades and elements of the 32d Army Tank Brigade only just managed to hold east of Knightsbridge. Due to troop exhaustion, the 21st Panzer did not attack with its usual spirit and did not really get started until noon. On the other hand, British armor was even slower, and some of their tanks were running out of ammunition. As a result, Bismarck was able to destroy another twenty-five British tanks and overrun part of the 2d Scots Guards on Rigel Ridge. The 6th South African Anti-Tank Battery, which was supporting the Scots, fought until all eight of its guns had been knocked out. The battery commander and half of his men were killed or wounded, and only one damaged gun and fifteen men escaped. Fortunately for the Guards, the 7th Royal Tank Regiment charged to their rescue and retook part of the ridge. Lieutenant Colonel H. R. B. Foote, the regimental commander, was awarded the Victoria Cross for this action. Only the northern part of the position could be held, however, and the Scottish Guards were forced to withdraw into the Knightsbridge Box.

At nightfall, the 15th Panzer Division finally reached the Trigh Bir Hacheim. The 2d Armoured Brigade was holding the northern edge of the Rigel feature (but only with difficulty), while the 4th Armoured was withdrawing toward Acroma. By now Knightsbridge was clearly threatened with a double envelopment, so General Gott ordered the 201st Guards Brigade to abandon it. Brigadier Marriott successfully evacuated the box that night. Rommel wasted no time ordering a pursuit.

Only on Rommel's right flank did the battle go badly. That afternoon the 90th Light, which had been engaged against the numerically superior 29th Indian Brigade Group at the El Adem Box, with the 7th Motor Brigade operating in its rear, was finally defeated and forced to withdraw in confusion, under the cover of a sandstorm.

Tank-repair efforts on both sides were remarkable. Up to 13 June, the British had recovered no fewer than 417 damaged cruiser tanks. Of these, 201 had been repaired, 122 had been sent to base workshops in the rear, and the rest were being repaired locally. In addition, 138 damaged "I" tanks had been recovered as of 12 June (the records for 13 June are missing), for a total of at least 555 tanks recovered. Those damaged tanks repaired by their own crews are not part of this record. The German mechanics' performance was equally impressive. Despite the efforts of the men in his motor pools and workshops, however, and in spite of the fact that he had already received at least 300 replacement tanks, Ritchie reported that he had only 50 cruisers and 20 infantry tanks on 14 June. This represented a decline of some 200 cruisers and 60 "I" tanks since the evening of 10 June.[10]

That morning, General Gott ordered Operation "Freeborn," the evacuation of the Gazala Line, to begin. The evacuation of Number 4 Forward Base at Belhamed also began, but Tobruk, with its 3,000,000 rations, 2,500,000 gallons of fuel, and 270,000 rounds of artillery ammunition, as well as tons of other supplies, could not be evacuated. And the British were still undecided about what to do about the fortress. Auchinleck wanted Ritchie to hold the Acroma, El Adem, and positions to the south, as shown in Map 10, p. 126,

AUCHINLECK'S PROPOSED LINE OF JUNE 14, 1942

while he brought up reinforcements from the frontier. He did not believe that the Germans would be physically capable of continuing the offensive much longer. However, if Eighth Army were not able to hold this line, he ordered, Ritchie was to abandon Tobruk and retreat to the frontier. The C in C, Middle East Command, categorically declared that under no circumstances was he to allow the Germans to invest Tobruk; nor was he to allow any part of Eighth Army to be surrounded there.

Had he heard these instructions, Admiral Cunningham would have uttered a loud "Amen." Sir Andrew had already told Churchill to his face, and in no uncertain terms, that the Mediterranean fleet would not resupply Tobruk through a second siege. The prime minister did not seem to believe him, however.

Sir Neil Ritchie also disagreed with Claude Auchinleck and Admiral Cunningham. He conferred constantly with General Gott, who had considerable influence over him, and Gott convinced him that he must accept the investment of Tobruk if he were to hold the place at all. The commander of the XIII Corps believed that the loss of the fortress, with its vital harbor, its installations, and its huge quantities of supplies and ammunition, need not occur, and he convinced the Eighth Army commander that the garrison could hold out for two months without difficulty, even without the help of the Royal Navy. As a result, General Ritchie began making preparations for a siege.

William H. E. Gott was famous for his fearlessness. "Men felt that in him they could rely on a rock-like stability, a certainty of touch and judgment which convinced them that their cause was sure, allayed against their anxieties, and gave them courage for the future," Agar-Hamilton wrote later.

What they valued in him was his appearance of complete serenity in troublesome times, his unfailing good humour, his indefatigable energy, his intense and very real human sympathy, his readiness always to propose a solution when others could not decide what to do, his integrity, his charitable ability to forgive.[11]

"Perhaps he was too great a man to be a really great soldier," one British officer wrote later. "There was nothing small or mean about him. He had all the Christian virtues in abundant measure. I have never met another soldier whom I would rank as his equal."[12]

Meanwhile, as Ritchie and Gott prepared for a second siege of Tobruk, General Auchinleck summoned the Headquarters, X Corps, and the rebuilt 2d New Zealand Division from Syria to Egypt, and sent elements of the 10th Armoured Division from Egypt toward Libya, to create a mobile reserve. In addition, there were at least 150 tanks which could be made operationally ready in just a few days.[13]

The hard-pressed Eighth Army had the promise of a great deal of help in the near future.

THE EVACUATION OF THE GAZALA LINE

At 7:00 A.M. on 14 June, General Pienaar, the commander of the 1st South African Division, received orders to begin the evacuation of the Gazala Line at 6:00 P.M. that evening (three hours before dark). Its rearguards were to be clear of Tobruk by 7:00 A.M. on 15 June.

The division began to move out that afternoon, but was soon attacked by Stukas. The Transvaal Scots were struck near the pass known as Fig Tree or Agheila West. The battalion's history recorded:

> Some of the battalion are down the pass, others still jammed in the bottleneck at the top, when the first Stukas arrive. The trucks at the foot of the pass stop. The men run for cover. At the top, the men fling themselves down beside their trucks. The Stukas scream down . . . into the path of the Bofors [antitank gun] fire, up and off . . . The gun at the top ceases to chatter; dead men hang over it and lie among torn sandbags . . .
>
> . . . As the battalion vehicles try to regain their places, convoy discipline begins to go: a panicking few are breaking up the disciplined many; each small group of trucks is becoming an isolated unit. . . . This road from Gazala to the Acroma Monument is relentlessly machine-gunned and bombed. Trucks blaze. Men run; ambulances howl towards the hospital in Tobruk; dead men lie in blood and oil and broken glass.[14]

The British plan called for the 1st South African Division to escape via the Coastal Road, while the 50th Division escaped via the desert, after breaking through the Italian XXI Corps. The 2d South African Division, supported by the 1st Armoured Division, was ordered to hold the line of minefield running generally north to south from El Mrassas to Acroma, to keep the Coastal Road open. The key positions, however, were the line of strongpoints south of the coastal escarpment, including Elwet et Tamar (Best Post), Point 187, William's Post, Commonwealth Keep (also known as Point 209), Point 208, and Acroma Keep (see Map 11). The 22d Armoured Brigade and the 3d South African Reconnaissance Battalion formed a screen in front of these positions.

At Best Post, which was named after the garrison commander, Lt. Col. J. B. Bester, the British XIII Corps deployed three companies of South African infantry, three troops of two-pounder antitank guns, and a troop of AA guns. Point 187 was held by the 1st Worcestershire Battalion, with the 62d Field Battery and several antiaircraft guns in support, all under Lieutenant Colonel Knight. William's Post was held by Lieutenant Colonel Minnaar, with two reinforced companies of South African infantry and the 3d South African Field Battery. In the area between Best Post, Point 187, and Acroma lay the remnants of the British 1st Armoured Division, including the 32d Army Tank Brigade, which concentrated between Acroma and Commonwealth Keep. Most of the rest of the division concentrated around Point 208 (Hagfet el-Anebo), which was garrisoned by "Stopcol." A squadron of the 3d South African Reconnaissance Battalion lay behind Elwet et Tamar, while "Tonycol" (elements of the 2d South African Field Regiment) lay east of Acroma. The artillery of the 201st Guards Brigade took up positions just west of Acroma, while the 11th Royal Horse Artillery was positioned at Point 189 (Bir et Tmer). The Allied defense thus had a considerable depth, but it lacked armor and cohesion. The 1st Armoured Division, for example, had no liaison officers with the posts to which it was supposed to provide mobile support. Best Post and William's Post were under the command of the 1st South African Division, while Point 187 (the Worcesters) were under the 2d South African Division.

Rommel, of course, realized that the Eighth Army had to hold the line of strongpoints between the Gazala Line through Tamar to Medawar, or everything west of Tobruk would be lost to the British. He therefore ordered an attack along a narrow front with all of his available forces. By now, the Afrika Korps had 140 runners and outnumbered the British two to one in armor, but its performance was becoming increasingly sluggish. Rommel urged his men on, as usual, but many of them were so tired after two weeks of more or

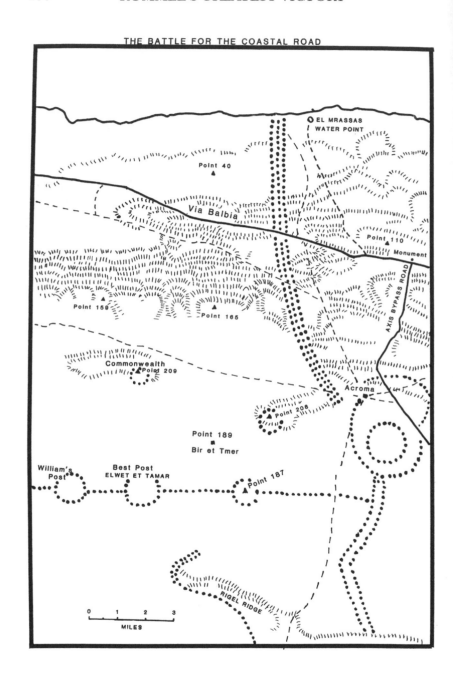

THE BATTLE FOR THE COASTAL ROAD

EL MRASSAS
WATER POINT

Point 40

Via Balbia

Point 110
Monument

Point 159

Point 165

AXIS BYPASS ROAD

Commonwealth
Point 209

Acroma

Point 208

Point 189
Bir et Tmer

William's
Post

Best Post
ELWET ET TAMAR

Point 187

RIGEL RIDGE

0   1   2   3
MILES

less continuous combat that they had little left to give. "When he [Rommel] saw his chance," Wolf Heckmann wrote later, "he became a restless and ruthless thruster, who did not ask of his men any more than he asked of himself—which was to be superhuman."[15] His men were not superhumans, however, and it was almost 7:00 A.M. on 14 June before the DAK could form up in the sector north of the Rigel and Raml Ridges. Here it was spotted by the 3d South African Reconnaissance Battalion, which called the Allied artillery, and soon the Afrika Korps was under a heavy bombardment from British and South African guns. The 15th Panzer Division nevertheless managed to push forward, where it was engaged by the 22d Armoured in front of Point 187. The "Africans" pushed the depleted 22d back, but the British armored brigade significantly slowed the German advance and generally held its own. It was 9:50 A.M. before Colonel Crasemann was able to launch a frontal attack on Point 187 with about thirty tanks and a battle group of panzer grenadiers. The Worcesters, however, were well supported by the 62d Field Battery, RA, which knocked out five or six panzers. The attack quickly bogged down and remained held up at Point 187 all morning.

To the east, it was almost noon before the 21st Panzer Division reached the minefield linking Tamar and Point 187. General von Bismarck called for his engineers, but, to his great exasperation, they did not arrive for two and a half hours. The German attack did not begin again until 2:00 P.M., when the 15th Panzer struck the Worcesters again, and the 21st Panzer attacked Best Point. An hour later, Colonel Crasemann signaled that he had broken the strongpoint, but it did not fall until 5:20 P.M. All of the guns of the 62d Field Battery were knocked out, and the Worcesters were forced to abandon all of their equipment. They lost 200 men in the process.

The 21st Panzer continued to be dogged by bad luck until 5:30 P.M., when a sandstorm descended on the battlefield. Taking advantage of the cover offered by the blowing dust, Bismarck's troops closed in on Best Point and broke into the perimeter, only to be beaten back by machine-gun and artillery fire. Meanwhile, the 200th Panzer Engineer Battalion had at last breached the minefield east of the box and had gotten behind it. The stubborn South Africans continued to hold out, however, despite being nearly surrounded.

It was 6:00 P.M. before the 15th Panzer managed to push its way through the minefield. General Nehring ordered Bismarck to take the Tamar Box (Best Post) forthwith and began a general attack on the British armor, using only the 15th Panzer.

Despite the odds against them, the British 2d and 22d Armoured Brigades were ordered to hold Point 208 and Acroma until dark, no matter what the cost. They were both smashed and, by the end of the day, the 2d Armoured was reduced to two Grants and eight Crusaders. It did, however, hold its positions, if only barely. This stand, and those of the strongpoints to the south, enabled the 1st South African Division and the 201st Guards Brigade to escape. Eighth Army finally ordered a general retreat at 8:30 P.M. The remnants of the 2d Armoured (a brigade that was now less than the size of a company) fell back to positions several miles west of Gambut and proceeded back to the Egyptian-Libyan frontier the next day. The 4th Armoured Brigade, which had not been seriously engaged all day, had already departed for Sidi Rezegh, and the 22d Armoured had already retreated in the direction of Tobruk. There was now very little to prevent Rommel from cutting the Coastal Road, except for the exhaustion of his own troops. For once this proved to be enough. The frustrated Desert Fox threatened, exhorted, and raged, but nothing worked. After more than two weeks of combat, his men were now bone tired—they simply could not go on. Not even Rommel was able to get them to move.

On the Coastal Road, meanwhile, the British withdrawal had deteriorated into a precipitate retreat, which the troops even at the time referred to as the "Gazala Gallop."[16]

"I had never seen such chaos," Capt. Faure Walker of the Coldstream Guards wrote later.

> Lorries all over the road, sideways, forwards and backwards, all motionless, most of the drivers half asleep, having given up the struggle to get through. In the end I took my company . . . off the road and went across country just in sight of the road. Most of the battalion were doing the same.[17]

Tanks, vehicles, and stragglers on foot blundered down the escarpment and intermingled with the 1st South African, which was now retreating to the west. They were joined (in no particular order) by the 201st Guards Brigade, the surviving Worcesters, "Stopcol," "Tonycol," and the garrisons of Commonwealth Keep, Best Post, and William's Post, among others. Had Rommel been able to get one more major effort from his men, he would have bagged quite a prize. But this time Rommel had exceeded even the endurance of the Afrika Korps. Even so, the forces which entered the fortress of Tobruk were not exactly the most organized formations in military history.

During the night of 14–15 June, the British rearguard consisted of the small garrison at Acroma Keep (now reduced to one infantry company) and the 32d Army Tank Brigade, with thirty-six operational Valentines and Matildas. General Lumsden ordered Brigadier Willison, the commander of the 32d, to act as the rearguard commander for the entire Eighth Army and to hold the escarpment until daylight. Willison, however, left the 4th and 8th Royal Tank Regiments to serve as the rearguard and withdrew to Tobruk with his headquarters and the 7th RTR. He was fortunate indeed that Rommel was unable to complete his drive to the Coastal Road.

General Pienaar was also fortunate. His retreat was well planned and, except for disorganization, interference from the Stukas, stragglers, and the usual confusion of a night move, was conducted in the same manner. Even here he was fortunate, for one of the most important Malta convoys—"Vigorous"—was passing between Crete and Cyrenaica, and it diverted the bulk of Air Command Afrika away from the Coastal Road. General Ramsden, the commander of the 50th Infantry Division, had the most difficult time, for it was already too late for him to retreat down the Via Balbia. He would have to break out through the Italians. He decided to strike just after dark. Ramsden divided his command into two main groups: one under Brigadier L. L. Hassell (commander of the 69th Infantry Brigade Group) and the other under Brigadier J. S. Nichols (151st Infantry Brigade Group). His plan called for one battalion from each group to smash a gap into the Italian positions and hold it open, while the rest of the brigade, in self-contained columns, passed through.

A dust storm that afternoon helped conceal Ramsden's preparations and the surprise was total. The 5th Battalion, East Yorkshire Regiment, and the 8th Battalion, Durham Light Infantry, made the gaps, and the columns ran through them (or over the Italian positions) and into the open desert. They all then made a wide sweep to the south before turning east and north, heading for the wire, a huge barbed-wire fence separating Libya and Egypt. All, that is, except for the 9th Battalion, Durham Light Infantry. It was cut off to the west so its commander, Lieutenant Colonel Percy, decided to follow the South Africans down the Coastal Road instead.

Colonel General Rommel arrived at the Headquarters, 15th Panzer Division, at 8:00 A.M. on 15 June. He assumed that the British had escaped, so he ordered the 21st Panzer to pull out of the drive to the north and make a long sweep in the direction of El Adem. The 15th Panzer continued to push to the Coastal Road alone.

At 9:00 A.M., the 33d Panzer Artillery Regiment took up positions on top of the escarpment, where it fired on the main bodies of the 2d and 3d South African Brigade Groups as they streamed across the Via Balbia and the coastal plain below. The panzers, however, were not able to negotiate the escarpment at this point, so little damage was done. It was around 11:30 A.M. before the 3d Battalion, 115th Panzer Grenadier Regiment, finally managed to scramble down the escarpment at Mrassas and block the Coastal Road, cutting off the escape route of the South African rearguard (two companies of armored cars, one from each of the 2d and 3d South African Brigades, plus a company from the 3d South African Recon Battalion and the 9th Durhams). Lieutenant Colonel Percy quickly took charge of the trapped forces, however, and launched an immediate breakout attempt. The 8th Panzer Regiment was still on top of the coastal escarpment and was unable to intervene as Percy pushed aside the 3d/115th Panzer Grenadiers, recaptured Mrassas, and continued on to Tobruk, followed by most of the South Africans. During the retreat, Pienaar's division lost a total of 27 killed, 133 wounded, and 233 missing, as well as seven armored cars, thirteen field guns, a troop of antitank guns, and four antiaircraft guns.[18] The 50th Infantry Division also escaped with relatively minor losses except in terms of heavy equipment, which it had to leave behind.

The Gazala Line was lost, but the damage could have been much, much worse.

CHAPTER VI: Breaking the Gazala Line

"The battle has been won, and the enemy is breaking up," Erwin Rommel wrote to his wife on 15 June. "This was unpleasantly near the truth," the British Official History recorded. "He was now almost within reach of his objective, which was Tobruk; moreover, he was quite clear as to his object, which was to capture it quickly. The British, on the other hand, were by no means clear what they meant to do, and were soon to pay the penalty."[1]

There was, indeed, considerable confusion in the higher levels of the British command. Ritchie made it clear that he preferred a second siege to abandoning Tobruk without a fight, although, as of 14 June, he was by no means sure that a second siege was going to be necessary, i.e., he thought he might even now be able to stop Rommel short of the Tobruk perimeter. For this reason he gave XXX Corps command of all of the Eighth Army forces outside the perimeter, including the 7th Armoured Division, the 29th Indian Infantry Brigade (at El Adem), and the 20th Indian Infantry Brigade (at Belhamed), and ordered General Norrie to halt the panzer army. He also placed XIII Corps (General Gott) in charge of operations inside the perimeter, even though he did not yet have permission to hold the place; in fact, just the opposite was true.

This, too, was subject to change. Unlike Auchinleck, Cunningham, and Tedder, the commanders in chief, Middle East, Prime Minister Winston Churchill passionately wanted to hold Tobruk. The decision to evacuate the two divisions from what was left of the Gazala Line naturally aroused his interest, and, on 14 June, he signaled Cairo and asked Auchinleck what he intended to do. "Presume there is no question in any case of giving up Tobruk," the prime minister added. This, of course, was a major change of strategic policy, for the C in Cs had specifically and emphatically informed London on 19 January—six months before—that there should never be a second Siege of Tobruk.

Early on the morning of 16 June, Auchinleck signaled back that Rommel's army was now superior to Eighth Army in armor, that he was recovering and repairing his damaged tanks, and that the Long Range Desert Group (a commando and reconnaissance force operating behind German lines) had reported large tank reinforcements coming up from Tripoli. (This was the Italian Littorio Armored Division.) His orders to Eighth Army (issued at 8:00 A.M.) gave Ritchie some latitude, but Auk insisted that he not allow the garrison at Tobruk to be invested, because Tobruk could not withstand another siege. There followed an exchange of signals, during which the C in C weakened. It was certainly not the first time in history an officer yielded to pressure from his head of state and took or permitted military actions to be taken which went against his better judgment, and it would not be the last. Although Auchinleck never changed his position that Ritchie should not allow Tobruk to be invested, he did give in to Churchill by granting Ritchie permission to allow Tobruk to be isolated for short periods of time, which was virtually the same thing. When a fortress is isolated, it is up to the enemy whether or not he wishes to invest it—the friendly side no longer has any say in the matter.

And Rommel very much wanted to invest it.

The stage was set for another disaster.

Tobruk did have some hope of early relief. The very tough 2d New Zealand Division (which had been badly shot up during the winter battles of 1941–42) had been rebuilt and was on its way from Syria, and the 8th Armoured Brigade was en route from the Nile delta. (The 8th Armoured, however, had been partially cannibalized to provide replacements during the Gazala fighting and still lacked transport.)[2] In addition, the 8th Armoured Division would reach Suez from the United Kingdom at the end of June, and the 44th Infantry Division would arrive by mid-July. Several workshop units, as well as

7,600 individual RAF and 1,000 naval replacements, had already disembarked at Suez, and more than 3,000 other replacements would arrive with the 8th Armoured Division. In addition, a convoy bringing 7,500 Army, 1,000 RAF, and 900 naval replacements was due to arrive on 22 June, and another 8,000 Army, 1,300 RAF, and 800 naval replacements were scheduled to arrive on 18 July. The convoy bringing the 44th Division also contained eleven antiaircraft regiments and several other units, as well as 3,000 Army and 2,800 RAF draftees.[3]

Meanwhile, General Norrie tried to halt Rommel south of Tobruk. The key position in this effort was El Adem, and Auchinleck demanded that Ritchie hold it. Unfortunately, Ritchie had little to hold it with. El Adem was defended by the 29th Indian Brigade under Brigadier Denys W. Reid, who was described by one author as "a tough, fearless Scot" who had survived some of the most bitter fighting of World War I.[4] His brigade had two battalions in place, while its third, Lt. Col. H. W. Dean's 3d Royal Battalion, 12th Frontier Force Regiment, held a detached position three miles to the northwest at the Batruna Box (Point B.650). The brigade as a whole was excellent, and its morale was high, and it was well supported by the 3d Field Regiment, RA, under Lt. Col. P. H. Teesdale. A second auxiliary box to El Adem was established at Point 187, thirteen miles northwest of El Adem and just south of Acroma, on 8 June. It was garrisoned by Lt. Col. J. C. O. Knight's 1st Worcestershire Battalion, with a battery of the 3d Field Regiment and a troop of Bofor antiaircraft guns attached.

The other major static position Ritchie desperately needed to hold was the huge supply dump at Belhamed and the RAF bases around Gambut. Belhamed was defended by the 20th Indian Infantry Brigade under Brigadier L. E. Macgregor—a newly created formation that had not been trained as a brigade. It had arrived from Iraq in the first week of June and by 10 June was holding Number 4 Forward Base at Belhamed, with a battalion at Sidi Rezegh. It included the 1st Battalion, South Wales Borderers; the 1/6th Rajputana Rifles; the 3/18th Royal Garhwal Rifles; and the 97th (Kent Yeomanry) Field Regiment, RA.

While the two Indian brigades might be able to hold key static positions, only mobile forces could, in the long run, prevent Rommel from rounding the southern flank of the XIII Corps and forcing the Eighth Army to either abandon Tobruk or accept a siege of the fortress. The only mobile force left to XXX Corps, however, was the 7th Armoured Division, which consisted of little more than the battered 4th Armoured and 7th Motor brigades, and the 3d Indian Motor Brigade, which had been mauled on 26 May. Norrie, therefore, had two simultaneous problems: (1) hold off Rommel, and (2) rebuild his mobile strength. For the second mission, he was given the 2d and 22d Armoured Brigades, which were hastily rebuilding along the Libyan-Egyptian frontier. They were receiving about twenty-five tanks per day from the XXX Corps repair shops and the maintenance facilities in Tobruk, as well as about nine replacement tanks per day from Egypt. At this rate, the two brigades would be reequipped within a week or so. But the Desert Fox was not about to give the XXX Corps that much time.

Rommel outmaneuvered Norrie almost immediately. (There is no implied criticism of Norrie here; not even a military genius like Alexander the Great, Napoleon, or Robert E. Lee could have prevented this with the forces Norrie had.) On the morning of 15 June, Rommel ordered a sweep to the east, telling 21st Panzer Division to advance to Bir Lefa, and then on to El Duda and Gambut, with the eventual objective of isolating Tobruk. At the same time, the 90th Light Division was to pin down the 29th Indian at El Adem and capture the place, if possible, while the 15th Panzer Division left the Acroma sector and headed for El Adem. The 20th Indian, of course, was tied down with the mission of defending the Belhamed supply depot. Map 12, p. 139, shows the situation at nightfall on 15 June.

The 90th Light had already invested El Adem on 12 June and blasted the place, destroying all but six of Reid's twenty-five-pounders and seriously wounding Colonel Teesdale, the artillery commander. On 15 June, however, the German division attacked El Adem three times and was three times repulsed. During this battle, the British hurried a battery of 3.7-inch heavy antiaircraft guns down from the nearby airfield and fired about 200 rounds in a ground support role. They were so effective that no German armored-car commander

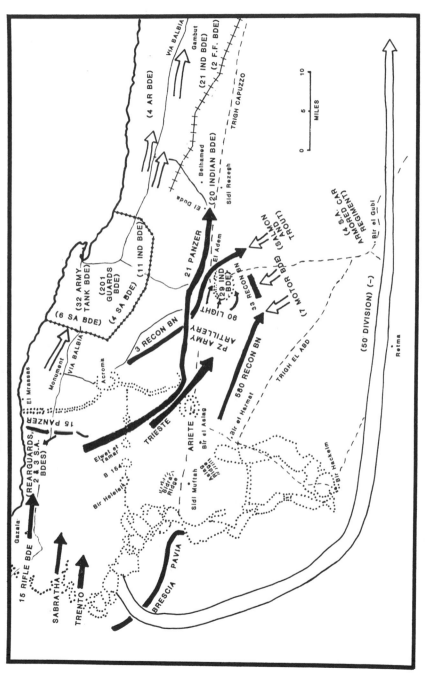

GAZALA LINE: Situation at Nightfall, June 15, 1942

would venture anywhere near them.[5] Unfortunately, however, Eighth Army ordered that they be withdrawn and then evacuated to Egypt. Meanwhile, the three German reconnaissance battalions struck the 7th Motor Brigade southeast of the El Adem Box and were also checked. General von Bismarck, on the other hand, was more successful against the Batruna Box (Point B.650), the strongpoint located on the Batruna escarpment where the Axis Bypass Road (also called the Acroma Road) climbs up to El Adem. That afternoon he began a heavy bombardment and knocked out every gun in the box; then, just after darkness fell, he surged forward with his panzers and panzer grenadiers. They overwhelmed the 3/12th Frontier Force Regiment on the first rush. Only a few survivors managed to escape into the darkness. Colonel Dean was among the prisoners.[6]

Meanwhile, against heavy odds, the 1st Worcesters made a determined stand at Point B.187. On 15 June they knocked out seventeen panzers. There were no major attacks on 16 June, but the isolated British battalion was the target of constant probes, continuous shelling, and several raids from Stuka dive-bombers. Casualties mounted and ammunition ran low. That afternoon, General Lumsden—who recognized that the position was hopeless in the long run—ordered Colonel Knight to evacuate the place. The gallant colonel was immediately awarded the DSO, but there was no time for a formal ceremony; the Worcesters were busy falling back into the fortress of Tobruk.

With Points B.650 and B.187 in German hands, Rommel was now in a better position to threaten Gambut, the major RAF base. But Air Vice-Marshal Arthur Coningham, the commander of the Desert Air Force, knew that if he withdrew his fighters the thirty miles to Sidi Azeiz, it would seriously limit the support they could give at El Adem. The army had given him four infantry battalions and three and one-half antiaircraft batteries for the defense of the Gambut airfields, plus the remnants of the 4th Armoured Brigade, which would probably not be enough if a panzer division attacked, but he nevertheless decided to keep Gambut open for the time being.

By nightfall, it was obvious to Norrie that Rommel (like Auchinleck) appreciated the strategic importance of El Adem and was concentrating the bulk of his mobile forces to take the place. General

Norrie felt that he had too few mobile troops to guarantee support for the garrisons at El Adem and Belhamed, and he did not believe the casualties they could inflict on the Germans would be worth the loss of the two Indian brigades. Eighth Army, however, did not seem to share his view on any of these issues, so the battle of El Adem was fought on 16 June. Rommel advanced with the Ariete Armored Division on the right and the 90th Light on the left. All Norrie could throw against them was the 29th Indian (two battalions), and the 7th Armoured, which now had only one available brigade: the 7th Motor, which consisted of little more than the King's Dragoon Guards and the 4th South African Armoured Car Regiment. All Gott's XIII Corps contributed to the battle were two columns from the 11th Indian Brigade, "Salmon" and "Trout," each with South African transportation.

General Norrie was taken out of the battle almost immediately, when he learned that German tanks were approaching his headquarters. He was forced to move back to the frontier. (HQ, Eighth Army, also moved that afternoon—although more leisurely—to Halfaya Pass, on the Egyptian side of the wire.)

While Ariete (with the German reconnaissance battalions) pinned down the 7th Motor Brigade on the right, and the Trieste Motorized Division advanced down the Coastal Road and contained the XIII Corps at the northern and western ends of the Tobruk perimeter on Rommel's deep left flank, the 90th Light again attacked the El Adem Box on the morning of 16 June, but again without success. At noon General Kleemann, the commander of the 90th Light, who no doubt knew that the 15th Panzer Division was coming up from Acroma, asked for tank support, but Rommel refused. He intended to use the 15th Panzer against the 20th Indian Brigade at Belhamed (with an eye to capturing the huge supply dump there), but still demanded that El Adem be taken. After renewed protests from the division, however, he weakened his requirements somewhat and ordered that El Adem be surrounded. Meanwhile, the bulk of Krause's Panzer Army artillery arrived and turned its full attention on the two battalions at El Adem, while the 90th Light struck again. Brigadier Reid turned back every assault, but it grew more difficult every time. Map 13, p. 143, shows the situation on the afternoon of 16 June.

As the 90th Light closed in on El Adem, Brigadier Reid needed to evacuate his more seriously wounded to a true surgical hospital. Unfortunately, the only one anywhere close was in Tobruk, and the road to the fortress had already been cut. Reid loaded his wounded into ambulances anyway and, under a flag of truce, sent a note written in German, Italian, and English, asking that they be permitted to pass through Axis lines. He added that he would be even more grateful if they would be allowed to return. The German 90th Light not only allowed them to pass, but they cleared paths for them through two minefields they had just lain across the road. Later, they also allowed the ambulances to return.[7]

By early afternoon, General Messervy was convinced that the garrison would not be able to hold out another twenty-four hours, but, at 2:25 P.M., General Ritchie dictated that El Adem be held at all costs. Accordingly, Messervy ordered the brigade to fight to the last man. This order was greeted with enthusiasm by the men of the 29th Indian, which was still full of fight. At 7:00 P.M., however, Ritchie reversed himself and gave Reid permission to break out, although he said it would probably be better to reorganize and break out the next night. Messervy passed the order and Ritchie's comments on to Reid and told him to act as he saw fit.

Brigadier Reid realized that he could not hold out another day and broke out to the south and northeast at midnight, taking the bulk of his command with him. About 150 men from the 1/5th Mahrattas were killed or captured in the darkness; the 3/2d Punjab lost about fifty. All of the antitank guns and all but six of the twenty-five-pounders were also lost.[8] The 90th Light moved into the box at 3:00 A.M. on 17 June. The German soldiers were delighted; the Indians had left most of their provisions, which included a large amount of rice.

Rommel was also delighted. The southern cornerstone of the Tobruk defenses had been conquered.

Meanwhile, the 21st Panzer Division, using the 2/5th Panzer Regiment and the 39th Anti-Tank Battalion, threw an antitank/panzer screen to the east, to check the 4th Armoured Brigade at Gambut, and doubled back to take the Sidi Rezegh Box, the southeastern cornerstone of fortress Tobruk. It occupied El Duda early that morn-

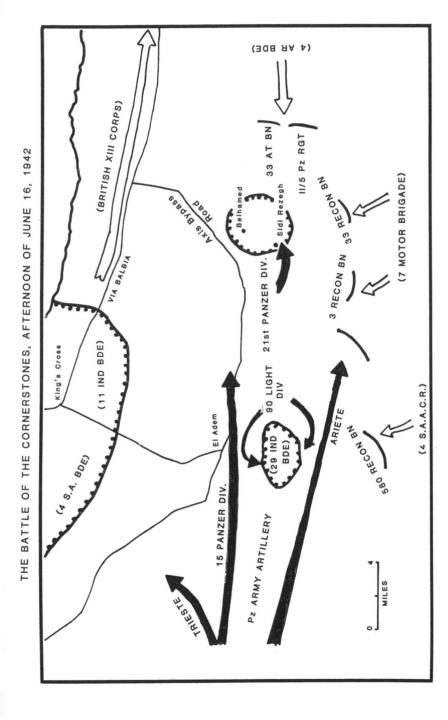

THE BATTLE OF THE CORNERSTONES, AFTERNOON OF JUNE 16, 1942

ing without any trouble, but, from 9:30 A.M. on, was subjected to repeated air strikes by the RAF, which was now using new tactics and
was attacking tanks with 20mm guns. It also had the double-edged
advantage of having bases very near the front; ground crews would
load a fighter-bomber with bombs and then have the strange sensa-
tion of hearing those same bombs explode on German positions less
than five minutes later. The 21st Panzer suffered significant casualties and was not able to attack the Sidi Rezegh Box until 4:00 P.M.
When it did strike, however, it did so with its customary style. The
defenders, the 1/6th Rajputana Rifles, fought well, but were crushed.
Only a tiny remnant of the battalion fell back to Belhamed that night.

With Number 4 Forward Base at Belhamed now practically on the
front line, the Indians began to destroy it on the night of 16–17 June.
But supply dumps take much longer to destroy than most people re-
alize, and this one contained nearly 1,000,000 rations, 1,500,000 gallons of fuel, and tons of ammunition, clothing, and other items. The
process would be far from complete when the Germans arrived.
British provisions would supply the Afrika Korps for weeks after the
base was "destroyed."

Rommel intended that his attacks against El Adem and Sidi
Rezegh convey the impression that he was still trying to destroy the
Eighth Army; in reality, his objective remained what it had always
been—Tobruk. Only two obstacles remained to prevent him from
investing the fortress: the strongpoint at Belhamed, and the British
4th Armoured Brigade, which lay ten miles southeast of the tomb of
Sidi Rezegh.

Brigadier Richards's 4th Armoured Brigade was no longer the
well-equipped and well-trained force that it had been when the battle began. It now had more than one hundred tanks, but the newly
acquired vehicles had not been run in and their guns had not been
adjusted. The crews were improvised, disorganized, and unfamiliar
with each other, and in at least two cases consisted entirely of officers. It now had two composite regiments: the 1st/6th and the
3d/5th Royal Tank Regiments, as well as the 9th Lancers (two
squadrons), and a composite squadron from the 3d and 4th County
of London Yeomanry battalions. The brigade also controlled the 1st

Royal Horse Artillery and the 1st Battalion, King's Royal Rifle Corps (KRRC). Teamwork was decidedly lacking in all units. Simultaneously, the 1st Armoured Brigade had been broken up. The 1st RTR had been allocated to the 4th Armoured Brigade on 3 June, and the 6th RTR had been transferred to the same unit four days later. "It has been suggested," Field Marshal Lord Carver wrote later, "that it would have been preferable to keep the [1st Armoured] brigade together as a fresh formation, perhaps replacing the 4th Armoured Brigade, the performance of which had not been impressive."[9]

In addition to its other problems, the 4th Armoured Brigade was short of artillery on 17 June. That morning, General Messervy sent two columns (each with a battalion from the 1st Royal Horse Artillery and an infantry company) to reinforce the 20th Indian Infantry Brigade. He assigned most of the rest of the brigade's guns to various harassing columns, sent out to annoy and confuse the Germans. Then he instructed Richards to take the rest of the brigade and advance to a position south of the Trigh Capuzzo, between Sidi Rezegh and El Adem, with an eye toward striking the enemy in the flank. Richards objected on the grounds that the terrain here was tactically unsuitable for such an operation but was overruled. The rest of the 7th Armoured Division (the 7th Motor and 3d Indian Motor brigades) was ordered to patrol the area from Harmat on the west to Gambut on the east.

Richards would have no air support during his maneuver. Air Vice-Marshal Coningham had already noticed that he was getting numerous requests for air support, but none of them came from the 29th Indian Brigade. Finally, at 3:00 P.M., the Desert Air Force received the news that El Adem had been evacuated—twelve hours after the event! This was enough for Coningham. He knew that Rommel was very, very close, and, if Gambut were not next on his list, it would be near the top, and his spearheads were only a few miles away. Since 15 June, the bases around Gambut had been operating with skeleton crews who were ready to move on an hour's notice. The fighter-bombers had dropped more than 100 tons of bombs since then, but now the Germans were entirely too close. He ordered the immediate evacuation of the airfields, and the fighters and fighter-bombers flew back to safety at Sidi Azeiz, while the bombers continued on to Baheira or to bases near Mersa Matruh. Tobruk had lost most of its air cover.

On the afternoon of 17 June, the German Afrika Korps turned southeast, to deal with the last of the British armor and, by 3:30 P.M., a mile or so to the south of Sidi Rezegh, the 9th Queens Royal Lancers was in trouble again.

It will be recalled that this gallant armored regiment had fought with great courage during the first five days of the campaign and had lost 85 percent of its tanks as a result. Sent back to Capuzzo to rebuild, it had been given the last reserve tanks from the Tank Delivery Regiment, which was now falling back into Egypt. It now had twelve Grants, nineteen cruisers, and three Stuarts—thirty-four tanks in all. This was enough to equip two of its three squadrons. On 17 June it was attached to the 4th Armoured Brigade and was given the job of holding the ridge south of the long Sidi Rezegh feature, near Hareifet en Nbeidat. When the regiment arrived, it found sixteen well-sited antitank guns and a battery of twenty-five-pounders on each flank. Brigadier Richards, the commander of the 4th Armoured, asked Lt. Col. Ronald Macdonell, the regimental commander, to "keep a fatherly eye on the guns," and, apparently feeling that the position was secure, left the area.

Shortly thereafter, the Lancers saw forty-five Mark III and IV panzers coming straight for them at maximum speed. It was the spearhead of the 21st Panzer Division. Macdonell could not understand why the artillery did not open fire; then, to his horror, he saw that the AT guns and twenty-five-pounder batteries were limbering up. They took off and disappeared beyond the horizon without a word; apparently the 4th Armoured had left the Lancers "holding the bag."

The Grants opened up at a range of 1,500 yards. The first two panzers burst into flames while the others halted and returned fire. "The air was filled with flying metal and cordite fumes," one survivor recalled. Soon six or seven panzers were on fire and two Grants were blazing, while a third disappeared in a great explosion—apparently it had been hit in the ammunition compartment. Twice the Germans charged, and twice they were turned back. Colonel Macdonell, meanwhile, contacted HQ, 4th Armoured Brigade, but got "no coherent reply." The colonel then suggested that a tank squadron from the 3d/5th RTR on his left, which he knew to be nearby, should be used to reinforce him. Brigade Headquarters replied that they were very well placed where they were. Colonel Macdonell and his Lancers were left alone to face what turned out to be the bulk of the Afrika Korps. By now, General von Bismarck had reported stubborn resistance and was calling for help. General Nehring immediately ordered the 15th Panzer Division to come up on their flank and to provide support. In the dust and confusion, the 15th initially fired on the 21st, but the situation was soon corrected. By this point, the Germans had identified Macdonell's positions, and about a dozen tanks (apparently from the 15th Panzer) worked their way around his right flank. With the Grants of B Squadron engaged in the center, all that defended this sector was A Squadron, which was equipped with inferior cruiser tanks. Their two-pounder main battle guns were no match for the 75mm guns of the Panzer Mark IIIs. Meanwhile, to the front, Bismarck's panzers had pushed to within 700 yards of the Grants, which they outnumbered at least three to one. They were, as usual, accompanied by the panzerjägers—the antitank gunners, who used the terrain well, kept as low as possible, and skillfully kept the sun behind them. "The sun was, as usual, in our eyes," Captain Bright recalled.[10] Had the British artillery remained in the area, the antitank gunners would have been vulnerable, but they were nowhere to be seen. One by one the British tanks were being knocked out. To make matters much worse, the British could see that, behind the panzers on the Sidi Rezegh Ridge but well within range of their positions, more German antitank crews had arrived and were hurriedly unlimbering their 88s. Colonel Macdonell realized if he did not do something in a matter of minutes, his entire regiment would be wiped out. The fact that his main tank was the Grant presented him with a very difficult problem. Unlike the case with the panzers, and many of the Allied tanks, the 75mm gun of the Grant had a limited traverse—so when you turned the tank to the rear, you also turned your main battle gun to the rear. It was therefore impossible for him to simply "turn tail."

Macdonell handled the dilemma brilliantly. He ordered all units to reverse slowly and load smoke shells. Then, on command, after retreating about a mile, they all fired smoke at once, quickly pivoted 180 degrees, and sped across the desert at full speed, pursued by the panzers. A couple of Grants were hit by 88mm shells (killing at least three crewmen), and a cruiser was destroyed by a direct hit, but the Lancers quickly outdistanced their pursuers, who soon turned back—much to the relief of the Lancers, who were running dangerously low on fuel.[11]

Meanwhile, the 3d/5th Royal Tank Regiment was finally sent into action to the southwest. It was too late, however, and now they were just reinforcing failure. The German antitank gunners turned on them as well, so soon they also suffered heavy casualties. The 1st/6th RTR was ordered to help its hard-pressed sister regiment, but, due to a misunderstanding, only part of it ever got into action. Before long, the 4th Armoured had lost half of its strength. Brigadier Richards finally began to retreat at 7:00 P.M., pursued by the Afrika Korps. By nightfall, Richards had only twenty operational tanks left.[12] After the sun set, Richards took the remnants of his brigade to a field maintenance center south of the Trigh el Abd. Here he would be resupplied, some of the tanks he had managed to tow off the battlefield could be repaired, and he would be in a position to attack the flank of any enemy advancing eastward the next day. But the Afrika Korps (which had finally broken off the action on Rommel's orders) had already turned north, to cut the Coastal Road.

Colonel Macdonell's skillful handling of a bad situation and his brilliant escape did not alleviate the most important facts of this battle, which were: (1) another British armored brigade had been mauled; (2) it could have been prevented; and (3) the British commanders' grasp of combined-arms tactics was still very poor. Had the artillery and antitank guns of the 4th Armoured Brigade remained in their original positions, and had Macdonell received the reinforcements he requested when he requested them, it is quite conceivable that the Afrika Korps would have received a very bloody check. As it was, 9th Queen's Lancers returned with nine Grant tanks—none of which was still operational, because every gun was out of action. Only one could be repaired locally; the rest were sent to workshops in Egypt.[13] Meanwhile, the remnants of the 9th returned to the Tank Delivery Regiment (now at Ikingi, Egypt) to be rebuilt—again.

After this fight, which was dubbed the Battle of Sidi Rezegh, the British armor was no longer a factor in the campaign. The 4th Armoured Brigade spent 18 and 19 June reorganizing and making repairs, and building itself up to a strength of fifty-eight tanks. Then it was ordered back to the Egyptian frontier.

Meanwhile, late in the day on 17 June, Eighth Army urgently ordered the 21st Indian and 2d Free French Brigades, which had been in reserve at Gambut during the Battle of Sidi Rezegh, to fall back to the frontier. To the south, about 7:30 P.M., Erwin Rommel came up with his *Kampfstaffel* (his personal mobile battle group, which was about the size of a battalion), placed it at the head of the Afrika Korps, and personally led the advance to the north. His object was obvious: drive to the sea and cut the Coastal Road, isolating the fortress of Tobruk.

That night, General Norrie correctly concluded that the 20th Indian Brigade at Belhamed was nearly cut off; however, instead of instructing it to retire to Tobruk, which it easily could have done, and where it would have formed a much-needed reserve, he ordered it to break out to Sollum and the frontier. Unfortunately, two of its three infantry battalions ran directly into Rommel and the Afrika Korps near Gambut. The 1st South Wales Borderers and the 3/18th Royal Garhwal Rifles were quickly surrounded and, after launching some uncoordinated breakout attempts, surrendered. Almost no one from either battalion managed to get away. The brigade headquarters, the 1/6th Rajputana Rifles, and 97th Field Regiment, which had taken other routes, made good their escape. The 90th Light Division occupied the undefended Belhamed Box at 8:00 A.M. on 18 June, and seized the partially destroyed supply depot.

Meanwhile, half an hour past midnight on 18 June, the 21st Panzer Division reached the Via Balbia near Gambut, cutting Tobruk off from the rest of the Eighth Army. For the second time in fourteen months, the fortress was isolated.

CHAPTER VII: Rommel's Greatest Victory

Tobruk, a little city of about 4,000 people who lived in battered white houses, was important because it was the only good harbor between Alexandria and Sfax, and there were a few springs of brackish water in the nearby wadis. Its extreme eastern and western flanks were well covered by deep wadis, but most of the thirty-three-mile perimeter ran across flat plains eight to nine miles from the town. Within the fortress, the ground rose rapidly from sea level to 500 feet via a series of three escarpments, each commanded by the one above. The final and most prominent escarpment was Pilastrino Ridge (which was really an escarpment, not a ridge). Just north of that lay the Solaro escarpment. The southwest corner of the perimeter bulged into a salient, which encompassed the low hill mass of Ras el Medawar, where Rommel had launched his main attack in 1941. In 1942, the outer perimeter consisted of a double line of prepared strongpoints, with concrete dugouts and barbed wire, protected by an anti-tank ditch, a perimeter minefield, and several secondary minefields within the fortress. There were also a number of obsolete Italian fortresses within the defenses, but they were of little value.

About two miles inside the outer perimeter lay the inner perimeter, which had been dubbed the "Blue Line" by the Australians. It included the main internal minefields, which were designed to break up, channelize, and localize any breakthrough. The Blue Line also covered King's Cross, the major road junction within the fortress.

The defenders of 1942 labored under several major handicaps. Many of the mines and wire entanglements that had defended the fortress had been lifted, initially to accommodate the garrison's breakout in 1941, and later to strengthen the Gazala Line. Also, the antitank ditch, which had originally been dug by the Italians, was partially silted up and was of little value in places, and the fortress was now characterized by a tangled labyrinth of minefields. Over the last three years, mines had been laid by Italians, Australians, the British, Poles, New Zealanders, and Germans. Most of the maps had been lost, so no one knew where they all were, which naturally had an inhibiting effect on the defense. In fact, Major Sainthill of the Coldstream Guards later recalled: "Our greatest difficulty was our restricted movement. The place was a mass of minefields . . . and there were no minefield maps. Routes had to be cleared by sappers [engineers] with mine detectors causing, of course, an interminable delay and preventing the reconnaissance for the counterattack roles from ever being completed."[1] The only maps available dated back to the time of the previous siege, and Brigadier Willison was annoyed to discover that they showed minefields which he himself had lifted for the breakout the previous November. The Royal Engineers (514th Field Survey Company, RE) had conducted a fresh survey in May and June, but the new maps would not be ready for another three months.

The picture was further complicated by the fact that there were three CREs (Chief, Royal Engineers) in Tobruk: Lieutenant Colonel Henderson of the 2d South African Division; Lieutenant Colonel Butler of the 88th Sub-Area, a territorial and base command; and Lieutenant Colonel Baker of Eighth Army. Brigadier Gaussen, the chief engineer of XIII Corps, had told Colonel Henderson that very little dismantling of the perimeter minefields had taken place. Brigadier Kisch, the Eighth Army chief engineer, had warned him that the minefields had been largely denuded. Henderson tended to believe Gaussen and acted upon his guidance; however, Kisch was right. The New Zealanders alone had lifted 19,000 mines from the Tobruk perimeter for the defense of El Adem,[2] and many more had been moved to the Gazala Line. The South Africans and Indians on the front lines had no idea to what extent the minefields had been depleted. Against the Germans, many of them had no tactical significance whatsoever.

• • •

The Tobruk garrison, which was under the command of Maj. Gen. H. B. Klopper, consisted of units in every stage of disorganization and which—generally speaking—had never worked together. They included the 2d South African Division (4th and 6th SA Brigades and the 11th Indian Brigade), the 201st Guards Brigade (a motorized infantry unit), the 32d Army Tank Brigade, and the Headquarters, 88th Sub-Area, which controlled the docks, harbor installations, workshops, the water distillation plant, supply facilities, and so on.

The 6th South African Brigade (Brigadier F. W. Cooper) was responsible for the coast and the northwest sector of the perimeter, as far as the Derna Road. It included the 2d South African Police Battalion (on the northern coast) and the Transvaal Scottish (in the perimeter), with the 1st South African Police Battalion in reserve.

The 4th South African Brigade (Brigadier A. A. Hayton) held the perimeter from the Derna Road Gap to a point about a mile west of the El Adem Gap on the southern face of the perimeter. It included the 2d Durham Light (south of the Derna Gap), the Umvoti Mounted Rifles in the Medawar corner (which now included Carrier Hill), and the Blake Group and the Kaffrarian Rifles along the southern perimeter. (Blake Group was an ad hoc force, consisting of elements of the 1st Royal Durban Light Infantry, the Imperial Light Horse, and the Rand Light Infantry, under the command of Lt. Col. E. H. R. Blake. These forces had been detached from the 1st South African Division and were less than a battalion in strength.)

The 11th Indian Brigade, which held the southeastern and eastern sectors of the perimeter, was a unit with an excellent reputation. Its leader, Scottish brigadier A. Anderson, the former commander of the 2d Cameron Highlanders, was also held in high regard. He and his men, however, had thirteen miles of perimeter to defend—about three times more than what a single brigade could reasonably be expected to hold. In addition, many of the mines in the brigade's sector had been lifted for the 1941 breakout and for the construction of the Gazala Line, and the antitank ditch in its sector had never been completed by the Italians. According to one witness, "it would hardly have interfered with the progress of a garden roller."[3] Right to left, the 11th Indian included Beer Group, the 2d Cameron Highlanders (rated by many as the best battalion in the Eighth Army), 2/5th Mahrattas, and 2/7th Gurkhas, which anchored the fortress's defenses on the east coast. (Beer Group was another composite force from the 1st South African Division. It included companies from the Royal Natal Carabineers, the Duke of Edinburgh's Own Rifles, and the 1st Transvaal Scottish, all under Lt. Col. J. M. de Beer.) The brigade also controlled the 18th Field Company, the Royal Bombay Sappers and Miners (an engineer unit), and the 19th Field Ambulance Battalion. Map 14, p. 155, shows the major units of the Tobruk defenses as of dawn on 20 June.

The excessive length of the defensive sector made the placement of the garrison's mobile reserves a matter of vital concern. They centered around the 32d Army Tank Brigade, which had fought in the earlier siege and which had lost almost all of its original tanks in the November 1941 breakout attempt. The 32d had again suffered heavy losses during its futile 5 June attack during the battle of the Cauldron, when it was smashed by the 21st Panzer. It had also fought at Acroma on 14 June, and came into the Tobruk perimeter with only thirty-six tanks. Here its survivors were reformed into two units, the 4th and 7th Royal Tank Regiments. Due to replacements from the workshops, the brigade had fifty-four tanks on 19 June, and sixty-one the following day. All were Matildas and Valentines, mounting the old, inferior two-pound gun. The 4th RTR (three squadrons with thirty-five fit Valentines) camped in a wadi below the escarpment that runs from King's Cross to Pilastrino. Two miles to the west of Pilastrino lay the brigade headquarters and A Squadron, 7th RTR. B Squadron lay about a mile to the north, beyond the Derna Road. The 7th RTR (which had been reinforced by elements of the 8th and 42d Royal Tank Regiments) had only two squadrons and twenty-six operational "I" tanks. Although the tanks of the 32d Brigade were a good distance from the perimeter, they occupied the same positions they had held in 1941. Brigadier A. C. Willison, the commander of the 32d Army Tank, was a man of great experience and energy. He had led the brigade in the previous siege.

Brigadier H. F. Johnson's 201st Guards Brigade had also suffered heavy losses during the battles before Tobruk; in fact, of the original brigade, only the headquarters and the 3d Coldstream Guards

Battalion remained in the fortress. The 2d Scots Guards had suffered such high casualties and equipment loss at Rigel Ridge that it was sent back to Egypt to rebuild, and the 9th Rifle Brigade had been detached some time before. Although the 3d Coldstream had lost its commander, Lt. Col. Tom Bevan (killed at Knightsbridge), it was still in reasonably good condition. The 1st Sherwood Foresters and 1st Worcesters Battalions were attached to the brigade on 15 June. The Sherwood Foresters were in good condition and had a number of the excellent six-pounder antitank guns; the 1st Worcestershire, on the other hand, had lost many men and most of its equipment on 14 June. To make matters worse, Brigadier Johnson was completely new to his command. He had only arrived in the Middle East on 12 June and was not given command of the brigade until June 16—just four days before the Desert Fox struck.

Although Johnson was new to the theater and to his command, he knew his job and positioned his brigade well. His mobile units (the Guards brigade headquarters, the Coldstream Guards, and the Sherwood Foresters) took up old defensive positions (originally part of the Italian inner perimeter) forward of Pilastrino Ridge. The virtually immobile Worcesters he disposed in the vicinity of the derelict Fort Pilastrino, which commanded one of the two vital passes descending the coastal escarpment toward Tobruk. The other pass was 4.5 miles east of Pilastrino, where the roads from Bardia and El Adem converged at an important road junction known as King's Cross. Here lay a number of headquarters, supply units, a tank workshop, a hospital, a POW compound, and a South African post office. Strangely, even though King's Cross was of the greatest importance, it had no permanent defenders. The South Africans had had no time to restore the inner defenses of the fortress; King's Cross was covered by the 25th Field Regiment, Royal Artillery, and the 201st Guards could be called for infantry support if the situation became critical, but that was all.

The Allies were well supported by field artillery, including the 2d and 3d South African Field Regiments and the 25th Field Regiment, RA. There were also two regiments of medium artillery in the garrison: the 67th and 68th Medium Regiments, RA, each armed with eight 4.5-inch guns and eight 155mm howitzers, the largest guns in

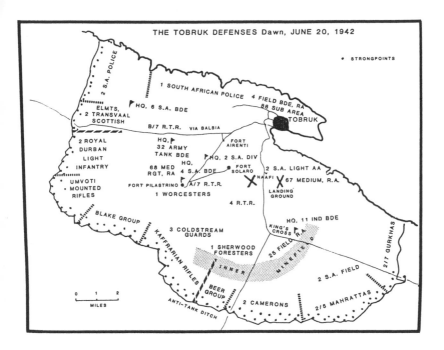

THE TOBRUK DEFENSES Dawn, JUNE 20, 1942

the fortress. Headquarters, 67th Medium Regiment, was located at the northeast corner of the main Tobruk airfield, near the Navy, Army, and Air Force Institute (NAAFI), with its batteries supporting the western half of the fortress, including the 11th Indian Brigade. The 68th Medium Regiment was headquartered just west of Fort Solaro, with batteries located a mile northwest of Fort Pilastrino, near the position known as "Fig Tree"; other guns were positioned two miles to the east. The 68th was responsible for general artillery support in the western half of the fortress. Unlike the case with the smaller guns, both medium artillery regiments faced a serious ammunition shortage. There were only 450 rounds available per gun, and the CRA (Commander, Royal Artillery) rationed it at a rate of five shells per gun per day. This would not make much of an impression on the Afrika Korps when it attacked.

The rest of the Allied artillery was quite formidable in numbers and well supplied with ammunition. It included the 2d and 3d South

African Field Regiments, the 25th Field Regiment, RA, and the 12th and 21st South African Field Batteries. The 2d and 3d SA Field Regiments were assigned to support the South African brigades. The 25th Field Regiment was attached to the Indian brigade. The problem the field artillery units had, according to Major Tower, a battery commander in the 25th Field, was that "far too much ammunition was still at the main dumps and not at the guns. We had much difficulty in getting permission to dump 200 rounds per gun and fired it all on June 20th."[4] In addition, the artillery's chain of command was vague, communications were poor to indifferent, and fireplans were complicated and obscure. Also, the CRA, Col. H. McA. Richards, who had commanded a sector of the Gazala Line during the battles there, arrived in Tobruk on 12 June. During the next few days many units came and went, and Richards could never get anyone to clearly state what units would be available for the defense. The general fireplan was never brought up to date.

There was no antitank regiment in Tobruk, but the AT units and seventy-odd antitank guns were scattered throughout the garrison. The 4th Field Brigade, RA, was in charge of antiaircraft defense and controlled eighteen 37mm guns and some Bofors—40mm automatic cannons that were called "Pom-Poms" because of their distinctively paced rate of fire. Some of these were part of the permanent defense of Tobruk and were located in fixed sites, to protect the harbor area. The 2d South African Light Anti-Aircraft Regiment had several mobile batteries distributed throughout the fortress, but the heavy flak batteries had been disassembled and sent back to Alexandria.

Finally, General Klopper also inherited the 88th Sub-Area, which was under the command of Brigadier L. F. Thompson. It controlled 10,000 base and rear area troops, about which the South Africans knew little. Gott left behind Col. G. E. R. Bastin, a tactics instructor at the South African Military College before the war, to coordinate between the 88th and General Klopper. Brigadier Thompson, however, had been the CRA during the first siege and knew the fortress well. Klopper signaled Eighth Army and requested that Thompson be named his deputy commander, but Ritchie did not move quickly and his appointment was never confirmed.

• • •

Major General H. B. Klopper, the commander of the 2d South African Division and fortress commander, Tobruk, had been director of the Infantry and Armoured Fighting Vehicle Training at Pretoria during the Union of South Africa's mobilization in 1939. Later he served as acting director of Military Training. He was noted for being a good administrator and for getting the best out of a mixed team. As a colonel, Klopper served as G-1 (chief of operations) of the 2d South African during the Siege of Bardia, when the division was commanded by Maj. Gen. I. P. de Villiers. Then he was promoted to brigadier and given command of the 3d South African Infantry Brigade, which he led for four months, before receiving his final promotion and command of the division on 14 May. He had only been in the job a few weeks, had only been a general a month, and had limited experience in mobile warfare as conducted by Erwin Rommel. Many of his staff officers were also newcomers, and there were serious temperamental differences and personality conflicts within the staff.

Klopper headquartered in the Pilastrino Caves, where the road from Pilastrino to Tobruk crossed the lower (Solaro) escarpment, and it was from here that he fought the first phases of the battle. The general and his senior staff officers lived one hundred yards away, in a pink house called the "Pink Palace."

General Klopper never forcefully established his personal command of the garrison. "Tobruk," Barnett wrote, "was commanded, in the current British manner, by a debating society."[5] Klopper called in his brigadiers at 2:00 P.M. on 15 June and announced that he was assuming command of the fortress. No tactical matters were discussed, although Willison did approach him afterwards and told him that the troop dispositions were not satisfactory. He pointed out that, in 1941, all three infantry brigades held the perimeter—not two on the perimeter and one along the coast. Furthermore, as overall armored commander (Royal Tank Commander, or RTC), he requested that all armored cars be placed under his command. He also objected to the placement of the artillery (most of it, he felt, was too far back, and the rest was too far forward), and he complained that the transport was not camouflaged and was scattered all over the place. Klopper thanked him politely for his observations but took no immediate action.

On the morning of 16 June, General Ritchie flew into Tobruk in a captured Fieseler Storch and conferred with Klopper and Gott. General Gott was now convinced that the fortress could hold out four to five months without help from the Royal Navy and even went so far as to suggest to the Eighth Army commander that he (Gott) take command of it himself. Auchinleck, however, had other plans. He had placed XXX Corps in general reserve in the Matruh area of Egypt, where it was to form and train a striking force which would eventually resume the offensive. Gott's XIII Corps was given control of the mobile forces, including the 7th Armoured Division (4th Armoured, 7th Motor, and 3d Indian Motor Brigades)—sixty-six tanks in all—plus six Jock-columns, and one brigade each from the 50th Northumbrian and 1st South African Divisions. It was to plan for two eventualities: a German attack against the Egyptian frontier, or a German attempt to storm Tobruk. Auchinleck considered the second case more likely. Klopper was told to prepare to hold the fortress in case Rommel invested it; he was also assured that El Adem and Belhamed on his southern flank would be held.

As the generals talked, the remnants of the XIII Corps continued to pass through the Tobruk sector, heading west. At the same time, the corps staff moved several transportation companies into the fortress, bringing the total number of vehicles in the garrison to 700—enough to move the entire command. This indicates that someone thought a breakout was an extremely likely possibility.[6]

After the 1st South African Division passed through Tobruk, Gott remained in the city another twenty-four hours, to check the defenses with the less experienced Klopper. During that period, anything considered unnecessary for a siege was sent out. Among other things, XIII Corps sent out eighteen 37mm guns—half of the heavy antiaircraft artillery available to the garrison. The 37s also made excellent antitank guns, and the garrison staff questioned the wisdom of sending them east. The last six Grant tanks in Tobruk were also sent to Egypt, leaving Klopper with only Matildas and Valentines. The 2d Regiment, Royal Horse Artillery, which had been attached to the 201st Guards Brigade, was also sent to the land of the pharaohs.

On the afternoon of 16 June, XIII Corps Headquarters announced that it was pulling out, and Gott and his staff departed Tobruk via the Gambut Road that same evening, leaving a very optimistic Klopper behind. He wrote to his friend, Major General Theron, the South African liaison officer in Cairo: "Things are going very well indeed with us here, as spirits are very high, and I do not think morale could be better. . . . There is a general feeling of optimism, and I think there is every reason for it. . . . We are all looking forward to a good stand, and we are supported by the very best British troops."[7]

Initially, it seemed as if this optimism was justified for, on 16 June, the garrison won the opening round against Panzer Army Afrika. The Germans' target was Acroma Keep, a position that dominated the Axis Bypass Road, which had been built for Rommel by the Italians in 1941. It was garrisoned by a reinforced company of the 2d Transvaal Scottish, including mortars and a machine-gun platoon from Die Middellandse Regiment (a South African heavy-weapons battalion). The Keep garrison also boasted a captured German 88mm gun and four Italian 47mm guns, all without sights. The garrison was supported by the 68th Medium Regiment, RA.

The battle began when the Keep was shelled by the 104th Artillery Command; then Colonel Menny's 15th Rifle Brigade tried to lift the protective mines, but was beaten back by the garrison. The next day's battle was a repeat of the day before. In addition, an Italian motorized infantry column attacked from the south, but came too close to the Keep in its trucks and was smashed. The Transvaal Scots killed about eighty men and took two hundred prisoners.

Later that day, an ominous development occurred. The Umvoti Mounted Rifles on Ras el Medawar noticed an unusual stillness at El Adem, fifteen miles away. They sent a patrol to investigate and found the position in German hands. One of the two cornerstones to the Tobruk defense had been lost. The other, Belhamed, was also in grave danger. That same day, 17 June, Tobruk was placed directly under the command of Eighth Army, while XIII Corps was made responsible for building up a strike force on the frontier to rescue the garrison. That afternoon the Afrika Korps made its move to the north, and reached the Coastal Road thirty minutes after midnight. Tobruk was surrounded.

On 18 June, Rommel completed the second investment of Tobruk. On the Allied right flank, the Trieste Motorized Division and the German 33d Panzer Reconnaissance Battalion advanced down the Coastal Road and closed in on the perimeter from the west, while the Italian X Corps took positions south of the fortress, above El Adem. General Navarini's Italian XXI Corps and the German 15th Rifle Brigade closed in from the south and east, despite the resistance from Acroma Keep, while the Afrika Korps and 90th Light Division pressed beyond Gambut. The DAK deployed as if it intended to invade Egypt and made sure that Eighth Army was out of the picture for the final assault on Tobruk, while the Italian XX Motorized Corps, including the Ariete and newly arrived Littorio Armored Divisions, took up positions around Sidi Rezegh and El Adem respectively, to guard against British interference from the south. The 90th Light, meanwhile, reported the capture of "enormous" quantities of fuel, rations, water, and ammunition in the Gambut sector.[8] The German *Feldgrau* ("field gray," the companion in misfortune to the American GI or the British "Tommy") enjoyed all of the captured booty (Allied food was of a much higher quality than that produced by the field kitchens of the German Army), but seemed to be particularly fond of the fruit, especially the canned peaches from California.

Early on the morning of 18 June, Rommel reported to OKW that Tobruk was now invested and the area forty miles east and southeast of it had been cleared of the enemy. He had succeeded in giving the British the impression that he was going to continue his advance to the east and only intended to besiege Tobruk. Simultaneously, he had captured enough maneuvering room to attack the place. He also captured several huge supply dumps in and around Gambut, and now had plenty of fuel, rations, and ammunition for his attempt to storm the fortress. Much of this ammunition fit the British twenty-five-pound gun—an excellent weapon which was now a mainstay of the Panzer Army Artillery. In addition, he seized fifteen Allied airplanes intact and forced the South Africans to burn four Boston bombers, in order to prevent their capture. Several British motor convoys were also captured on the Via Balbia, while smaller groups of Allied soldiers were run down and taken prisoner in the desert to the south.

While the Afrika Korps made as if it intended to continue the attack to the east, Rommel doubled back to the west with his battle staff and his Kampfstaffel. He was almost killed near El Adem by a British column, which included a troop of twenty-five-pound guns. The Kampfstaffel drove them off, but the British gunners redeployed and forced an irritated Desert Fox to seek safety in the El Adem box, which had housed Norrie's XXX Corps Headquarters just a few days before.

Rommel was especially concerned that Acroma Keep had not yet fallen. On 18 June, the 15th Rifle Brigade attacked it again and was again repulsed. It was then joined by the Italian XXI Corps and a group of tanks, but they were also checked. At 3:30 P.M., the 15th Rifle attacked again and began to gain ground slowly, but by 5:30 P.M. was bogged down in a minefield. Rommel himself apparently accompanied this attack, because he was also pinned down. The South Africans also knocked out a PzKw II, which was the victim of a lucky hit by a mortar bomb.

When night fell and darkness at last restored his freedom of maneuver, an impatient Rommel demanded that the Italian XXI Corps capture the Keep with all possible speed. The garrison, however, realized that its position was growing increasingly untenable, so it evacuated the place at ten-thirty that night. It had lost only one man killed.

There was very little Luftwaffe activity on 18 or 19 June, because the German Air Force was preparing for a maximum effort on 20 June. The RAF, meanwhile, was gone. Eighth Army could provide the British fighters no security at Sidi Azeiz, and the fast-moving Germans—including the Afrika Korps—were known to be east of Tobruk. Air Vice-Marshal Coningham therefore withdrew his fighters back to the airfields near Sidi Barrani. The entire fighter arm of the Desert Air Force was now out of range of Tobruk except for Number 250 Squadron—a few Kittyhawks equipped with long-range tanks. The last British airplane departed on 19 June, and just in time at that: the Germans arrived the next day.

• • •

Rommel issued his plans for the final assault on Tobruk on 17 June (see Map 15). The Afrika Korps and 90th Light would deploy as if to continue their drive into Egypt; then, on the night of 19–20 June, they would turn around and head west, directly into the assault. The main attack would begin at 5:20 A.M., when dozens of Stukas would pound Allied lines, with especially heavy concentrations in the zone of the 11th Indian Brigade. At the same time, Group Menny (the 15th Rifle Brigade) would launch a diversionary attack against the southeastern perimeter. As soon as the aerial bombardment ended, the engineers would push into the defenses and bridge the antitank ditch, while Menny rejoined the DAK for the main attack. As soon as the AT ditch was bridged, the Afrika Korps and the 15th Rifle Brigade would charge across, breach the perimeter between Points R.71 and R.59, and break through the Allied defenses in the zone of the 2/5th Mahratta Light Infantry, with the 21st Panzer Division on the right, Group Menny in the center, and 15th Panzer on the left. They would then drive into the British rear, where the main body under General Nehring would turn west, in the direction of Fort Pilastrino, while a strong secondary force (21st Panzer Division under General von Bismarck) captured the harbor, to prevent a Dunkirk-like embarkation. At the same time as the main attack, the Italian XX Motorized Corps would breach the perimeter between Points R.57 and R.49 (in the zone of the Cameron Highlanders) and drive through the Allied rear toward Fort Pilastrino. Meanwhile, the Italian X Corps would mop up and consolidate behind the panzers, while the XXI Corps feinted an attack from the west, using smoke screens, strong artillery, and a few tanks. While the assault took place, the 90th Light Division (with Special Unit 288 and the 155th Grenadier Regiment) would take up positions between Sidi Rezegh and Belhamed, while the 3d and 33d Panzer Reconnaissance Battalions (still under the command of the 90th Light) pushed into the desert forward of the line Sidi Rezegh–Bir el Gubi, to form a screen and an early warning system, in the unlikely event Eighth Army's armor became aggressive again. The Italian Trieste, Pavia, and Littorio Divisions would cover Rommel's deep southern flank.

The Germans continued to probe British defenses on the fron-

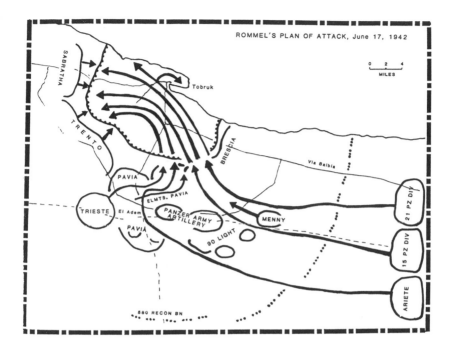

tier throughout 19 June, and a battalion from the 90th Light even managed to capture the minor port of Bardia that afternoon. The Afrika Korps began to disengage from the Eighth Army near the Egyptian frontier at 4:00 P.M. on 19 June. When darkness fell, it headed for Tobruk, while Ariete came up from the desert south of Sidi Rezegh and tied in with the DAK on its right just before the attack. Meanwhile, the 90th Light established a screen from the sea to south of Trigh Capuzzo, and the Littorio Armored Division (fresh from the mainland) and the Pavia Infantry Division faced south, to guard against interference from the British 7th Motor Brigade.

Despite the fact that a complicated night maneuver of this nature invites problems and confusion, especially when employing overworked troops, everything went according to plan except for Colonel Menny's diversionary attack. The Desert Fox canceled it, mainly because General Nehring objected to it and was anxious that the infantry support he had been promised might not be there when he needed it. (The Afrika Korps was desperately short of infantry.) Even this worked out to Rommel's advantage. As luck would have it, the garrison staff regarded the southeast and southwest sectors of the perimeter as equally likely targets for Rommel's attack. They assumed he would feint against one side, then launch the main attack against the other—which is exactly what he intended to do. When he did not feint, Klopper and his closest advisors assumed that the first attack was not the major offensive and did not react quickly. By the time they committed their reserves, it would be too late.

For the big attack, the Afrika Korps had about 130 operational tanks. As of the morning of 19 June, Crasemann's 15th Panzer Division had six PzKw IIs, thirty-four PzKw IIIs, six PzKw III Specials, two PzKw IVs, and one Panzer Mark IV Special—forty-nine tanks in all. At the same time, the 21st Panzer had fifty-three "runners"—ten PzKw IIs, twenty-nine PzKw IIIs, nine PzKw III Specials, a pair of PzKw IVs, and three PzKw IV Specials. The headquarters company of the Afrika Korps had three PzKw IIIs, giving the DAK a total tank strength of 105 operational panzers (excluding captured tanks). By evening, however, the tank strength of the 15th Panzer Division had increased to sixty, thanks to the efforts of the men in the workshops, and the 21st Panzer's strength must have increased to about the same number. Work continued throughout the night; the exact number of tanks available on 20 June was not reported, but it was considerably higher than that of the 32d Army Tank Brigade, the only armored unit present in the Tobruk pocket.

At 3:30 A.M., General von Bismarck reported that the 21st Panzer Division (which had left the frontier at 5:00 P.M. the previous afternoon) was fully ready to attack Tobruk. Neither the garrison nor the Eighth Army was yet aware of Rommel's redeployment, because it had been so rapid and the fortress did not have the luxury of aerial reconnaissance. Most of the garrison slept a peaceful sleep during the night of 19–20 June, unaware that they were about to be pounded by a vastly superior enemy. The majority of the soldiers did not even believe Rommel would attack them; they thought he would strike the rest of the Eighth Army instead.

Field Marshal Rommel, on the other hand, was wide awake before 4:30 A.M. As was his custom, he wrote a prebattle letter to his wife. "Today's the big day," he said. "Let's hope Lady Luck stays faithful to me. I'm dog-tired, otherwise okay."[9] The fatigue that had affected the Afrika Korps earlier was not a factor in this battle, however. "To every man of us, Tobruk was a symbol of British resistance, and we were now going to finish with it for good," Rommel wrote later.[10] Determination, excitement, and professional competence would be much more in evidence than fatigue on 20 June.

Promptly at 5:20 A.M., just as dawn was breaking, the aerial bombardment began. "Kesselring had been as good as his word and sent hundreds of bombers in dense formations," Colonel von Mellenthin recalled. "They dived on the perimeter in one of the most spectacular attacks I have ever seen."[11]

Captain Faure Walker of the Coldstream Guards recalled: "Never have I seen such a mountain of dust and smoke that towered in the sky after those bombers had done their work. They came again and again, and I realized that from now on we should get this hourly, for their aerodrome was only ten miles off and we were never going to see a British fighter."[12]

Although his effort would pale by comparison to the Anglo-American air raids of 1944 and 1945, Kesselring did, in fact, throw into action every fighter and bomb carrier he could lay his hands on. Every bomber and dive-bomber in Africa was in the Tobruk sector, and airplanes joined the attacks from as far away as Crete and Greece. In all, Second Air Fleet committed about one hundred fifty bombers and Stuka dive-bombers, as well as fifty German and more than a hundred Italian fighters. The nearness of the landing grounds at Sidi Rezegh, Gazala, and El Adem made "shuttle bombing" possible. German airplanes flew no less than 580 bombing sorties on 20 June (thirty of them from Crete), and the Italians flew 177. In all, the Luftwaffe dropped more than 300 tons of high explosives on the fortress, and the Italians added about sixty-five tons more. Kesselring lost only three aircraft: two Stukas (destroyed in a midair collision) and a Me-110 twin-engine fighter, smashed in a crash landing. The Italians suffered no losses at all.

"The air attack was extraordinarily effective," the Afrika Korps *Schlachtbericht* (battle report) stated. "It shattered strongly fortified positions, in particular the infantry wire obstacles, and had a profound effect on the fighting morale of the 11th Indian Brigade . . ."[13]

"I myself watched the astounding effect of the attack," Rommel wrote later. "Great fountains of dust rose from the fortifications occupied by the Indians, whirling entanglements and weapons through the air. One direct hit after another tore the wire obstacles to bits."[14] Due to the intensity of the bombardment, Allied forward observers had difficulty picking up targets and, in the confusion of shellbursts, in identifying and adjusting the fire of their own guns. The Panzer Army artillery, on the other hand, had no trouble putting down a heavy and concentrated fusillade on the area around Strongpoint R.63, in the Mahratta sector.

After the artillery barrage had been in progress for some time, clouds of orange smoke were seen. This was the signal to the engineers that the range was being lengthened. It was time for them to move forward to breach the minefields, the wire, and the antitank ditch. Even though an irritated Georg von Bismarck relieved the leader of the 200th Engineer Battalion of his command at 6:13 A.M. (because he thought inadequate progress was being made on bridging the antitank ditch), the panzer engineers, in fact, did their usual good job in pushing into the British perimeter. At 6:35 A.M., the vanguard of the 15th Rifle Brigade reported to the headquarters of the DAK that the wire in front of Strongpoint R.69 had been cut, and Colonel Menny asked that the artillery increase its range. The weakness of the initial resistance surprised the Germans, and, at Indian brigade headquarters, it was greeted with disbelief. When a forward observer from the 2d South African Field Battery reported that the garrison of one of the strongpoints had surrendered and marched out as a body, the Indian brigade staff officers coldly informed him that they were obviously preparing for a counterattack.[15] Yet the Indians had not been taken by surprise. Of all of the units trapped inside Tobruk, the 11th Indian Brigade alone seems to have realized that an attack was imminent, and it was going to be deeply involved. Its leader, Brigadier Anderson, was a tough and competent officer who had joined the army as a private in the 2d Cameron Highlanders and had risen to command of the battalion before he took charge of the brigade.[16] He had already sent out patrols and established listening posts, and they had heard the sounds of considerable movement in the Axis rear, especially tracked vehicles coming from the direction of Belhamed. They had also noted an unusual display of flares and signal lights. Once the Germans attacked, Anderson promptly committed his reserve into the correct sector, and by 7:30 A.M. had ordered the Gurkha reserve into the counterattack as well. The truth was that the Stuka bombardment had simply broken the morale of the 11th Indian, especially the Mahrattas.

Following closely behind their artillery bombardment, the German infantrymen took many prisoners without much difficulty. The garrisons of several posts were driven underground by the air and artillery bombardment and were not able to determine what was happening on the surface above them until they were suddenly called upon to surrender. During the 1941 siege, Jan Yindrich asked the Australians why they were not using the elaborate underground concrete dugouts built by the Italians. They told him that they could see nothing from the inside. Yindrich wrote: "'You could get caught like a rat in a trap down one of those,' one rawboned private told me. 'The enemy could advance and overrun your position. You wouldn't know anything about it.'"[17] This happened to hundreds of Indians on 20 June.

At 6:58 A.M., the 104th Panzer Grenadier Regiment reported the fall of a strongpoint, while the commander of the 155th Panzer Artillery Regiment reported that R.62 and R.65 had fallen. Five minutes later, Colonel Menny reported the capture of an entire Indian company. Just after 7:00 A.M., Lieutenant Colonel Lancaster, the commander of the 2d Mahrattas, reported that the Germans were within 400 yards of his command post and that he was launching an immediate counterattack with his last reserves.[18] But he simply did not have enough men to make much of an impact. By 7:15 A.M., 21st Panzer Division had penetrated the first belt of fortifications, and Group Menny had captured a bridge crossing the antitank ditch. By 7:45 A.M., most of the strongpoints between R.58 and R.69 had fallen, and 15th Panzer Division signaled that it had captured a good crossing point between R.63 and R.58. Nehring ordered the tanks to advance.

By 7:55 A.M., the AT ditch was bridged, a bridgehead a mile in depth had been formed, and the panzers were pouring into the opening. Group Menny had not been able to take R.71, a strongpoint 400 yards from the Mahratta headquarters, due to the strong supporting fire of its neighbor, R.73. This, however, was on the extreme flank of the German penetration and was the only place they were halted.

Brigadier Anderson knew that his brigade would not be enough to block the entire German Afrika Korps. Early on, he realized the scale of Rommel's offensive and was calling for help from the fortress reserves. About 7:00 A.M., General Klopper ordered a battalion of tanks from the 32d Army Tank Brigade to counterattack, supported by infantry and antitank guns from the 201st Guards Brigade. This order was sent to Brigadier Willison, who was instructed to coordinate the attack with the Indians.

Anderson intended to use the tanks to check the German infantry and to use the infantry and antitank guns to counterattack and plug the gap in the perimeter. He realized it was critical to employ the Matildas and Valentines before the panzers and German antitank gunners could establish themselves. It was therefore essential that the tanks be thrown into battle at once. But it was about 8:00 A.M. before Brigadier Willison summoned Lieutenant Colonel Reeves, the commander of the 4th RTR, to his command post and ordered him to send one of his squadrons (i.e., battalions) against the German penetration. Reeves, however, concerned himself only with his tanks; he did not feel any responsibility for coordinating his activities with those of the Indians or the 201st Guards.

The two squadrons of the 4th RTR were well dispersed and well dug in, and it took some time for the regiment to get the first one moving. In the interval, the decision was made (apparently by Klopper) to send in the other squadron as well. They moved off one behind the other and made the slow climb up the escarpment, and, at 9:30 A.M., the leading elements reached King's Cross, where they met the liaison officer from the Mahrattas, who was supposed to guide them to the battalion headquarters at R.72. (Brigadier Anderson, who had waited for Reeves at King's Cross for some time, had already lost patience and returned to his own HQ, where he continued to put pressure on Klopper for his tanks.) By the time the "I" tanks reached King's Cross, it was already under heavy shell fire. Colonel Reeves met briefly with the detachment commander from the 201st

Guards but did not seem to grasp that they were supposed to cooperate. Without waiting for the infantry or their antitank support, Reeves and the 4th RTR advanced down the Bardia Road, but did not make contact with the 11th Indian Brigade or the Mahrattas. They were already more than an hour too late.

Rommel's first tanks (part of the 21st Panzer Division) crossed the antitank ditch under light artillery fire at 8:31 A.M. The Desert Fox himself was in one of the forward panzers. Fourteen minutes later, Crasemann's 15th Panzer crossed the ditch, accompanied by Walter Nehring, the commander of the Afrika Korps. Ariete crossed the ditch about ten minutes later, but then bogged down in front of R.53 and would not take the strongpoint until after 2:00 P.M. Meanwhile, however, the panzers of the Afrika Korps poured into the breach. At 9:45, Mueller's 8th Panzer Regiment (of the 15th Panzer Division) reported the first clash with British tanks. (They were probably not tanks at all, but the Bren carriers of the 11th Indian.) Bismarck's division joined the action about ten minutes later. The panzers were now on the southern edge of the second minefield (i.e., the inner perimeter minefield), where they were fired upon by the 25th Field Regiment, Royal Artillery. Despite the shelling, the 15th Panzer continued to advance smoothly, but the 21st Panzer Division (on the right flank of the advance) bogged down in a minefield. General von Bismarck came up personally, reconnoitered the area, and discovered a gap in the minefield, through which he led his tanks. As usual for him, he directed his troops from the sidecar of a motorcycle.

By 10:00 A.M., Bismarck had gotten the advance of the 21st Panzer back on track. Colonel Lancaster reported that panzers were approaching his headquarters, and he was about to destroy his radio set. Then there was silence. The Mahrattas battalion was finished. The "Africans" pressed on toward their next victim: an artillery troop from the 2d South African Field Battery about a mile and a quarter north of R.68. First they fired heavy machine guns on the pieces, forcing the gunners to take cover; when they did, they ran over the guns with their tanks.

Meanwhile, Colonel Reeves and the 4th RTR reached the gap in the inner minefield on the Bardia Road. Its original orders (to cooperate with the Mahrattas) were no longer valid, since the battalion no longer existed. Reeves positioned his two squadrons in hull-down positions, each covering one of the two gaps in the inner (Blue Line) minefield. Meanwhile, about 10:00 A.M., Lieutenant Colonel Foote, the commander of the 7th RTR, was ordered to move up and to concentrate west of King's Cross. He came up much more quickly than had the 4th RTR and soon was at one of the gaps in the inner minefield, where he met with Colonel Reeves. They agreed that Foote should bring his tanks up on the right of the 4th RTR, to engage the greatest number of guns against a large German tank formation was heading west (this turned out to be the main body of the 15th Panzer Division). On his way back to his regiment, Foote called HQ, 11th Indian Brigade, and informed Anderson that the situation was in hand. This was news to the brigadier, who expressed concern about the Cameron Highlanders, into whose rear the 15th Panzer was advancing. Foote agreed to send B Squadron of the 7th RTR to the Camerons' command post, while A Squadron moved up to the left gap, where the 4th RTR had already suffered heavy casualties.

While the tanks, panzer grenadiers, and antitank gunners of the Afrika Korps dealt with the unsupported British armor, two companies and an antitank platoon from the Coldstream Guards sat down and waited 1,000 yards west of King's Cross. Reeves and the tanks had left them far behind. "The detachment commander reasonably decided that as there was no plan his small force could do nothing but await events," the British Official History recorded later.[19]

Shortly after 10:00 A.M., a lull in the advance occurred. The German Panzertruppen mistakenly thought they had entered a heavily mined area, so they halted and called for the engineers with mine detectors. They would not discover their mistake until almost 11:00 A.M., giving the British the chance to at least partially regain control of the battle, but the opportunity was wasted. About the time the panzers halted, Colonel Richards, the commander, Royal Artillery, told Major Pope, the commander of the 25th Field Regiment, RA, that Fortress Headquarters was uncertain as to the principal direction of the German attack and (misled by initial reports that only two companies of German infantry were involved in the first strike) would send no artillery reinforcements until that direction was determined. Richards, however, did reinforce Pope with the 95th Anti-Tank Battery, RA. Colonel Tuck, the commander of the medium artillery forces, rang up CRA twice during the morning and suggested that the 68th Medium Regiment be moved forward to fire on the threatened sector, but was told not to change his dispositions.

The German blitzkrieg resumed at 11:00 A.M., when the 21st Panzer attacked on the right flank and overran the remaining troops of the 2d South African Battery. The Headquarters, 25th Field Regiment—which earlier had been refused permission to withdraw—was pinned down and could not retreat. Major Morris, the regimental commander, was wounded and was carried to a first-aid station, where he was captured when the Germans overran the place at 12:20 P.M. Meanwhile, at 11:00 A.M., 15th Panzer Division claimed the destruction of fifteen tanks and the capture of 150 prisoners of war. Seven minutes later it reported that it was through the second minefield and advancing rapidly. Meanwhile, the Brescia Infantry Division followed the Afrika Korps into the breach, to mop up scattered pockets of resistance which had been left behind by the infantry-poor DAK.

At noon, the 21st Panzer cut the Via Balbia at Kilometer Marker 13, which was inside the inner minefield. By now, roughly fifty British tanks had been destroyed. At this point, the 4th RTR finally gave way and fell back from the inner minefield with its six remaining tanks. The three surviving guns of the 25th Field Regiment got away about the same time. At this moment someone cut a field telephone wire, and communications between Fortress Headquarters and the 11th Indian Brigade failed completely.

Colonel Foote also fell back toward King's Cross and signaled for B Squadron to join him there. It tried, but was ambushed by Nehring and the 15th Panzer Division about 12:45 P.M. and was completely destroyed.

Reeves arrived back at King's Cross at 1:00 P.M. and told the Coldstream Guards officers that his command had been destroyed. He handed his last six tanks over to Colonel Foote and returned to brigade headquarters, to report to Brigadier Willison.

The Afrika Korps approached King's Cross in three columns shortly after 1:00 P.M. On the right, 21st Panzer advanced westward along the Bardia Road. On the left, 15th Panzer drove on the vital crossroads from the south, while about forty to fifty panzers moved up from the southeast. They came abreast for the final attack on the crossroads, which was to be an all-out assault.

With their tank forces largely destroyed, the British concentrated several artillery units to defend King's Cross. These included elements of Headquarters Battery and three troops from the 6th South African Light Anti-Aircraft; a troop of the 287th Field Battery, RA; two antitank guns from the 95th AT Battery; D Troop, 5th South African Field Battery; 31/58th Field Battery, RA; and 12/25th Field Battery, RA. The bulk of the 3d Coldstream Guards, now led by Maj. W. D. H. C. "Willie" Forbes, a handful of tanks under Colonel Foote, and a few miscellaneous units also joined the battle. But they had to hold a line more than four miles long against two panzer divisions and the equivalent of an infantry brigade. They destroyed several panzers, but the unequal battle did not last long, and most of the Allied guns were heaps of scrap metal by 1:30 P.M. About the same time, the Headquarters of the 11th Indian Brigade and the HQ, 25th Field Regiment, which were situated in a wadi in the escarpment just within the inner minefield, were overrun by the "Africans." Brigadier Anderson fled just in time and escaped with a few members of his staff. Major Pope of the 25th Field—who had put up a very gallant fight—blew up his last two guns and hid in the wadis, along with several of his men. "Willie" Forbes and the Coldstream Guards fought with great courage, as usual, but were overwhelmed. Forbes was captured and half of his battalion was either killed or taken prisoner. Maj. H. M. "Tim" Sainthill, the former commander of Number 2 Company (the antitank company) took charge of the remnants and led them off the field in the general direction of Fort Pilastrino. Meanwhile, several administrative and supply units were also overrun or scattered by the DAK, and the hospital was captured. By 2:00 P.M., all of the Allied artillery on and in front of the Blue Line had been destroyed, with the exception of a few isolated detachments.[20] Map 16 shows the German penetration as of 2:00 P.M.

At 1:30 p.m., Rommel signaled that the dominating heights four to five miles from the harbor (i.e., King's Cross) had been taken. The Germans were struck by the patchy nature of the defense and re-

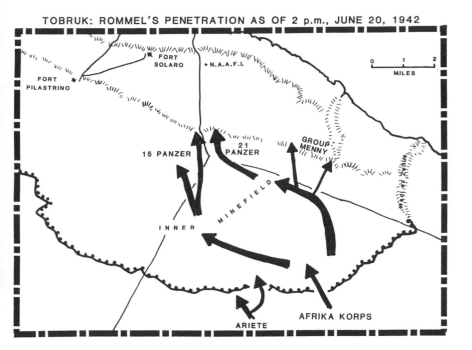

TOBRUK: ROMMEL'S PENETRATION AS OF 2 p.m., JUNE 20, 1942

ported that the "enemy reacted violently but locally." Major General Count Folchi-Vici, the commander of the Ariete Division, felt that the defending forces were too few to cover the long perimeter adequately.[21]

Meanwhile, at 1:45 P.M., Bismarck signaled that he was about to attack the aerodrome. He had reached the escarpment east of King's Cross and was ready to descend to the plain beneath, and asked Nehring to protect his flank with elements of the 15th Panzer—all the way to the harbor.

A few minutes later, Group Menny (with the 100mm batteries of the 21st Panzer Division attached) branched off to Chteita, from which it could bring direct fire on the harbor.

Rommel himself was at King's Cross by 2:00 P.M., standing up in his car and looking for the first time at the harbor of Tobruk—the objective that had eluded him for so long. Here he briefly talked with the commander of the 6th South African Light AA, who was now a prisoner of war, and made his preparations for the final push.

A few miles away, General Klopper was also issuing orders, but—unlike Rommel—was too far away from the point of action to have much effect on the battle. For example, about 2:00 P.M., he ordered that the El Adem Road and the inner perimeter be held with the Guards Brigade, the 7th RTR, and the artillery. By this time, however, all but a remnant of the 7th RTR had ceased to exist, and most of the artillery was also gone.

Klopper had not had a clear and timely picture of how the battle was progressing since it began, but he experienced a growing sense of uneasiness all morning. Finally, about 11:00 A.M., he complained that he was "completely in the dark" and decided to go see for himself, but—unfortunately—he was talked out of it by Colonel Bastin (the Eighth Army liaison officer) and his own chief of staff, Lieutenant Colonel Kriek, who told him that his place was at headquarters.[22] He did not get a firm idea of the extent of the disaster that was about to overwhelm him until after 3:00 P.M., when Brigadier Willison reported to Fortress Headquarters that his entire command had been destroyed. He asked for and received permission to break out. About the same time Brigadier Anderson arrived at the Pink Palace, but left shortly thereafter. He still hoped to reach the Camerons, which were holding the El Adem gate.

From his own experience as chief of staff at Bardia, Klopper realized how easily a strong position could be overcome, even by inferior numbers, once its perimeter had been penetrated. Klopper advised Colonel Bastin to leave by sea and began to organize a new defensive line running north to south, generally along the El Adem Road. He ordered Brigadier Hayton to take command of the remnants of the 11th Indian Brigade and to organize the southern section of the new line. He also ordered the 4th and 6th South African Brigades to each detach a reinforced company (with antitank guns) for night counterattacks against the German laagers.

Meanwhile, between 2:00 P.M. and 3:00 P.M., the 21st Panzer descended the escarpment a mile and a half east of King's Cross and captured the main airfield, scattering the handful of "I" tanks Colonel Foote had left in the process. There was now nothing between Rommel and Tobruk except the 9th South African Field Battery, a troop of the 5th, a troop of the 231st Medium Battery, RA, and four guns of the 277th Heavy Anti-Aircraft Battery, RA. They put up a stiff fight, destroyed several panzers, and delayed the advance until 4:00 P.M., when they were finally destroyed or pushed off the battlefield to the west. (Unfortunately, German records of tank losses for 20 June are missing.) Rommel later had nothing but praise for their "extraordinary tenacity."[23]

The fortitude of the artillery allowed Brigadier Thompson, the commander of the 88th Sub-Area, to start his demolition program, which he initiated sometime after 3:15 P.M. Soon the smoke from the large fuel tanks could be seen twenty miles away. But the Tobruk depots and supply dumps contained 3,000,000 rations, 7,000 tons of water, 1,500,000 gallons of gasoline, and more than 130,000 rounds of artillery. It would take days to destroy it all, and Thompson had but hours.

At 4:00 P.M., the 21st Panzer Division began descending the last escarpment before the harbor—and approached the Pink Palace. At that moment, the Fortress Headquarters was informed that enemy tanks were nearby. The staff hurriedly destroyed their papers and fled, most of them turning up later at the Headquarters, 6th South African Brigade. Meanwhile, the 15th Panzer Division turned toward Pilastrino Ridge, to deal with Klopper's last significant mobile reserve, the 201st Guards Brigade.

General von Bismarck captured the last airstrip between 4:00 and 4:30 P.M., halted, and signaled General Nehring, asking that the 15th Panzer Division be required to capture Fort Solaro before 21st Panzer finished its advance to the harbor. DAK relayed the request to Crasemann, who replied that he would first have to dispose of the Guards Brigade, on the high ground between King's Cross and Pilastrino. Soon Rommel interjected himself into the argument, for he was not about to allow the advance to be held up because of a minor tactical disagreement. At 5:00 P.M., Georg von Bismarck asked that the artillery fire on the harbor be lifted, and the drive for Tobruk resumed about 5:15. There was little left to stop him. The Headquarters, 88th Sub-Area, located just outside the city, was overrun at 5:40. Five minutes later, the staff of the Senior Naval Officer, Inshore Squadron, began executing his demolitions plan. Staff officers and sailors, armed only with rifles, valiantly tried to halt the advance of the panzers, while others wrecked petroleum tanks, water tanks, the distillation and refrigeration plants, and some of the motor transport. It was too late to do much damage, however, and the base supply depot near the ruined Fort Airente was captured virtually intact.

Meanwhile, the panzers and veteran Afrika Korps infantry crushed the courageous but futile resistance of the sailors and base personnel, and pushed to the water's edge. As several British lighters full of men tried to escape, Lt. Heinrich Dammann, commander of the nearest 88mm battery, hesitated to fire until Rommel himself rushed up. "Get on with it, Dammann," he cried in his native Swabian dialect, into which he always lapsed when he was excited. "Shoot, man, shoot! You can almost spit into the harbor!"

The 88s opened up at once. Capt. Frank Montem Smith, the Naval Officer in Charge, Tobruk, had fought until the Germans pushed to the water's edge. Then he jumped onto a large lighter and tried to escape. Smith's lighter was smashed by 88mm shells; soon the engine compartment was on fire and another shell burst on the bridge, killing or wounding all of the officers. The lighter, out of control, drifted back to land. Captain Smith's arm was smashed by shrapnel, and he died the following night.[24] Captain Walter, the Senior Naval Officer, Inshore Squadron, was also seriously wounded, and Brigadier Thompson was firing a machine gun from the roof of a house when he was captured by the DAK. Most of the landing craft and motor launches of the Inshore Squadron were sunk, either by airplanes or panzers, before they could weigh anchor. With their decks full of refugees, the South African antisubmarine vessels *Bever* and *Parktown* cast off at 8:00 P.M. and managed to reach open sea, despite heavy fire from German tanks and self-propelled guns. The *Parktown,* however, was sunk by German E-boats (motorized patrol boats) the next day. In all, two minesweepers and thirteen other craft of various sorts escaped. Twenty-four tugs, launches, schooners, and landing craft were lost in the harbor or en route to Alexandria.[25]

At 7:00 P.M., 21st Panzer announced the capture of the town and harbor of Tobruk. Meanwhile, it pushed some distance to the west, across the Solaro Plain, overrunning several transportation companies and the "B" echelon of the 32d Army Tank Brigade. Most of the German troops then halted, to sleep the sleep of exhaustion. Rommel ordered that the attack be continued at first light. Map 17 shows the situation outside the Tobruk perimeter as of nightfall on 20 June. Meanwhile, at 3:12 P.M., the 15th Panzer Division engaged in a tank battle west of the airfield and northwest of King's Cross. Here it claimed the destruction of thirty tanks (probably from the 7th RTR) in the last serious tank encounter of the operation. The main resistance after that was put up at Fort Solaro, which was defended by fifteen South African twenty-five-pounders and three British 37mm antiaircraft guns. They fought hard but were soon overwhelmed.

The 201st Guards Brigade deployed along Pilastrino Ridge, from a point about a mile southwest of King's Cross to Fort Pilastrino, four miles away. East to west, it deployed the Sherwood Foresters, the Brigade Headquarters, the remnants of the Coldstream Guards, and the Worcestershires at Fort Pilastrino. There was practically no natural cover here and the rocky ground made digging all but impossible.

Crasemann's division attacked about 5:00 P.M. and overran the two easternmost companies of the Sherwood Foresters, taking another 300 prisoners. Half an hour later, 15th Panzer Division signaled that the 33d Anti-Tank Battalion had taken Gabr Gasem, along with 300 prisoners and several guns captured or destroyed. Fifteen minutes later, the division reported the capture of another 200 prisoners from the escarpment. About the same time, a dozen panzers approached the headquarters of the 201st Guards. Apparently someone had told them where it was. One of the German tanks drove up to the headquarters dugout, flying a white flag, and a German officer began a discussion with Brigadier Johnson. Shortly thereafter, word was sent out to the subordinate units to lay down their arms: the 201st Guards had surrendered. Only Tim Sainthill, the commander of the 3d Coldstream Guards, refused to comply. He extricated his Number 4 Company, about fifty survivors from other units, and six antitank guns, and withdrew to positions near Fort Pilastrino. The Germans did not follow him but headed for the fort itself. The fort reportedly surrendered to the 15th Panzer shortly after 7:00 P.M.

And what was happening at Eighth Army while all of this was going on? Very little, actually. Ritchie had promised that if the Panzer

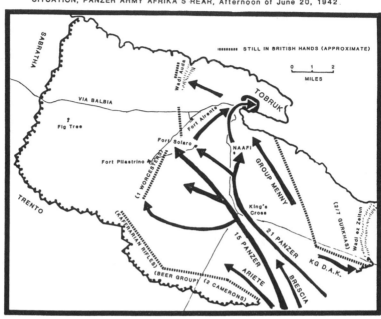

SITUATION, PANZER ARMY AFRIKA'S REAR, Afternoon of June 20, 1942.

Army did attack Tobruk in strength, a strike force of 116 guns and sixty-six tanks would seize Ramy Ridge and make a feint into the Belhamed-Sidi Rezegh sector, in the rear of the assaulting divisions, as soon as they were decisively engaged. Nothing of the sort was done, however—partially because Ritchie was away from his headquarters, visiting his corps commanders, and did not return until 3:00 A.M. on 21 June; and partially because no one in the fortress seemed to know what was going on, especially after the Pink Palace was overrun. It was unlikely that anything would have been done in any case. On 19 June, the day before Rommel unleashed his attack, Ritchie ordered Norrie to sack Maj. Gen. Sir Frank Messervy, a move that was probably overdue. Norrie nevertheless declared that he did not support this decision and, if the Eighth Army commander wanted Messervy relieved, he would have to do it himself. Ritchie therefore summoned the unfortunate general to Eighth Army Headquarters and, in an amiable manner, relieved him of his command.[26] That same day, Sir Frank handed the leadership of the 7th Armoured over to Brigadier Renton. Ritchie instructed the new divisional commander to harass the southern flank of the Panzer Army, but not to become decisively engaged. With 7th Armoured under such orders, it obviously posed no threat to General Rommel.

As we have seen, the Desert Fox had posted considerable forces below Tobruk to cover his southern flank, including all three of his reconnaissance battalions, part of the 90th Light Division, and the Italian Trieste Motorized, Pavia Infantry, and 133d Littorio Armored Divisions.[27] Few of them were engaged. The 580th Reconnaissance Battalion did turn back a British column fourteen miles northwest of Bir el Gubi, and the Pavia Division reported coming under fire as it covered the El Adem crossroads, so it was reinforced with the San Marco Battalion and a battery of 100mm howitzers. At 6:45 P.M., the Littorio Division (which was farther east) reported being under artillery fire, but none of this activity in any way disturbed Erwin Rommel. In fact, the Germans on the frontier gave as good as they got. The 3d Panzer Reconnaissance Battalion harassed the Allied forces between Bardia and Capuzzo all morning, and, late that afternoon, the 90th Light Division captured another supply dump, full of "new underwear, tents, trousers, shoes, and towels."[28] Map 17, p. 178, shows the movements and probes in the rear of Panzer Army Afrika on 20 June.

As night fell, confusion reigned inside the fortress of Tobruk. On the extreme eastern side of the original perimeter, the 2/7th Gurkha Rifles were resisting attempts to mop them up, while in the south, the Cameron Highlanders, Beer Group, and the Kaffrarian Rifles—all of which had been bypassed—prepared their sectors for an all-around defense. The Coldstream Guards, a company of Worcesters (who had been attached to the South African brigade when Fort Pilastrino surrendered), and most of the remaining South African artillery were preparing to give battle in the vicinity of Pilastrino. The 4th and 6th South African Brigades, which had hardly been engaged, continued to hold their positions, but they had neither the tanks nor the guns to restore the situation. Klopper's attempt to place Brigadier Hayton, the leader of the 4th South African Brigade, in charge of the 11th Indian as well had backfired, because Hayton and his staff had been forced to flee German tanks, and could not reestablish command of their own brigade until around 7:00 P.M. The 11th Indian remained effectively leaderless. Brigadier Willison, with

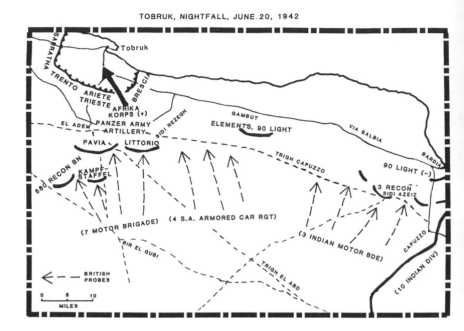

TOBRUK, NIGHTFALL, JUNE. 20, 1942

General Klopper's permission, was planning to break out with the survivors of his brigade, using wheeled transport, since there were no tanks left. There was a mass of chaos and confusion in the administrative areas around the town, and a steady stream of miscellaneous stragglers who made their way into the western perimeter. A similar situation existed in the eastern perimeter, where the Derna Road (i.e., the Coastal Road west of Tobruk) was clogged with refugees. Divisional headquarters had clearly lost control of the situation. The flow of stragglers intensified as the night wore on. Many groups of men with assorted types of guns and vehicles—or on foot— headed west and joined up with "friendlies" wherever they could. Many of these had been overrun or bypassed by the 15th Panzer and had lain low much of the day. They were completely disorganized, and were frequently without food, water, or weapons of any kind. This was especially true of the thousands of administrative and supply personnel in the Tobruk area, and of the many "native" truck drivers from South Africa, who had never been given weapons. Like their white counterparts, they were governed by only one emotion: escape!

But there was no escape.

Meanwhile, the 15th Panzer fell back to King's Cross (called the Road Triangle by the Germans), where it laagered for the night and slept the sleep of exhaustion. Several refugees who made their way back through enemy lines actually passed through the camps of the 15th Panzer, and some actually stepped over sleeping German soldiers. They were not challenged. One party of South African engineers visited the supply depot, which had been captured by the Afrika Korps, and took away a truckload of mines, in the middle of the 21st Panzer Division.

Erwin Rommel, on the other hand, was too excited to sleep. He visited Colonel Bayerlein, the acting chief of staff of the panzer army. "You know," he declared, "it's not just leadership that produces a triumph like this. You've got to have troops who will accept every imposition you put on them—deprivation, hardship, combat and even death. I owe everything to my soldiers."[29]

During this, the Allied generals back in the western perimeter were not asleep either, but were desperately trying to formulate any kind of a plan that might have any chance of working. Brigadier Hayton met with his subordinates at 8:00 P.M. and discussed a breakout, but the conclusion was virtually unanimous: such an action was out of the question because they lacked the transport. Most of it was already in the hands of the Afrika Korps. After this council of war ended, Hayton left for Fortress Headquarters (now reestablished at Belhamed), to impress his views on Klopper. Here the arguments for and against a breakout continued until early morning. Brigadier F. W. Cooper was solidly in favor of making the attempt, but Hayton, Colonel Cooper (the CRA), and others considered the situation hopeless. They suggested that the mobile forces alone try to escape.

Beginning at 9:00 P.M., Klopper and Brigadier Whiteley, the Brigadier General Staff at Eighth Army, exchanged a series of messages by radio-telephone. Whiteley asked if the situation was in hand and how long the garrison could hold out. Klopper signaled back: "Situation not in hand . . . All my tanks gone. Half my guns gone. Do you think it advisable I battle through? If you are counterattacking let me know." At 2:00 A.M. on 21 June, Klopper signaled that he was sending his mobile troops out and that he intended to "resist to the last man" with the rest of his command. At 4:50 A.M., he ordered his men to fight it out where they stood; however, he shuddered to think what would happen to the refugees when the Stukas returned. Crowds of unarmed fugitives clustered together, but, for them, all discipline was gone; they were a disorganized and panicky mob.

Shortly before dawn, Klopper received a report that 150 panzers were preparing to attack the 4th South African Brigade. This was not true, but it made up Klopper's mind. Correctly concluding that the advantages he could gain for Eighth Army by continuing the resistance would not be worth the casualties he would suffer, he sent representatives to the Germans under a white flag at 6:30 A.M. Before they left, he gave his staff car to six young South Africans who were determined to break out. "I wish I could go with you," he said with a wan smile.[30]

The order to cease fire and destroy all equipment was greeted with shock and amazement by many, especially those in the 4th and 6th South African Brigades, which had hardly been engaged. When one young South African heard the cry "They've surrendered!" he responded: "But why? We haven't beaten them yet!"[31]

The South Africans did destroy much of their equipment. Armored cars were pushed down the cliffs into the sea, trucks were burned, and rifles were smashed. Meanwhile, Rommel reentered Tobruk at 5:00 A.M. He found almost every building was a heap of rubble, and burning vehicles lined both sides of the road leading to Derna. A few minutes thereafter he accepted the surrender of the survivors of the 32d Army Tank Brigade—a headquarters without a command. All of its tanks had already been destroyed. Rommel set up his own headquarters in the Albergo Tobruk, where he attended to the details of the capitulation. He met with General Klopper that morning, and the surrender became effective at 9:40 A.M. Scattered fighting continued, however. The Gurkhas continued to resist, and the Bardia Road was not opened until 10:30 A.M. The last unit to surrender was the 2d Cameron Highlanders. It held out against Ariete throughout 21 June, but finally surrendered to the 15th Panzer Division at 5:00 A.M. on 22 June—and only after annoyed German officers informed them that they would wipe out the battalion if they did not put an end to their defiance. They had already held out twenty-four hours longer than the rest of the garrison. Lieutenant Colonel Colin Duncan paraded his men along the El Adem road before they handed over their weapons and marched into captivity, led by their own bagpipers. About 200 of the Camerons tried to escape, but almost all of them were picked up by the Germans or Italians in the open desert.

Numerous small parties did try to escape. Brigadier Anderson was captured as he tried to make his way through German lines. Brigadier Willison and his personal staff succeeded in getting through Axis front lines, but were captured in a cave several miles east of the perimeter. The most successful escape attempt was led by Major Sainthill of the Coldstream Guards, who assembled 199 men from his battalion and 188 men from other units. He put them in trucks and led his column single file through the southwest corner of the perimeter, reached the Axis Bypass Road, and began working his way through Rommel's supply columns. "One felt thankful then that they had so much captured British equipment . . . ," Captain Walker wrote home later, "for none of them seemed to guess what we were and there were even cases of columns slackening speed to let us through."[32] The Sainthill column continued east until it made contact with South African armored cars, which were serving as the rearguard for the 7th Armoured Division.

Major Pope of the 25th Field also made good his escape, taking sixty-four of his men with him. When he finally reached friendly lines several days later, they were more than 200 miles east of Tobruk.

The Germans reported taking 35,000 prisoners at Tobruk. The British estimated their losses at 19,000 British, 10,000 South African Europeans (i.e., whites), 3,400 South African Natives and Coloureds, and 2,500 Indians. In addition, the Panzer Army captured more than 2,000 tons of fuel at Tobruk and Belhamed (1,400 tons at Tobruk alone), as well as large quantities of ammunition, about 2,000 operational vehicles, and about 5,000 tons of provisions.

One group of South African officers demanded that they be housed in separate POW compounds from blacks. Rommel curtly rejected this demand, pointing out that the blacks were Union of South Africa soldiers too; if they were good enough to wear the same uniform and fight side by side with whites, they were entitled to the same prisoner-of-war facilities as their white counterparts.[33]

German losses had also been high during the Gazala Line–Tobruk battles. Although the Germans did not report their losses in the Battle of Tobruk separately, their total losses since 26 May stood at 300 officers, 570 NCOs, and 2,490 enlisted men—15 percent of their strength.

Like most of Nazi Germany, Adolf Hitler was ecstatic about Rommel's amazing triumph. On 22 June, he promoted the Desert Fox to the rank of field marshal. At age fifty, he was the youngest man to reach this, the German Army's highest rank. "To have become a field marshal is like a dream to me," he wrote later. He celebrated in a typically restrained fashion. He ate a can of pineapple and had a small glass of well-watered whiskey, recently liberated from the British. After dinner, he became more somber. "Hitler has made me a field marshal," he wrote to his wife. "I would much rather he had given me one more division."[34]

Rommel did not rest long at Tobruk. The 21st Panzer Division set out for Gambut on the afternoon of 22 June, followed the next day by the 15th Panzer.

"The fall of Tobruk came as a staggering blow to the British cause," the British Official History recorded. "For South Africa it was particularly tragic, since about one-third of all her forces in the field went into captivity."[35]

Coming on the heels of the Singapore debacle and the near loss of Malta, Tobruk nearly toppled the Churchill government. He was forced to face a vote of confidence, but, as on many other occasions, he mastered the political storm, and went on to master Hitler as well.

"The Afrika Korps was entitled to its hour of glory," the South African Official History remarked. "The capture of Tobruk crowned what was probably the most spectacular series of victories ever gained over a British army."[36]

Epilogue

After the Battle of Tobruk, the participants were scattered to the four winds. General Klopper went to Italy as a prisoner of war, along with most of his men. Most of the rest headed east, in the direction of El Alamein. But some of them did not make it that far.

General Ritchie was finally sacked by Sir Claude Auchinleck on 25 June 1942. Auchinleck personally assumed command of the Eighth Army and, on 6 July 1942, relieved General Norrie of his command, in favor of General Ramsden, the former commander of the British 50th Infantry Division. A good army commander, Auchinleck was able to check—but could not defeat—Erwin Rommel in the First Battle of El Alamein. On 8 August 1942, he was replaced as C in C, Middle East, by Gen. Sir Harold Alexander, and as commander of Eighth Army by General Gott. That same day, Lt. Gen. T. S. Corbett was sacked as Chief of the General Staff, Near East, along with his deputy, Dorman-Smith; and Ramsden was replaced as commander, XXX Corps, by Gen. Sir Brian Horrocks.[1]

On 7 August 1942, William Henry Ewart Gott boarded a transport aircraft to make the short flight from the front to Cairo. He never made it. Unescorted by fighters, his airplane was jumped by Messerschmitts and was shot down into the desert. Gott escaped uninjured, but returned to the crashed airplane to help rescue survivors. At that moment the German fighters reappeared and strafed the wreckage, killing the Eighth Army commander. He was replaced by Gen. Sir Bernard Law Montgomery. "Strafer" Gott was survived by his wife and two daughters, the youngest of which he never saw.[2]

Sir Claude Auchinleck was deeply hurt by his dismissal and refused to be relegated to the backwater command of Persia and Iraq. As a result, he returned to India, where he remained unemployed until 18 June 1943, when Wavell was named Viceroy to India. Wavell immediately named "the Auk" C in C, India, effective 20 June. In this role he "bore the burden of the vast expansion of the Indian Army and its war industry"[3] and rendered valuable support for Lord Mountbatten's Southeast Asia Command, as well as for the 14th Army in Burma, and for the Americans and Chinese in China. By 1945, he had built the Indian Army to a strength of 2,500,000 men. He was promoted to field marshal in 1944.

Auchinleck's wife, Jessie—whom he loved very much—left him for another senior officer in 1946. She felt that the long hours he spent at work made continuation of their marriage intolerable. They had no children.

Sir Claude was forced to step down for political reasons on 1 December 1947. He left India bitter after forty-four years of service and occupied a flat at Rapallo, Italy. Later he declined a peerage. In the late 1940s he moved to London, where he was still active and— among other activities—served as president of the London Federation of Boys' Clubs from 1949 to 1955. His last years, however, were lonely ones. In 1968, he moved to Morocco, partly because he could live there more cheaply and partly because the Atlas Mountains reminded him of the northwest frontier of India. His unpretentious one-bedroom flat at Marrakech was filled with photos and mementos of his Indian days. He led a quiet life of painting, reading, and walking alone in the mountains.[4]

Field Marshal Sir Claude Auchinleck died quietly at home in Marrakech, Morocco, on 23 March 1983.[5]

After he was relieved, Sir Neil Ritchie took a brief rest in Palestine and returned to Britain, where he was received by a sympathetic Churchill. He voluntarily accepted a demotion to the rank of major general to obtain command of the 52d (Lowland) Division, which was training for mountain warfare. Ritchie loved his new command and proved to be an excellent divisional commander. In 1944, he was again promoted to lieutenant general and given command of the XII

Corps, which fought with Dempsey's Second Army in northwest Europe. "Montgomery never gave him the glamorous jobs; always the steady, hard-slogging ones, which suited Ritchie well," Field Marshal Lord Carver wrote later.[6] Sir Alan Brooke, the CIGS, later said that Ritchie was "a very fine man, who did a wonderful 'come back' after suffering a serious blow."[7] After the war, Ritchie was appointed GOC Scottish Command. In 1947, as a full general, he returned to his boyhood home of Malaya as commander in chief, Far East Land Forces. Three years later he was posted to Washington, D.C., as head of the British Army Staff in the Joint Service Mission to the United States. In 1951 he retired to Canada, where he engaged in commerce. He died on 11 December 1983.[8]

After he was relieved of his command on 19 July, Sir Frank Messervy also made a very fine professional "come back." He returned to India, where he was ordered to raise the 43d Indian Armoured Division. After he trained this unit for six months, it was disbanded and its units used to reinforce other divisions. Messervy was sent to New Delhi, where he was named director of armored fighting vehicles at the General Headquarters, Indian Army, in March 1943.

In July 1943, Messervy succeeded Tom Corbett as commander of the 7th Indian Infantry Division. Corbett had done a good job as divisional commander, but had been sacked due to a security breach. Sir Frank led the 7th with great success, fighting against the Japanese in Burma and smashing their forces in the Battle of Arakan.

In 1944, young Rosemary Messervy underwent a major operation in the Wingfield Hospital, Oxford, England. It was brilliantly successful, and General Messervy's "little girl" recovered completely. A few days later, in October 1944, her very happy father was given command of the IV Corps. No longer under a cloud, he led his new command against the Japanese and was completely successful, capturing Rangoon on 2 May 1945. With the memory of his days as the unfortunate commander of the 7th Armoured Division behind him, Messervy went on to command the Fourteenth Army in Malaya, where he accepted the surrender of 100,000 Japanese. He remained there until October 1946, when he was named GOC in C, Northern Command, India. The next year he became commander in chief of the Pakistan Army, a post he held until mid-February 1948. He then retired with the honorary rank of general and took up residence at Wiltshire Farm, United Kingdom.[9] He died at home in Heyshott, near Midhurst, on 2 February 1974.[10]

Denys Reid, who so courageously commanded the 29th Indian Brigade at El Adem, was captured when the Afrika Korps overran his headquarters at Fuka Pass on 26 June 1942. Sent to Italy, he remained a prisoner of war until November 1943, when he escaped and managed to reach the lines of the U.S. Fifth Army. Shortly thereafter, he was given command of the 10th Indian Division.

Lieutenant Colonel J. Ronald Macdonell, the commander of the 9th Queen's Royal Lancers, whose tactical skills saved his regiment at Sidi Rezegh, was promoted to colonel in September 1942, and was named second in command of the 2d Armoured Brigade. He thus left the 9th Lancers after twenty-four years of service with the regiment. He was killed in action during the Battle of San Savino on the Italian front on 5 September 1943, when a German artillery shell hit his command tank.[11]

Lieutenant Colonel Douglas Thorburn, commander of the 2d Highland Light Infantry, recovered from his wounds and resumed command of his battalion. He was killed in action on 10 July 1943, during the Allied landings in Sicily.[12]

Lieutenant Colonel Michael Carver, the XXX Corps staff officer who correctly analyzed Rommel's moves on 26–27 May, went on to have a most distinguished military career and eventually reached the highest rank in the British Army. During World War II, he commanded a tank battalion and an armored brigade while still in his twenties. After the war he served as a brigade and division commander (both in the infantry) and, after a number of staff assignments, became commander in chief, Far East (1967–71), Chief of the General Staff (1971–73), and Chief of the Defense Staff

(1973–76). Field Marshal Lord Carver retired in 1976 and became a military historian. His books include *The Seven Ages of the British Army, Dilemmas of the Desert War,* and *Twentieth Century Warriors.*[13]

G. W. Richards, the commander of the 22d Armoured Brigade, later commanded the 23d Armoured Brigade. He ended the war as a major general and director of Armoured Fighting Vehicles at Headquarters, 21st Army Group.

Major John Hackett, who commanded a Stuart squadron in the 8th Hussars during the Battle of the Gazala Line, also went on to have a distinguished military career. During World War II, he fought in Syria (where he was wounded), in the Western Desert (wounded again), and Italy, where he was also wounded. In September 1944, he commanded the 4th Parachute Brigade during the Battle of Arnhem. Later he served as GOC in C, Northern Ireland, Deputy Chief of the General Staff, commander in chief of the (British) Army of the Rhine, and commander of NATO's Northern Army Group. He retired from the service in 1968 and spent the next seven years as principal of King's College in the University of London, where, at last report, he was still visiting professor in classics. He has written at least three books, including the best-selling novel *The Third World War.* General Sir John Hackett was still alive in 1989.[14]

After being relieved as commander of the XXX Corps, Gen. Sir Willoughby Norrie became governor of South Australia. He made international news in March 1950, when he took a fishing trip off Winceby Island and caught a 2,225-pound white pointer shark.[15]

Siegfried Westphal was promoted to colonel shortly after the fall of Tobruk and returned to North Africa, where he served as Rommel's chief of staff during the decisive Battle of El Alamein. He was later chief of staff of the 1st Italian-German Panzer Army (1942–43), chief of the operations staff of OB South (the Supreme German Headquarters in Italy) (1943), and chief of staff of OB South (later OB Southwest) during Kesselring's Italian campaign of 1943–44. He suffered a nervous breakdown on 5 June 1944, the day after the

Allies captured Rome, and did not return to active duty until 9 September, when he was named chief of staff of OB West under Rundstedt. He did an excellent job at this post, which he held until the end of the war. Westphal was promoted to major general (1 March 1943), lieutenant general (1 April 1944), and general of cavalry on 1 February 1945 at the age of forty-three. Released from the POW camps in 1948, Westphal moved to Dortmund and had a highly successful career in the West German steel industry. He also wrote a book about the German western front in World War II, which was entitled *Defeat in the West*. He died at the family estate near Celle in Lower Saxony on 2 July 1982.[16]

General of Panzer Troops Ludwig Cruewell was released from a prisoner-of-war camp in 1947 and returned to Germany. He reportedly died in Essen at the age of sixty-six (i.e., in 1954 or 1955).[17]

Georg von Bismarck, the commander of the 21st Panzer Division, was killed in action during the Battle of Alam Halfa Ridge when the panzer in which he was riding suffered a direct hit from a British anti-tank gun on 31 August 1942. He was posthumously promoted to lieutenant general.[18]

Colonel Hans Hecker, the panzer army engineer who was largely responsible for the capture of Bir Hacheim, soon recovered from his wounds and remained at his post until 1 December 1942. Apparently he was wounded during the retreat from El Alamein; in any case, he did not return to duty until the spring of 1943, when he was assigned to the 29th Panzer Grenadier Division, a "Stalingrad" unit then in the process of building. He assumed command of the 3d Panzer Grenadier Division on the Italian front in March 1944 and was promoted to major general on 1 June 1944. He was assigned to the OKH staff in late 1944 and remained there until the end of the war. He was living in Münden in 1958.[19]

Major General Richard Veith, who was relieved of the command of the 90th Light Division on 10 April 1942, later served as general on special assignment with Army Group North (1942–44) and Army

Group Center (1944) on the eastern front. He was promoted to lieutenant general effective 1 August 1942. General Veith was living in
Dietramsried in 1957.[20]

Like Rommel, Walter K. Nehring was rewarded for the capture of
Tobruk. In his case, this meant a promotion to general of panzer
troops, effective 1 July. He continued to command the Afrika Korps
until 31 August 1942, when his command vehicle was attacked by a
fighter-bomber during the Battle of Alam Halfa Ridge and he was
seriously wounded. Evacuated back to Europe, he was ordered to return to North Africa on an emergency basis in November 1942, when
Eisenhower's forces landed in Morocco and Algeria. Even though
he had not fully recovered from his wounds, he rushed to Tunis,
quickly organized the ad hoc XC Corps, and saved the Axis bridgehead—barely. Recognizing that the Axis situation was hopeless in the
long run, however, Nehring called for a timely evacuation of all German forces from North Africa—earning the censure of Hitler and
Goebbels, who labeled him a defeatist. As a result he was passed over
for command of the Fifth Panzer Army (as the upgraded XC Corps
was called) and he was never promoted again. He was still recognized
as a brilliant tactician, however, so he was sent to the Russian front
as commander of the XXIV Panzer Corps. He was wounded again
in the autumn of 1943 and in September was decorated with the
Wounded Badge in Gold, which was only given to men who had been
wounded five or more times (Rommel received his in the fall of
1944).

Except for a five-week stint as deputy commander of the Fourth
Panzer Army, Nehring led the XXIV Panzer Corps until 1945, fighting in the Donets, at Kiev, across the Dnieper and the Mius, at
Kharkov, Zhitomir, Vinnitsa, Brody, and in the Carpathians. In January of that year, his corps alone held together against Stalin's winter offensive, which pushed Hitler's legions back virtually to the gates
of Berlin. Outnumbered seven or eight to one, Nehring—who had
been joined and reinforced by the Grossdeutschland Panzer Corps
in the middle of the battle—established a "floating pocket"—i.e., he
kept his perimeter intact while moving west at the same time, saving
tens of thousands of German civilians from rape and/or murder in

the process. Eventually he fought his way through to the Oder and reestablished contact with the rest of the Wehrmacht.

Nehring's floating pocket was arguably the most incredible feat of tactical genius performed by the German Army in World War II and one not even Hitler could ignore. He awarded Nehring the Swords to his Knight's Cross with Oak Leaves and, on 23 March 1945, gave him command of the First Panzer Army on the eastern front—although without his much-deserved promotion to colonel general.

Hitler committed suicide on 30 April 1945. Nehring surrendered to the Western Allies on 9 May 1945. Released from POW camp on 30 September 1947, Nehring retired to West Germany, where he wrote a number of books on his experiences, including *Der wandernde Kessel (The Wandering Pocket)* (1959) and *Die Geschichte der Deutschen Panzerwaffe, 1916–1945 (The History of the German Armored Force, 1916–1945)* (1969). As of 1979 he was still alive, residing in an apartment in Düsseldorf. All that appeared on his door was his card, which simply said: WALTHER K. NEHRING.[21]

Ulrich Kleemann, who succeeded Veith as commander of the 90th Light Division, led his command with considerable distinction until he was wounded during the battle of Alam Halfa Ridge on 31 August 1942. Evacuated back to Europe, he recovered his health and took charge of Assault Division Rhodes in the Aegean sector in 1943. He later led the IV Panzer Corps on the eastern front (late 1944–1945), fighting in Hungary and in the retreat into Austria. Kleemann was promoted to lieutenant general on 1 April 1943, and to general of panzer troops on 1 September 1944. In 1958 he was living in Oberursel.[22]

Gustav von Vaerst, the commander of the 15th Panzer Division, returned to North Africa after the fall of Tobruk but was wounded again during the retreat from El Alamein in December 1942. He did not return to active duty until March 1943, when he was promoted to general of panzer troops, and was given command of the Fifth Panzer Army in Tunisia, even though he had only been promoted to lieutenant general four months before and had never commanded a corps. He nevertheless led the army as well as was possible, given the overwhelming odds against him. He was captured on 9 May 1943, three days before resistance in Tunisia ended. General von Vaerst was still alive in 1957.[23]

Eduard Crasemann, the commander of the 33d Panzer Artillery Regiment and acting commander of the 15th Panzer Division during the Gazala Line campaign, led the 15th Panzer until 25 August, when he also was wounded. Crasemann did not return to active duty until 1 September 1943, when he assumed command of the 143d Artillery Command (Arko 143), which was attached to Walter Nehring's XXIV Panzer Corps on the eastern front. Apparently Crasemann was wounded again (or fell ill) in the spring of 1944, for he was unassigned for more than three months. Still a colonel, he led the 26th Panzer Division on the Italian front from early July 1944 to 29 January 1945, when he was named acting commander of the XII SS Corps on the western front, even though he was never an SS officer and never expressed the slightest interest in being one. (By this stage of the war, Heinrich Himmler was commander in chief of the Replacement Army, and several SS corps were created, even though most of the staff officers and some of the commanders were army officers.) Crasemann was promoted to major general on 1 October 1944, and to lieutenant general on 27 February 1945 (with a date of rank of 1 December 1944). General Crasemann was captured in the Ruhr Pocket on 16 April 1945. A holder of the Knight's Cross with Oak Leaves, he was released from the prisoner-of-war camps in 1947 or 1948 and died in Gefaengnis in 1950.[24]

The brilliant Luftwaffe general Otto Hoffmann von Waldau, the leader of Air Command Afrika, was promoted to general of fliers on 1 January 1943, and was given command of the X Air Corps in the Balkans. He was killed in an air accident on 17 May 1943.[25]

After the Gazala Line–Tobruk battles, Gerhard Mueller, the commander of the 5th Panzer Regiment, was transferred to OKH, where he remained until 1944, when he was named commander of the 116th Panzer Division. He was not a successful divisional commander, however, and his staff demanded that their previous leader be returned. Mueller was demoted to deputy commander of the 9th Panzer Division in September 1944, but was simultaneously promoted to major general. He was nevertheless not given any more important commands. He was deputy commander of the Pilsen garrison at the end of the war. He was living in Landau in 1958.[26]

Fritz Bayerlein returned to his old post as chief of staff of the Afrika Korps after Westphal recovered from his wounds in the fall of 1942. Later he became German chief of staff of the First German-Italian Panzer Army (1943), but was wounded in the last days of the Tunisian campaign and evacuated back to Europe. After he recovered, he commanded the 3d Panzer Division on the eastern front (October 1943–early January 1944), and the Panzer Lehr Division in the West (1944–45). He was named acting commander of the LIII Corps in 1945, and was captured in the battle of the Ruhr Pocket in April 1945. Bayerlein retired to his hometown and died at Würzburg on 30 January 1970, of a kidney disease contracted in Africa.[27]

Colonel Fritz Krause, who had so distinguished himself as the commander of the Panzer Army artillery during the Gazala Line–Tobruk battles, was given a well-deserved promotion to major general in July 1942. He continued to direct the German gunners at El Alamein, with even greater distinction. Krause did not give up command of Rommel's artillery until 15 April 1943—less than a month before the surrender of Army Group Afrika. That day he was promoted to divisional commander of the 334th Infantry in Tunisia. This command he led until 9 May, when he was captured by the British. He returned to Germany in 1947 or 1948, and was living in retirement at Ingelheim in 1958.[28]

Baron Hans von Luck, the commander of the 3d Panzer Reconnaissance Battalion, returned to North Africa in September 1942, and resumed command of his battalion. He was sent back to Europe by Colonel General von Arnim. Later he commanded the 125th Panzer Grenadier Regiment of the 21st Panzer Division against the D-day landings, in the Normandy campaign, and on the western front. His division was transferred to the eastern front in the last days of the war and surrendered to the Russians. Luck was released from Soviet captivity in 1950. After the war, he went into the coffee business. He is married (for the second time) and has three sons. As of 1994, he was still alive.[29]

Friedrich Wilhelm ("F. W.") **von Mellenthin** was evacuated to Europe with dysentery on 12 September 1942. After he partially recovered, he served as chief of staff of the XLVIII Panzer Corps on the eastern front (late 1942–1944), and chief of staff of the Fourth Panzer Army (August–September 1944). He was then transferred to the West as chief of staff of Army Group G and briefly as commander of a regiment in the 9th Panzer Division. Promoted to major general on 1 December 1944, he was chief of staff of the Fifth Panzer Army in the Ruhr Pocket and was captured by the Americans in April 1945.

Mellenthin was released from the POW camps in 1947 or 1948, and struggled in postwar Germany. In 1950 he emigrated to South Africa and entered business. At the age of fifty, he founded his own airline company, Trek Air (now Luxavia) in Johannesburg. He also wrote two books, *Panzer Battles* and *German Generals of World War II*, published in 1956 and 1977, respectively. Colonel Carlson, the American who visited him at home in the upper-class suburb of Sandton, Johannesburg, in 1987, noted that "his energy and vitality made him appear taller than his 5 feet 6 inches," and "his tanned face was calm and serene, free of the worry lines normal to executives working under stress." At age eighty-three he still rode horses two hours a day and followed that with eight hours of work. He still did not wear glasses, even though he was an octogenarian. He still appeared as a guest speaker for NATO and allied war colleges, and served as an unpaid consultant to various charitable causes.[30]

Following his greatest victory, at Tobruk, Erwin Rommel was swept away by his success and believed that he could "finish off" the badly damaged Eighth Army in another blitzkrieg campaign, capturing Alexandria, Cairo, the Nile, and the Suez Canal in the process. He persuaded Hitler to forego the airborne assault on Malta (over the objections of Field Marshal Kesselring) and to let him invade

Egypt. This proved to be a fatal mistake. Panzer Army Afrika was checked by Auchinleck in the First Battle of El Alamein and crushed by Montgomery in the second. After the Anglo-Americans landed in Morocco and Algeria on 8 November 1942, Rommel called for the evacuation of North Africa. Instead, Hitler sent reinforcements on a massive scale. Rommel, meanwhile, conducted a masterful retreat into the Tunisian bridgehead (evacuating Tobruk in the process) and, in February 1943, turned on his tormentors and inflicted a major defeat on the American forces in the Battle of the Kasserine Pass. He was, however, unable to sustain the momentum of his offensive.

On 23 February 1943, Rommel turned his army (now designated the First Italian-German Panzer Army) over to General Messe, an Italian, and assumed command of Army Group Afrika, which included Messe's command and the Fifth Panzer Army, which was led by Col. Gen. Jürgen von Arnim. On 6 March, Rommel launched his last offensive in Africa against the British at the Mareth Line and was soundly defeated. Three days later, Rommel flew to Rome to again call for the evacuation of Tunisia. Instead, Hitler decorated him with the Diamonds to his Knight's Cross with Oak Leaves and Swords, and sent him on indefinite leave. A few weeks later the inadequately supplied Tunisian bridgehead collapsed, just as Rommel had predicted, and approximately 230,000 Axis soldiers surrendered.

Hitler appointed Rommel commander in chief of OB Southeast (i.e., the Balkans), but this command lasted only one day. On 25 July Mussolini was overthrown and the Desert Fox was recalled to the Mediterranean, where he commanded Army Group B in northern Italy. Eventually, however, Hitler decided to adopt Kesselring's Italian strategy instead of Rommel's, so the conqueror of Tobruk was unemployed again.

Hitler planned to give Rommel a command in the East, but first decided to use him and his HQ to inspect the Atlantic Wall; however, Rommel met with Field Marshal Gerd von Rundstedt, the C in C of OB West, and the two proposed that Rommel be given control of Rundstedt's most important armies: the Fifteenth and Seventh, as well as HQ, Armed Forces Netherlands. Hitler was taken aback, but approved the idea. Rommel had his last and most important command.

Rommel's task in western Europe was to repulse the Allied D-day invasion. Rommel did much to improve Germany's western defenses but was home on leave on 6 June 1944, when the Allies struck. He rushed back to France and managed to check the Allies in Normandy, but could not defeat them. Slowly but surely his Seventh Army and Panzer Group West (later Fifth Panzer Army) bled to death in the hedgerows, while Hitler and OKW maintained that the real invasion was yet to occur and would come to the north, in the Pas de Calais area, in the zone of the Fifteenth Army.

Meanwhile, Erwin Rommel learned of Hitler's atrocities in the East, including the mass murder of the Jews, gypsies, Slavs, and others. These actions violated his strong moral code, and he turned against Adolf Hitler at once. He was preparing to act against the Führer on 17 July 1944, when he was critically wounded by an Allied fighter-bomber. [For the full story of Rommel's defense of Normandy, see Samuel W. Mitcham Jr., *The Desert Fox in Normandy* [Westport, Conn.: Praeger, 1997].

Three days later, Col. Count Claus von Stauffenberg set off a bomb in Hitler's conference room; the Führer, however, was only wounded. At once the Gestapo was after "the conspirators of 20 July." Rommel's involvement was soon discovered and he was forced to commit suicide on 14 October 1944.

"Rommel merits the huge acclaim accorded to him," Martin Blumenson wrote later. "His devotion to the profession of arms was in the best tradition of the gentleman."[31] He was without question a great man and a great military commander. He deserved a better leader, a better cause, and a better fate.

Notes

Chapter I: Enter the Desert Fox

1. Italo Balbo was one of the few genuine heroes to come from Fascist Italy. He was born in Quartesana on 6 June 1896, the son of a schoolteacher. Noted for his boyish charm, he was a revolutionary from his youth, although he did not join the Fascist Party until 1921. He was a lieutenant in World War I, an aviation pioneer, and one of the founders of the Fascist Militia. After Mussolini rose to power, Balbo served as undersecretary to the minister of national economy, undersecretary of aviation, and minister of aviation (1929–33). In 1933, he directed a double crossing of the Atlantic with twenty-four seaplanes. He was named governor of Libya in late 1933, where he built the Coastal Highway (Via Balbia), rebuilt Tripoli, and promoted colonization. Although pro-German, he consistently and vociferously opposed Mussolini's anti-Semitic legislation and Italian involvement in World War II, although he never broke with the Duce. He assumed command of the Italian forces in North Africa when the war broke out, and was killed by Italian antiaircraft batteries over Tobruk on 28 June 1940. See Philip V. Cannistraro, ed., *Historical Dictionary of Fascist Italy* (Westport, Connecticut: Greenwood Press, 1982), pp. 57–59 (hereafter cited as "Cannistraro").

Pietro Badoglio (1871–1956) was a career soldier and political "operator," who had a talent for ingratiating himself with "the powers that be." He rose from the rank of lieutenant colonel in 1915 to lieutenant general in 1917, and became deputy chief of staff, despite the fact that his corps collapsed under German attacks at Caporetto. He nevertheless became chief of the General Staff in 1919, but was forced to resign by Prime Minister Ivanoe Bonomi in 1921. He opposed fascism and wanted to oppose Mussolini's march on Rome with force. Afterwards he "buttered up" Mussolini and was named ambassador to Brazil in December 1923. He returned to active duty as chief of staff of the Army in 1925, was promoted to marshal in 1926, and became governor of Tripolitania and Cyrenaica in 1928, while retaining his post of chief of staff. He suppressed the guerrilla movement in Libya by building the "wire" (a huge barbed-wire fence separating Libya and Egypt) and concentrating the natives in camps, where about 60,000 of them died. The guerrillas were pacified by the end of 1933. He intrigued to replace Gen. Emilio De Bono as Italian commander in chief in Ethiopia, a post he assumed in late November 1935. Employing tanks and mustard gas, as well as lavish artillery support, he was able to crush Haile Selassie's forces and capture Addis Ababa on 5 May 1936.

Badoglio was unimpressed by the German panzer units and failed to modernize the Italian Army prior to World War II. He nevertheless successfully intrigued to become chief of *Commando Supremo*, the Italian High Command, in 1940. After the Italian disaster in Greece, he was charged with incompetence by the Fascist press. Badoglio demanded a retraction, but the Duce refused to order one, and the king supported Mussolini, so Badoglio was forced to retire on 4 December. He nevertheless continued his intriguing and, when Mussolini was overthrown and arrested on 25 July 1943, Badoglio was named prime minister. In this post he tried to hoodwink Hitler into believing that he intended to continue the war on the side of Germany, while he simultaneously negotiated Italy's defection to the Allies, but was unsuccessful. When the Germans attacked Rome on 8 September, Badoglio fled behind Allied lines with the royal family. He resigned as premier in June 1944, after the Allies captured Rome, and held no further appointments. He died at Grazzano Monferrato on 1 November 1956. His memoirs (*Italy in the Second World War*) are highly unreliable. See Cannistraro, pp. 53–55.

2. Paul Carell, *Foxes of the Desert* (New York: E. P. Dutton and Company, 1960), pp. 109–10 (hereafter cited as "Carell"). Paul Carell is the pseudonym of Paul Karl Schmidt, who served as press chief in the German foreign ministry, 1940–45.

3. Reynolds and Eleanor Packard, *Balcony Empire* (New York: Oxford University Press, 1942), p. 25.

4. "The wire" was a large barbed-wire fence built by the Italians, separating Libya and Egypt.

5. W. G. F. Jackson, *The Battle of North Africa, 1940–43* (New York: Mason/Charter, 1975), pp. 15, 39 (hereafter cited as "Jackson"). Sir Richard O'Connor was born in Srinagar, Kashmir, India, the son of a major in the Royal Irish Fusiliers. After graduating from Welling-

ton College and the Royal Military Academy at Sandhurst, he was commissioned second lieutenant in the Scottish Rifles (Cameronians) in 1909. He served in France and Italy during World War I and, in the 1930s, was commander of the Peshawar Brigade in India. In 1938 he was promoted to major general and named commander of the 7th Armoured Division, and was military governor of Jerusalem when the war broke out. He became commander of Western Desert Force in June 1940. See Michael Carver, "O'Connor, Sir Richard Nugent (1889–1981)," in Lord Blake and C. S. Nicholls, eds., *Dictionary of National Biography, 1981–1985* (Oxford: Oxford University Press, 1990), pp. 302–03 (hereafter cited as "Carver, 'O'Connor'").

6. John Strawson, *The Battle for North Africa* (New York: Bonanza Books, 1969), p. 10 (hereafter cited as "Strawson").

Archibald Percival Wavell was born on 5 May 1883, the only son of Major (later Major General) Archibald and Lille Percival Wavell. Educated at Winchester College and the Royal Military Academy at Sandhurst, he graduated in 1900 and joined the Black Watch Regiment in time to see action in the Boer War. He was sent to India in 1903 and took part in the Bazar Valley campaign of 1908. He later spent a year with the Russian Army and, in June 1915, lost an eye in the Battle of Yprès. He finished World War I as a brigadier on Gen. Sir Edmund (later Viscount) Allenby's staff in the Middle East. Wavell rose rapidly in the British Army of the 1930s, being named commander of the 6th Brigade at Blackdown (1930), commander of the 2d Infantry Division at Aldershot (1937), C in C, Palestine and Transjordan (1937), and GOC in C, Southern Command (April 1938). He was appointed C in C, Middle East, in July 1939.

7. Richard Collier et al, *The War in the Desert* (Alexandria, Virginia: Time-Life Books, 1979), p. 28 (hereafter cited as "Collier").

8. Ibid, p. 27.

9. Ibid, p. 28.

10. C. N. Barclay, *Against Great Odds* (Liverpool: Blake and Mackenzie, Ltd., 1955), p. 55 (hereafter cited as "Barclay").

11. Ibid, pp. 69–70. Mario Berti (1881–1960) had fought in Spain, where he commanded the Italian forces after the disaster at Guadalajara. He was on leave in Italy when the British attacks began and did not return until five days after the start of Wavell's offensive. He was

unable to cope with the rapidly deteriorating situation and was sacked by Graziani.

12. Collier, p. 32.

13. Erwin Rommel, *The Rommel Papers*, B. H. Liddell Hart, ed. (New York: Harcourt, Brace & Company, 1953), p. 97 (hereafter cited as "Rommel").

14. This force included the 25th, 27th, and 55th Infantry Divisions and the 132d Ariete Armored Division, which was just arriving from Italy.

15. Desmond Young, *Rommel: The Desert Fox* (New York: Harper & Row, 1950), p. 82 (hereafter cited as "Young").

16. Wolf Keilig, *Die Generale des Heeres* (Friedberg: Podzun-Pallas-Verlag, 1983), p. 99 (hereafter cited as "Keilig"). Baron von Funck was born in Aachen on 23 December 1891 and entered the Imperial Army as a Fahnenjunker (officer cadet) with the 2d Light Dragoon Regiment in the summer of 1914. He was commissioned second lieutenant the following year. He was a colonel and military attaché to Madrid when World War II broke out. Returning to Germany in October, Baron von Funck commanded the 5th Panzer Regiment (1939–40), the 3d Panzer Brigade (1940–41), and the 5th Light Division (1941). Funck succeeded Rommel as commander of the 7th Panzer Division on 2 February 1941, and led it on the eastern front until August 1943. After briefly serving as acting commander of the XXIII Corps (December 1943–February 1944), Funck assumed command of the veteran XLVII Panzer Corps on 5 March 1944. As part of Rommel's Army Group B, Funck led the XLVII Panzer in Normandy, with considerable distinction. He was nevertheless sacked by Hitler on 4 September 1944. On his own initiative, General of Artillery Kurt von Berg, the commander of Wehrkreis XII (XII Military District), named von Funck commander of XII Panzer Command, a replacement and training unit, in October. He was relieved again in January 1945, largely because Keitel and Jodl had professional grudges against him. Never reemployed, he fell into Russian hands at the end of the war and was sentenced to ten years' imprisonment. Repatriated to West Germany in 1955, he died on 14 February 1979, at the age of eighty-eight.

17. Erwin was the third of five children of Erwin and Helena Rom-

mel (née von Luz). The first, Manfred, died young. The second, Helena, became a schoolteacher like her father and (like many female schoolteachers of her era) never married. The future field marshal seems to have been closest to her. Karl, the fourth child, became a reconnaissance pilot and fought in Egypt and Palestine in World War I, before being crippled by malaria. The youngest child, Gerhardt, the "black sheep" of the family, was an aspiring opera singer, but never achieved success on or off the stage. He outlived them all, however, and was still alive in 1977.

18. David Irving, *Trail of the Fox* (New York: E. P. Dutton and Company, 1977), p. 10 (hereafter cited as "Irving").

19. The senior Erwin Rommel died in 1913. His wife (the field marshal's mother) died in 1940.

20. Irving, p. 11.

21. Keilig, p. 282. For promotion purposes, Rommel was given a date of rank of 30 January 1912.

22. Lucie, the daughter of a West Prussian landowner and a dancer of some note, was in Danzig to study languages.

23. Young, p. 31.

24. Ibid, pp. 32, 41.

25. Ibid, p. 33. Rommel was the first lieutenant in his regiment to receive this award. He lost less than a dozen men in this exploit. See Erwin Rommel, *Attacks* (Vienna, Virginia: Athena Press, 1979), pp. 1–2 (originally published in Germany as *Infantry Grief an*, 1936).

26. Field Marshal Wilhelm Keitel was commander in chief of the High Command of the Armed Forces (*Oberkommando des Wehrmacht*) from 1938 until 1945. He was hanged at Nuremberg in 1946. See Gene Mueller, *The Forgotten Field Marshal, Wilhelm Keitel* (Durham, North Carolina: Moore Publishing Company, 1979).

27. Young, p. 63.

28. Heinz Werner Schmidt, *With Rommel in the Desert* (London: G. Harrap & Co., 1972; reprint ed., New York: Ballantine Books, 1972), p. 89 (hereafter cited as "Schmidt").

29. Georg Stumme, who had led the 2d Light/7th Panzer since late 1938, assumed command of the XL Panzer Corps on 15 February 1940. He was relieved of his command in the summer of 1942 and court-martialed for a security violation. He was named deputy

commander of Panzer Army Afrika in September 1942, and became acting commander of the army on 20 September, while Erwin Rommel returned to Europe to undergo medical treatment. He died on 24 October 1942, during the Battle of El Alamein, when he unexpectedly came under enemy machine-gun fire and had a heart attack. Stumme fell off the running board of his car during the excitement and his body was not recovered for some time. He had been promoted to general of cavalry on 1 June 1940. At his own request, his rank was changed to general of panzer troops on 4 June 1941. The 2d Light Division was created in 1936 and was redesignated 7th Panzer Division on 18 October 1939.

30. The original light divisions—the 1st, 2d, 3d, and 4th—were converted into the 6th, 7th, 8th, and 9th Panzer Divisions, respectively, after the Polish campaign.

31. Rommel, pp. 82–84; Young, pp. 76–77; Irving, p. 56.

32. Young, pp. 76–77.

33. Italo Gariboldi was born in Lodi on 20 April 1879. He commanded a division in the Ethiopian campaign and seized Addis Ababa. Later he commanded the Trieste Corps (1938–39), and the Fifth Army in Tunisia. He was acting commander of the Tenth Army when Wavell launched his offensive, but returned command of the army to Mario Berti when he returned from leave five days later. Gariboldi succeeded Graziani as commander of Italian forces in North Africa in February, but was relieved by Gen. Ugo Cavallero, the chief of Commando Supremo, for the inept manner in which he dealt with the Desert Fox. After several months in staff appointments, Gariboldi led the Italian Eighth Army in Russia. It was crushed in the Stalingrad campaign, and Gariboldi returned to Italy in March 1943, with the remnants of his command. He was arrested by the Germans in September 1943, and the Special Tribunal for the Defense of the State (a part of Mussolini's Salo Republic) sentenced him to ten years imprisonment in 1944. Released at the end of the war, Gariboldi died in Rome on 9 February 1970 (Cannistraro, p. 240).

34. United States Army Military Intelligence Service, "Order of Battle of the Italian Army" (Washington, D.C.: Military Intelligence Service, June 1943), pp. 36, 55–60 (on microfilm at the U.S. National Archives, Washington, D.C.).

35. Brauchitsch (commander in chief of the Army since February 1938) was sacked during the Battle of Moscow on 19 December 1941, and Hitler himself assumed the post of C in C of the German Army. Brauchitsch died in an American prisoner-of-war camp in 1947.

36. Sir Richard O'Connor escaped from an Italian prison camp in September 1943 and eventually made his way back to Allied lines. In January 1944, he was named commander of the British VIII Corps, which he led in Northwest Europe in 1944. In December 1944, he was named commander of India's Eastern Command, headquartered in Calcutta. In 1945 he became commander of the North West Army. Promoted to full general in April, he was named adjutant general in 1946, when Montgomery became chief of the Imperial General Staff (CIGS). Unhappy in this position, he retired in January 1948. He died in London on 17 June 1981 (Carver, "O'Connor," pp. 302–03).

37. Sir Claude Auchinleck was born in England at Aldershot, on 21 June 1884, the eldest son of Lt. Col. John C. A. and Mary Eleanor Eyre Auchinleck. Colonel Auchinleck was an Indian Army soldier and Royal House Artillery officer who fought in the Indian Mutiny of 1857, the Second Afghan War (1878–80), and the Third Burmese War (1885–95). He retired due to illness in 1890 and died in 1892. Claude entered Sandhurst in January 1902, at age seventeen. He graduated the following year and sailed for India, where he joined the 62d Punjab Infantry Regiment. He served in India, Tibet, and Sikkim.

During World War I, Auchinleck fought in Egypt, Mesopotamia, and Kurdistan, emerging from the conflict as Brigade Major, 52d Infantry. He returned to India in 1920, serving on the frontier.

Archibald Wavell became C in C, Southwest Pacific, in December 1941. In this post his forces lost Singapore and experienced little success in Burma. Wavell was nevertheless promoted to field marshal in January 1943, and was named Viceroy of India in June. The following month he was raised to peerage as Viscount Wavell of Cyrenaica and Winchester. Replaced by Lord Mountbatten in February 1947, he retired to London and became president of the Royal Society of Literature. He was also honorary colonel of the Black Watch. He died in London on 24 May 1950.

38. Brian Bond, "Auchinleck, Sir Claude (1884–1983)" in Lord Blake and C. S. Nicholls, eds., *The Dictionary of National Biography, 1981–1985* (Oxford: Oxford University Press, 1990), pp. 16–17.

39. Ibid, p. 16.

40. Auchinleck was succeeded as commander of the V Corps by Gen. Sir Bernard Law Montgomery.

41. Sir Alan Gordon Cunningham, the brother of the admiral commanding the Mediterranean Fleet, was born in Edinburgh on 1 May 1887, the fifth (and last) child of a professor of anatomy. Commissioned in the Royal Artillery in 1906, he served on the western front in World War I and, by 1938, was a major general, commanding the 5th Anti-Aircraft Division. After commanding several other divisions early in World War II, he was named GOC, East Africa, and performed brilliantly against the Italians in Somaliland and Ethiopia. He was named commander of the Eighth Army in June 1941.

42. F. W. von Mellenthin, *Panzer Battles: A Study in the Employment of Armor in the Second World War* (Norman: University of Oklahoma Press, 1956; reprint ed., New York: Ballantine Books, 1976), p. 63 (hereafter cited as "Mellenthin"); Rommel, p. 158; I. S. O. Playfair, et al., *The Mediterranean and Middle East* (London: Her Majesty's Stationery Office, 1966), Volume III, pp. 27–31 (hereafter cited as "Playfair"). These figures exclude the Italian L-3 and British Mark VIB light tanks, which were useless.

43. Sir Alan Cunningham accepted his dismissal with "staunch dignity." After a brief hospital stay he returned to England and was named commandant of the Staff College at Camberley. In 1943–44 he was GOC (General Officer Commanding), Northern Ireland, and was GOC, Eastern Command, 1944–45. In 1945 he became the last British High Commissioner to Palestine. He retired to Hampshire in May 1948 and spent most of his remaining years gardening and fishing. He died in a nursing home in Tunbridge Wells on 30 January 1983, at the age of ninety-five. John Strawson, "Cunningham, Sir Alan Gordon (1887–1983)," in Lord Blake and C. S. Nicholls, eds., *The Dictionary of National Biography, 1981–1985* (Oxford: Oxford University Press, 1990), pp. 103–04.

44. Wolf Heckmann, *Rommel's War in Africa* (New York: E. P. Dutton and Company, 1980), p. 226 (hereafter cited as "Heckmann").

45. Ibid.

46. Roger Parkinson, *The Auk: Auchinleck, Victor at Alamein* (London: Hart-Davis, MacGibbon, Ltd., 1977), p. 144 (hereafter cited as "Parkinson"), citing Rommel, p. 180.

47. Rommel, p. 181; Young, p. 91; Carell, p. 133.

48. Mellenthin, p. 104.

49. Playfair III, pp. 148–49; Carell, pp. 134–35.

Chapter II: Preparing for Action

1. C. N. Barclay, *Against Great Odds* (Liverpool: Blake & Mackenzie, Ltd., 1955), p. 5, has a somewhat different definition and places the western edge of the Western Desert on an imaginary line running due south from Gazala. The area thus delineated by Brigadier Barclay is about 150 miles north to south and some 260 miles east to west.

2. Strawson, p. 42.

3. Rommel, p. 104.

4. Parkinson, p. 160.

5. General Alan Brooke, the CIGS, expressed a low opinion of Lord Gort and recommended that Wavell be reinstated. This Churchill refused to do. "Jumbo" Wilson was also considered for the post.

6. Archibald Nye, who was noted for his quick mind, rose from the rank of private to lieutenant general in a class-conscious army. He was born in Ship Street Barracks, Dublin, Ireland, in 1895, the son of the regimental sergeant major of the Oxfordshire and Buckinghamshire Light Infantry. When his father died when he was ten, Archibald was sent to the Duke of York's Royal Military School at Dover. He joined the army as an enlisted man and volunteered for combat duty in 1914. Wounded in action in France as an NCO, he was selected for a commission in the Leinster Regiment (a southern Ireland unit) in 1915. He was selected for a regular army commission in the Royal Warwickshire Regiment in 1922. Because he lacked financial means, he paid for his mess bills by shooting billiards. He was nevertheless selected for Staff College in 1924. Later he commanded the 2d Royal Warwickshires (1937), and raised the Nowshera Brigade in India when the war broke out. After marrying the

daughter of Gen. Sir Harry Hugh Sidney Knox, he returned to the War Office in early 1940 as deputy director (and later director) of Staff Duties, an office that dealt with organization and coordination. When Sir Alan Brooke replaced Field Marshal Sir John G. Dill as CIGS, Nye became vice chief. He held this post until he retired in 1946. Sir Archibald Nye later served as governor of Madras (India) under Nehru and was appointed High Commissioner to Canada in 1952. He retired again in 1956 and died in London on 13 November 1967. Anthony Farrar-Hockley, "Nye, Sir Archibald Edward (1895–1967)," in E. T. Williams and C. S. Nicholls, eds., *Dictionary of National Biography, 1961–1970* (Oxford: Oxford University Press, 1971), pp. 801–02.

7. Parkinson, p. 165, citing Churchill IV, p. 264.

8. For a complete description of the Churchill-Auchinleck controversy, see I. S. O. Playfair, *The Mediterranean and Middle East*, Volume III, *British Fortunes Reach Their Lowest Ebb (September 1941 to September 1942)* (London: Her Majesty's Stationery Office, 1960), John Connell, *Auchinleck* (London: Cassell & Company, Ltd., 1959); pp. 428–80; and Parkinson. As of early May, Churchill was considering replacing Auchinleck with Gen. Sir Harold Alexander.

9. Parkinson, p. 101.

10. Ugo Cavallero was born at Casale Monferrato on 20 September 1880 and was commissioned second lieutenant in 1900. He fought in Libya (1912–13) and was assigned to the operations staff of the Italian Army in 1915. Two years later he became chief of operations of the army, where he planned the successful Piave and Vittorio Veneto operations against the Austro-Hungarians. Promoted to brigadier general at the extremely early age of thirty-eight, he was a member of the Italian peace delegation at Versailles. Cavallero left the army in 1920 and became a corporate executive, but returned to public service as Mussolini's undersecretary of war in 1924. (Mussolini held the minister of war post, so Cavallero, in effect, held cabinet level rank.) He was dismissed by Mussolini after the two had a public altercation in November 1928.

Marshal Cavallero returned to private industry as president of the Ansaldo Works. Here he was involved in a scandal when it was discovered that the firm was supplying the navy with ordinary steel instead of armor-plate steel. Although he may have been personally blameless, he never regained his reputation in the eyes of the Italian people. Cavallero nevertheless made up with Mussolini and secured command of the Italian forces in East Africa in November 1937. He became president of the Pact of Steel Coordinating Committee in May 1939, and informed the Germans that Italy would not be ready for war until 1942 at the earliest.

On 4 December 1940, Cavallero assumed command of the disintegrating Albanian front, which he helped stabilize with his organizational and logistical talents. He returned to Italy as war minister and chief of Commando Supremo in May 1941. In this post he supported the policies of the Duce, including the German alliance. He was nevertheless relieved of his post on 6 February 1943, due to the deteriorating Axis military situation in North Africa. Imprisoned by the Badoglio government after Mussolini was deposed, he was later freed by the Germans. Cavallero killed himself at Frascati (Kesselring's headquarters) during the night of 12–13 September 1943.

11. Conrad Seibt (born on 5 August 1892) was a logistical genius and was largely responsible for the success of the Luftwaffe operations against the British garrison on Crete and against the Royal Navy in the eastern Mediterranean in May 1941. He was, however, not fully appreciated by OKL (the High Command of the Luftwaffe) and was not promoted to major general until 1 September 1944. He died on 6 January 1973. Rudolf Absolon, comp., *Rangliste der Generale der deutschen Luftwaffe nach dem Stand vom 20. April 1945* (Friedberg: Podzun-Pallas-Verlag GmbH, 1984), p. 64 (hereafter cited as "Absolon").

Bernhard Ramcke (who was born on 24 January 1889) did not go to parachute school until he was fifty years old. He fought in Crete in 1941 and led the 2d Parachute Brigade at El Alamein. He later commanded the 2d Parachute Division and was commandant of Brest. He surrendered the fortress, which only fell after a fierce resistance in September 1944. Ramcke was nevertheless promoted to general of paratroopers, effective 1 September 1944. He died on 7 July 1968 (Absolon, p. 29).

12. Kurt Student, the "father" of the German parachute branch,

was born on 12 May 1890. He was a World War I flying ace, shooting down six enemy airplanes on the Eastern front. Remaining in the secret air force after the war, he commanded the 7th Air Division (the first German parachute division) in 1940, when he was seriously wounded at the end of the battle of Rotterdam. He returned to active duty in 1941 and led the XI Air Corps during the battle of Crete. He later commanded the First Parachute Army (1943–44) and Army Group H (1945). He was named C in C of Army Group Vistula in the last days of the war. General Student died on 1 July 1978. His only son, a fighter pilot, was killed in action during World War II.

13. KTB, Panzer Army Afrika, 28 April 1942.

14. Ettore Bastico was born in Bologna on 9 April 1876. A career officer, he led a division and then the III Corps in Ethiopia, and later commanded the Alessandria Corps. He led the Italian forces in Spain in 1937 but was relieved in October because he could not get along with Franco. He later commanded the Second Army in Albania (1938) and the Sixth Army in Italy (1938–late 1940), before becoming governor of the Dodecanese. He became governor of Libya in July 1941. Here he clashed repeatedly with Rommel over strategic and logistical matters. Promoted to marshal in August 1942, Bastico was relieved in February 1943, after Libya had been overrun by the British. He died in Rome on 1 December 1972. Cannistraro, p. 63.

15. KTB, Panzer Army Afrika, 2 May 1942.

16. The standard German Pak (Panzerabwehrkanone or antitank gun) of 1941, the 37mm, was still used in some units.

17. Joan Bright, *9th Queen's Royal Lancers* (Aldershot: Gale & Polden, Ltd., 1951), p. 65 (hereafter cited as "Bright").

18. German antiaircraft on Flak units (*Flugabwehrkanone*) were part of the Luftwaffe, but Rommel took charge of the AA units in North Africa by simply ordering the commander of the 135th Flak Regiment to place his units under panzer army command. The term "Flak," incidentally, referred to heavy antiaircraft guns and to light AA guns under regimental command. Nonregimental light antiaircraft battalions (normally equipped with 20mm guns) were referred to as "Fla" units. These included the mobile light AA battalions that were organic to panzer divisions and that were part of the army, not

the Luftwaffe. Each panzer division had one such battalion. See J. A. I. Agar-Hamilton and L. C. F. Turner, *The Sidi Rezeg Battles, 1941* (Cape Town: Oxford University Press, 1957) (hereafter cited as "Agar-Hamilton and Turner, *Sidi Rezeg*").

19. Heckmann, p. 92; Henry Maule, *Spearhead General: The Epic Story of General Sir Francis Messervy and His Men in Eritrea, North Africa and Burma* (London: Odhams Press, Ltd., 1961), p. 115 (hereafter cited as "Maule").

20. Sir Henry Maitland Wilson (born 1881) was GOC in C, Egypt, in 1939 and played a major supporting role in Wavell's winter offensive that swept the Italians out of Egypt. Later he commanded the British and Australian forces in Greece (1941), where he was defeated by much superior German forces. After putting down a revolt in Iraq (1941), he commanded the Ninth Army and was simultaneously C in C of the Persia–Iraq Command. In February 1943 he succeeded Alexander as C in C, Middle East, and in January 1944 replaced Eisenhower as Supreme Allied Commander, Mediterranean, a post he held until November 1944. He ended the war as head of the British joint staff mission to Washington (Tunney, pp. 207–08).

21. Michael Carver, *Dilemma of the Desert War: A New Look at the Libyan Campaign, 1940–1942* (Bloomington: Indiana University Press, 1986), p. 15 (hereafter cited as "Carver, *Dilemma*").

22. Hobart's superior, General Wilson, did not approve of his dogmatic ideas and recommended that he be relieved of his command. Wavell sacked him in November 1939. The ideas of Hobart were much more difficult to get rid of than the man himself, however, especially in the division that he had formed and trained (Carver, *Dilemma*, pp. 13–14). Hobart later commanded the 79th Armoured Division in Normandy and Western Europe.

23. G. M. O. Davy, *The Seventh and Three Enemies* (Cambridge: W. Heffer and Sons, Ltd., 1952), p. 144.

24. Agar-Hamilton and Turner, *Sidi Rezeg*, p. 35.

25. Maitland Wilson, *Eight Years Overseas* (London: Hutchinson and Co., Ltd., 1950), pp. 127–28.

26. Mellenthin, p. 93.

27. Major General Vyvyan V. Pope, a veteran RTC officer with considerable desert experience, had initially been commander of the

XXX Corps in 1941. He was killed in an air crash on 6 October 1941, and was succeeded by Norrie, the commander of the 1st Armoured Division. Norrie was a cavalry officer who had some experience in tanks in World War I (Carver, *Dilemma*, p. 30).

28. Playfair III, pp. 217–18.

29. Mellenthin, p. 63.

30. Correlli Barnett, *The Desert Generals*, 2d ed. (Bloomington: Indiana University Press, 1982), p. 144. Strictly speaking, some of the tanks classified as Grants were General Lees, an earlier but almost identical tank, named after the greatest commander in American history.

31. Heckmann, p. 19.

32. Ibid, p. 101.

33. Ibid.

34. J. A. I. Agar-Hamilton and L. C. F. Turner, *Crisis in the Desert, May–July 1942* (Cape Town: Oxford University Press, 1952), p. 10 (hereafter cited as "Agar-Hamilton").

35. Mellenthin, p. 93.

36. Ibid; Rommel, p. 197.

37. Walter Warlimont, "The Decision in the Mediterranean," in H. A. Jacobsen and J. Rohwer, eds., *Decisive Battles of World War II: The German View* (New York: G. P. Putnam's Sons, 1965), p. 190.

38. The 104th Artillery Command also controlled the 2d Observation, a battalion of forward observers. Georg Tessin, *Verbande und Truppen der deutschen Wehrmacht und Waffen-SS im Zweiten Weltkrieg 1939–1945* (Osnabrück: Biblio Verlag, 1979), Volume 6, p. 195 (hereafter cited as "Tessin").

39. Hoffmann von Waldau (born 1898) was a former deputy chief of the General Staff of the Luftwaffe, but was removed from his post because he annoyed Goering with his reports, which the Reichsmarschall considered to be too pessimistic. (They were, in fact, highly accurate.)

Froehlich (who was born in 1889) was also promoted to general of fliers in 1943. He commanded the Tenth Air Fleet (the replacement and rear-area forces in Germany) until it was dissolved on 28 April 1945 (Absolon, p. 27).

40. Carver, *Dilemma*, pp. 147–48.

41. Barnett, pp. 123–24.

42. Ibid, p. 130.

43. Maule, p. 164.

44. Ibid.

45. General Brooke, the CIGS, had suggested on 6 February that Auchinleck replace both Smith and Shearer; however, he would have preferred Gen. Sir Henry Pownall as chief of staff (Parkinson, p. 153). Brigadier Shearer, as Auchinleck admitted at the time, was "to some extent the victim of intrigue" (Connell, p. 479). He had served twenty-three months at his post without leave. He now returned to the United Kingdom, left the service, and went into management.

46. Godwin-Austen, an infantry officer, had commanded the 12th East African Division under Cunningham in the Italian East African campaign.

47. Barnett, p. 134. Godwin-Austen had succeeded Lt. Gen. Noel Beresford-Peirse as commander of the XIII Corps on 18 September 1941.

48. Messervy was named acting commander of the 1st Armoured Division on 2 January 1942, because Lumsden had been wounded. Maj. Gen. Francis I. S. Tuker succeeded Messervy as commander of the 4th Indian Division. Herbert Lumsden returned and reassumed command of the 1st Armoured on or about 6 February. The division had suffered considerable casualties in the meantime, and Lumsden held Messervy largely responsible.

49. R. G. Satterthwaite, "Messervy, Sir Frank Walter," in Lord Blake and C. S. Nicholls, eds., *The Dictionary of National Biography, 1971–1980* (Oxford: Oxford University Press, 1986), p. 566.

50. Maule, pp. 23–170. Sir Frank Messervy was born in Trinidad on 9 December 1893, the eldest son of a bank executive. A graduate of the Royal Military College at Sandhurst, he was commissioned second lieutenant in 1913 and served with Hodson's Horse in World War I. Later an instructor at the Staff College at Quetta (along with Montgomery), he commanded the Duke of Connaught's Own Lancers (1938–39) and saw them through mechanization before he became chief of operations of the 5th Indian Division (1939) (Satterthwaite, p. 566).

51. Gyles Isham, "Gott, William Henry Ewart (1897–1942)" in L. G. Wichham Legg and E. T. Williams, eds., *Dictionary of National Biography, 1941–1950* (Oxford: Oxford University Press, 1959), pp. 310–12.

52. Barnett, p. 143.

53. Brigadier (later Major General) Dorman-Smith had served as commandant of the Haifa Staff College for years and was the former director of military training in India under Auchinleck. Called "mercurial" by Field Marshal Lord Carver (*Dilemma,* p. 132), he was not friendly toward Ritchie, who, after the war, accused him of poisoning his relationship with Auchinleck.

54. Parkinson, p. 180.

55. The "Jock" column was invented in 1940 by Lt. Col. (later Major General) J. C. "Jock" Campbell, who was commander of the 4th Regiment, Royal Horse Artillery. It was designed to harass the enemy, to support armored car (scout) units, and later to keep the German reconnaissance battalions from discovering British intentions. It usually consisted of a company of motorized infantry and a troop or battery of field artillery. Its offensive capability was limited; however, the British developed an exaggerated idea of its value (a Jock column had blocked the retreat of the Italian Tenth Army at Beda Fomm).

56. Barnett, p. 135.

57. Ludwig Cruewell was born in Dortmund on 20 March 1892. He entered the Imperial Army as a Fahnenjunker in 1911 and was commissioned second lieutenant in the 9th Dragoon Regiment the following year. He fought in World War I and remained in the *Reichsheer* after the armistice. He transferred to the panzer arm in the 1930s and led the 6th Panzer Regiment (1938–39). He was a detachment chief in the General Staff of the Army when the war broke out. He became chief of operations of the Sixteenth Army in November 1939, and commanded the 11th Panzer Division from August 1940 until September 1941, when, at the request of General Rommel, he was given command of the Afrika Korps. General Cruewell's young wife died suddenly in the spring of 1942, and he returned home on emergency leave. He did not return to his post as deputy commander of Panzer Army Afrika until two days before the Gazala offensive began (Keilig, p. 63).

58. Walter K. Nehring was born in Stretzin on 15 August 1892. He joined the Imperial Army as a Fahnenjunker in 1911 and was commissioned Leutnant in the 152d Infantry Regiment in 1914. He fought in World War I and was retained by the Reichsheer, being promoted to captain and selected for clandestine General Staff training in 1923. A major when Hitler came to power, he rose rapidly in the next eight years, being promoted to lieutenant colonel (1934), colonel (1937), major general (1940), lieutenant general (1 February 1942), and general of panzer troops (1 July 1942). In the meantime, he was a key advisor to Oswald Lutz, the first general of panzer troops, in the early and mid-1930s; commander of the 5th Panzer Regiment (1937–39); and chief of staff to General Guderian when he commanded the XIX Motorized (later Panzer) Corps with such success in Poland, Belgium, and France (1939–40). Nehring assumed command of the 18th Panzer Division on 26 October 1940. Keilig, pp. 237–38; John Angolia, *On the Field of Honor* (San Jose, California: R. James Bender Publishing, 1979), Volume I, pp. 234–35.

59. Gustav von Vaerst was born at Meiningen on 19 April 1894. He joined the army as a Fahnenjunker in 1912 and was commissioned second lieutenant in the 14th Hussar Regiment in early 1914. He fought in World War I, remained in the Reichswehr, and was commander of the 2d Rifle Brigade when World War II began. On 1 September 1941 he was promoted to major general, and he assumed command of the 15th Panzer Division on 9 December (Keilig, p. 353).

60. Karl Boettcher was born in Thorn in 1889. He joined the army in 1909 and was commissioned second lieutenant in the 5th Foot Artillery Regiment in 1910. He fought in World War I, remained in the Reichsheer, and was commander of the 1st Artillery Regiment (1936–38), commandant of Katowitz (1938–39), and commander of Arko 104 (1939–42). He also served briefly as commander of the 21st Panzer Division. Promoted to lieutenant general in March 1942, Boettcher spent most of 1942 in Führer Reserve—probably due to health problems. After briefly commanding the 345th Infantry Division, he was named commandant of the GHQ troops of Army Group D in France in March 1943, and took charge of the 326th Infantry Division in May. Apparently his health cracked again,

however, and he was back in Führer Reserve by the end of the month. He briefly commanded the 347th Infantry Division (November–December 1943), returned to Führer Reserve (December 1943–March 1944), and was CO of the 305th Higher Artillery Command (March 1944–1945). He was living in Kiel in 1956 (Keilig, pp. 42–43).

61. Georg von Bismarck was born in Neumuehl on 15 February 1891. He joined the army in 1910 and was commissioned second lieutenant in the 6th Jäger Battalion in 1911. Remaining in the service after World War I, he was named commander of the 7th Rifle Regiment in 1938. He later led the 20th Rifle Brigade (December 1940–December 1941), before assuming command of the 21st Panzer Division (Keilig, pp. 35–36).

62. Richard Veith was born in Amberg in 1890 and was educated at various cadet schools. He entered the service in 1909, was commissioned in the 2d Bavarian Infantry Regiment in 1911, and was commander of the 135th Infantry Regiment when World War II broke out. Veith led the 90th Light Division from 30 December 1941 until 10 April 1942.

63. Kurt Mehner, ed., *Die Geheimen Tagesberichte der deutschen Wehrmachtführung im Zweiten Weltkrieg, 1939–1945* (Osnabrück: Biblio Verlag, 1988), Volume 4, p. 382.

Ulrich Kleeman was born in Langensalza, Thuringen, on 23 March 1892. He entered the Imperial Army as a Fahnenjunker in October 1911 and was commissioned second lieutenant in the 21st Dragoon Regiment in 1913. He fought in World War I, remained in the Reichsheer, and (as a major) was commander of the 1st Motorcycle Battalion in 1934. He assumed command of the 3d Rifle Regiment at the beginning of 1938, and was named commander of the 3d Rifle Brigade in January 1940, before assuming command of the 90th Light. He was meanwhile promoted to lieutenant colonel (1936), colonel (1938), and major general (1941) (Keilig, p. 171).

64. Fritz Krause was born in Jüterbog (a major German artillery base, located near Berlin) on 29 January 1895. He was commissioned in the 41st Field Artillery Regiment in 1914 and remained in that branch until 1943. He led the 36th Artillery Regiment on the eastern front, taking part in the drive on Leningrad. He later fought in

the Battle of Moscow, at Klin, and in the Rzhev battles of late 1941 and early 1942 (Keilig, p. 184).

65. Antony Brett-James, *Ball of Fire* (Aldershot: Gale & Polden, Ltd., 1951), p. 119.

66. Ibid.

67. Hans von Luck, *Panzer Commander* (Westport, Connecticut: Praeger, 1989), p. 89.

68. Verner R. Carlson, "Portrait of a German General Staff Officer," *Military Review,* Volume LXX, No. 4 (April 1990), p. 75 (hereafter cited as "Carlson").

69. Dal McGuirk, *Afrikakorps: Self-Portrait* (Osceola, Wisconsin: Motorbooks International, 1992), pp. 63–64 (hereafter cited as "McGuirk").

70. Luck, p. 89.

71. Heckmann, p. 126.

72. Special Unit 288 (*Sonderverband 288* or the 288th Special Duties Unit) was commanded by Colonel Menton, a World War I comrade of the Desert Fox and one of the few people he allowed to call him by the familiar "du." The 288th was formed in Potsdam on 28 July 1941 and included a company of the 800th Lehr Regiment z.b.V. ("for special purposes"), which was also called the 800th Special Duty Training Regiment—the Brandenburgers—a special German commando unit. It also included a mountain antitank company, a rifle company, a machine-gun company, an antitank company (which included an assault gun platoon), a light antiaircraft (or Fla) company, an engineer company, and a signal company. It was upgraded to Panzer Grenadier Regiment "Afrika" on 30 October 1942, and was destroyed during the German collapse in Tunisia in May 1943 (Tessin, Volume 9, p. 23).

73. Collier, p. 54.

74. Mellenthin, pp. 111–12.

Chapter III: The Desert Fox Strikes First

1. Erwan Bergot, *The Afrika Korps* (New York: W. H. Allen Publishers, Inc., 1975; reprint ed., New York: Charter Books, 1975), pp. 132–33 (hereafter cited as "Bergot").

2. Rommel, p. 206.

3. Bergot, pp. 133–34.

4. Carver, *Dilemma*, pp. 77–78.

5. Jackson, p. 208; Playfair III, p. 223. Lieutenant Colonel (later General Sir) Harold E. Pyman later served as Brigadier General Staff of the XXX Corps and Second Army in Northwest Europe (1944–45). He went on to become deputy chief of the Imperial General Staff (1958–61) and C in C Allied Forces Northern Europe (1961–63).

6. Ritchie intended that HQ, 4th Indian Division (Major General Tuker), be placed in charge of the screen, which was to include the armored cars, the 3d Indian Motor Brigade, the 29th Indian Infantry Brigade, and the 1st Free French Brigade. Ritchie intended to place Tuker under Norrie's command; however, Rommel struck before these arrangements could be completed.

7. Maule, pp. 175–76. Admiral Cowan was sent to Italy but was later repatriated to England because of his age. He nevertheless parachuted into Yugoslavia at the age of seventy-three. Later he was invited to Buckingham Palace, where he received the bar to his DSO, which he had been awarded forty-six years before. He wore the uniform of the 18th Cavalry, which had made him an honorary colonel.

8. Compton Mackenzie, *Eastern Epic* (London: Chatto & Windus, 1951), Volume I, pp. 542–45 (hereafter cited as "Mackenzie").

9. Playfair III, p. 223.

10. Barnett, p. 146, citing personal interview with General Renton.

11. Ibid.

12. Lieutenant Colonel Wilhelm "Willi" Teege later commanded the 8th Panzer Regiment of the 15th Panzer Division in the Battle of El Alamein, where he fought with great skill and extreme tenacity. On 2 November 1942, after two weeks of fierce and unremitting combat, he was killed in the Battle of Tel el Aqqaqir, where his regiment was virtually wiped out.

13. Maule, pp. 177–78.

14. Richard D. Law and Craig W. H. Luther, *Rommel* (San Jose, California: R. James Bender Publishing, 1980), p. 136. Gerhard Mueller was born in Breslau in 1896. He entered the service as a Fahnenjunker in 1915 and was commissioned second lieutenant in the 154th

Infantry Regiment in 1916. Discharged from the service in 1920, he joined the police in the Weimar era, and reentered the army as a captain in 1935. He was named commander of the 33d Anti-Tank Battalion in 1938, and took charge of the 1st Battalion, 33d Panzer Regiment, in 1941. He became commander of the 5th Panzer Regiment in early 1942 (Keilig, p. 232).

15. Maule, p. 178.

16. Wolf Heckmann, *Rommel's War in Africa* (New York: E. P. Dutton and Company, 1979), pp. 236–39 (hereafter cited as "Heckmann"). Unlike the twenty-liter German "jerrycan," the British eighteen-liter (four-gallon) canisters were so flimsy that they were always splitting. Fuel losses in transit across rough terrain sometimes reached 40 percent, and British fuel trucks could be followed by the trail they left, but the British never did adopt a decent fuel canister. The jerrycan, on the other hand, could be thrown off a truck without damage. Like the British, the Americans never developed a good fuel can, so they simply appropriated the German design for their five-gallon cans. They did not even bother to change the name. As late as the Vietnam era, the "jerrycan" was still being used by the U.S. Army.

17. Maule, p. 179.

18. Ibid, pp. 181–84.

19. Bergot, p. 140.

20. Mellenthin, p. 99.

21. Bright, pp. 70–71.

22. Ibid, p. 71.

23. Karl Alman, *Panzer vor: Die dramatische Geschichte der Panzerwaffe und ihrer tapferen Soldaten* (Rastatt: Erich Papel Verlag, 1966), pp. 272–73 (hereafter cited as "Alman").

24. Carell, p. 168.

25. Eduard Crasemann was born in Hamburg in 1891. He joined the Imperial Army as a Fahnenjunker in 1910 and was commissioned second lieutenant in 1911. He was not retained in the Reichswehr when it was reduced to 4,000 officers and received his discharge in 1919. In 1936, during the initial Nazi military expansion, he reentered the service as a captain and was assigned to the staff of OKH. When the war broke out in 1939 he was a battery commander in the 73d Artillery Regiment, but he rose very rapidly to battalion commander in the 78th Artillery Regiment (fall 1940) and to commander of the

33d Panzer Artillery Regiment the following spring (Keilig, p. 62). Certainly he was a highly competent officer, but his contacts in the High Command did not hinder his advancement at all.

26. Rommel, p. 130.

27. Playfair III, p. 225; Agar-Hamilton, p. 30.

28. Bright, p. 73.

29. Ibid.

30. Agar-Hamilton, p. 31, citing Rommel, p. 134.

31. Agar-Hamilton, pp. 33–34, citing Carel Birkby, *Saga of the Transvaal Scottish Regiment* (Cape Town: Howard B. Timmions, 1950), pp. 464–65.

32. Agar-Hamilton, p. 31.

33. Heckman, p. 251.

34. Bright, p. 75.

35. Ibid, p. 76.

36. Agar-Hamilton, pp. 33–34, citing B. G. Simpkins, draft MS of *History of the Rand Light Infantry*. This quote is not found in the printed version of the book.

37. Barnett, p. 149.

38. Playfair III, p. 228.

39. Rommel, p. 138.

40. Carell, p. 170.

41. Mackenzie I, p. 548.

42. Heckmann, pp. 251–52.

43. Ibid, pp. 252–53.

44. Playfair III, p. 229.

45. Ibid, p. 230.

46. Young, pp. 94–95.

47. Mackenzie I, p. 546.

48. Agar-Hamilton, p. 38.

49. Carell, p. 172.

50. Ronald Lewin, *Rommel as a Military Commander* (New York: Ballantine Books, 1970), p. 149 (hereafter cited as "Lewin").

51. Friedrich Wilhelm von Mellenthin, a Pomeranian who counted Prince August von Hohenzollern and Frederick the Great among his ancestors, was born in Breslau, Silesia, on 30 August 1904. His father, Lt. Col. Henning von Mellenthin, was killed on the Western Front in 1918. Friedrich Wilhelm (who later preferred to be

called "F. W.") entered the service as a Fahnenjunker in 1924 and was commissioned second lieutenant in the 7th Cavalry Regiment in 1928. A thin, short man (only 5' 6"), he had a passion for steeple-chasing, and spent the first eleven years of his career in the cavalry. He began General Staff training in 1937 and received his red trouser stripes (the symbol of the General Staff officer) in 1939. Mellenthin was a major on the staff of the III Corps in Berlin when World War II began. He became chief of operations of the 197th Infantry Division in January 1940; was transferred to the staff of the First Army in occupied France in August 1940; and was sent to North Africa in June 1941. He became Rommel's chief of intelligence (Ic) in August (Carlson, pp. 70–73; Keilig, pp. 221–22). Mellenthin's brother Horst, a general of artillery and a holder of the Knight's Cross with Oak Leaves, commanded the 205th Infantry Division and the XXXVIII Panzer and VIII Corps on the Eastern front.

52. Luck, p. 103. Baron Hans von Luck was born in Flensburg on 15 July 1911, the son of a German naval lieutenant who died in 1918. Luck's stepfather was a naval chaplain and a teacher at a cadet school who brought him up in the Prussian manner. He entered the Reichsheer as a Fahnenjunker (officer cadet) in a Silesian cavalry regiment in 1929, but he was transferred to the 1st Motorized Battalion in East Prussia shortly thereafter. Luck first met Rommel in 1931, when he was attending the infantry school at Dresden and Rommel was an instructor. Luck was commissioned in 1932 and assigned to the 2d Motorized Battalion at Kolberg, Pomerania. In 1939, he was in the 7th Panzer Reconnaissance Battalion of the 2d Light (later 7th Panzer) Division during the invasions of Poland and France; in the latter campaign, Major General Rommel was the divisional commander. After a tour as company commander, Luck became divisional adjutant under Baron von Funck and served in the Russian campaign. That summer he was named commander of the 7th Panzer Reconnaissance Battalion and took part in the drive on Moscow. In January 1942, however, he was transferred to North Africa (over Funck's objections) to command the 3d Panzer Reconnaissance Battalion at Erwin Rommel's request.

Captain Everth became acting commander of the 3d Panzer Recce Battalion when the legendary Lt. Col. Baron von Wechmar returned to Europe in November 1941. Due to the delays in Luck's transfer to North Africa (caused by General von Funck), he led the unit until early April 1942. He led it again until Hans von Luck returned in late September. In the meantime, Everth was decorated with the Knight's Cross. He fell ill during the Second Battle of El Alamein and had to be evacuated back to Europe, never to return.

53. Barnett, p. 150.

54. Jackson, pp. 216–17; Connell, p. 532.

55. Barnett, pp. 150–51.

Chapter IV: The Cauldron and Bir Hacheim

1. Carell, pp. 174–75. Siegfried Westphal was born in Leipzig in 1902. He entered the Imperial Army as a Fahnenjunker on 10 November 1918—the day before the armistice ending World War I went into effect. Westphal nevertheless remained in service as an enlisted man and was not commissioned until 1922. He was a member of the 11th Cavalry Regiment at the time. Westphal remained in the horse branch most of his career. He was Ia of the 58th Infantry Division when World War II began. Later he served as Ia of the XXVII Corps (1940) and Ia of Panzer Group Afrika (from 15 June 1941).

2. Heckmann, p. 253.

3. Fritz Bayerlein was born in Würzburg on 14 January 1899. He entered the army as a Fahnenjunker in 1917 but was not commissioned until 1922, when he was a member of 21st Infantry Regiment. By 1938 he was a major on the staff of the XV Motorized Corps. Bayerlein later served as Ia of the 10th Panzer Division (1939–40), Ia of Guderian's XIX Panzer Corps (1940), and Ia of the 2d Panzer Group (later Army) (1940–41). He became chief of staff of the Afrika Korps on 5 October 1941.

4. Marseilles (by then a captain) was killed on 30 September 1942, in an air accident not involving enemy contact. He had shot down 158 enemy airplanes by then—all British. He shot down more British aircraft than anyone in history. Had he lived another month, he would have reached his twenty-fourth birthday. See Samuel W. Mitcham Jr. and Gene Mueller, *Hitler's Commanders* (Latham, Maryland: Scarborough House, 1993).

5. Carell, p. 177.

6. Mellenthin, p. 103.
7. These figures exclude PzKw IIs.
8. Jackson, p. 219.
9. Agar-Hamilton, p. 42, citing *The Tiger Kills* (London: Her Majesty's Stationery Office, 1944), p. 123.
10. Heckmann, p. 31.
11. Bergot, p. 140.
12. Brett-James, p. 185.
13. Ibid, pp. 185–86.
14. Bergot, p. 140.
15. Brett-James, pp. 186–90.
16. Ibid, p. 192.
17. Mellenthin, p. 109; also see Playfair III, p. 232.
18. Playfair III, p. 233.
19. Brett-James, pp. 191–92.
20. Barnett, p. 151.
21. Ibid, pp. 198–99.
22. Ibid, p. 190.
23. Ibid, p. 196.
24. Playfair III, p. 234.
25. Sir John Hackett, "Foreword" in Wolf Heckmann, *Rommel's War in Africa* (New York: E. P. Dutton and Company, 1980), pp. xvi–xvii.
26. Maule, p. 191.
27. Alman, p. 274.
28. Maule, pp. 192–93.
29. Ibid.
30. Rommel, p. 143.
31. Agar-Hamilton, p. 49.
32. Barnett, p. 155.
33. Mackenzie, I, p. 552. At this time, the British also summoned Brigadier (later Lieutenant General) Sir Dudley Russell's 5th Indian Brigade from Palestine to Libya.
34. Carell, p. 179.
35. Heckmann, p. 259.
36. Agar-Hamilton, p. 49, citing Rommel, p. 143.
37. Irving, p. 177. Lieutenant Colonel Ernst-Guenther Baade was

a maverick and one of the most colorful characters ever to wear anyone's uniform. Fluent in English, he frequently carried on conversations with the British over their own radio nets and even occasionally called them up to wish them Merry Christmas or Happy New Year. Despite his eccentricities, however, he was an excellent combat commander, as he was to prove beyond a shadow of a doubt leading the 90th Panzer Grenadier Division in Italy in 1944. He was wounded in December 1944, and, as a lieutenant general, was named commander of the *Volkssturm,* the Nazi equivalent of the Home Guard, in 1945. Baade, however, was an anti-Nazi and was not at all interested in sending old men and children to their deaths in order to prolong Adolf Hitler's miserable life for a few more days. He released people from this duty on the slightest pretext, leading to a major row with his National Socialist Political Officer. According to reports, this argument ended when General Baade shot the Nazi to death and went into hiding. Tragically, he was killed by an Allied fighter-bomber in May 1945, a few days after Hitler committed suicide.

38. Playfair III, p. 237; Agar-Hamilton, p. 60.
39. Carell, pp. 182–83.
40. Lewin, pp. 149–50.

Chapter V: Knightsbridge and the Drive to the Coastal Road

1. Agar-Hamilton, pp. 61–62.
2. Playfair III, p. 240.
3. Agar-Hamilton, p. 62.
4. Barnett, p. 155.
5. Playfair III, p. 239.
6. Jackson, pp. 224–25.
7. Lewin, p. 151.
8. Barnett, p. 156.
9. Agar-Hamilton, p. 66.
10. Playfair III, p. 243.
11. Agar-Hamilton, p. 107.
12. Ibid.
13. Mackenzie I, p. 559.
14. Ibid, p. 82, citing *Saga of the Transvaal Scottish Regiment,* p. 487.
15. Heckmann, p. 39.

16. Barnett, p. 162.

17. D. C. Quilter, comp. and ed., *No Dishonourable Name: The 2nd and 3rd Battalions Coldstream Guards, 1939–1946* (London: William Clower and Sons, Ltd., 1947; reprint ed., London: S. R. Publishers, Ltd., 1972), p. 146 (hereafter cited as "Quilter").

18. Agar-Hamilton, p. 98.

Chapter VI: Breaking the Gazala Line

1. Playfair III, p. 252.

2. The 8th Armoured Brigade had belonged to the 10th Armoured (formerly 1st Cavalry) Division.

3. Playfair III, p. 260.

4. Maule, p. 34.

5. Heckmann, p. 39.

6. Mackenzie, I, p. 559; Brett-James, p. 206.

7. Maule, p. 196.

8. Brett-James, p. 210.

9. Carver, *Dilemma*, pp. 99–100.

10. Brett-James, p. 83.

11. Ibid, pp. 82–85.

12. Mackenzie I, p. 561.

13. Brett-James, p. 83.

Chapter VII: Rommel's Greatest Victory

1. Agar-Hamilton, p. 139.

2. Howard Kippenberger, *Infantry Brigadier* (London: Oxford University Press, 1949), p. 114.

3. Agar-Hamilton, p. 131; Mackenzie I, p. 563.

4. Agar-Hamilton, p. 134.

5. Barnett, p. 165.

6. Agar-Hamilton, p. 120.

7. Ibid, p. 129.

8. Ibid, p. 148.

9. Rommel, p. 230.

10. Collier, p. 92.

11. Mellenthin, p. 144.

12. Quilter, p. 147.

13. Agar-Hamilton, p. 161.

14. Rommel, pp. 160–63.
15. Agar-Hamilton, p. 162.
16. Mackenzie I, p. 562.
17. Jan Yindrich, *Fortress Tobruk* (London: Ernest Benn, Ltd., 1951), p. 77.
18. Mackenzie I, p. 564. Lancaster counterattacked with his own reserve company, his carrier platoon, and the carrier platoon of the 2/7th Gurkha Rifles.
19. Playfair III, p. 268.
20. Quilter, p. 147; Playfair III, p. 268; Agar-Hamilton, p. 173.
21. Playfair III, p. 267; Agar-Hamilton, p. 175.
22. Agar-Hamilton, p. 172.
23. Playfair III, p. 269.
24. Heckmann, p. 278.
25. Playfair III, p. 271.
26. Maule, p. 198.
27. The Littorio Armored Division had all but been destroyed in the Tenth Army disaster during the winter of 1940–41. It was supposed to reorganize and refit, but instead was cannibalized to create the Ariete and Trieste Divisions. In addition, its transport was taken to provide a central pool for several units. When it moved up to Tobruk, it was short many of its units—it had no engineers or supply service units, for example. The Italian generals sent it forward reluctantly and only because Rommel insisted (Playfair III, p. 265).
28. Agar-Hamilton, pp. 205–06.
29. Irving, p. 182.
30. Heckmann, p. 276.
31. Agar-Hamilton, p. 215.
32. Quilter, p. 148.
33. Irving, p. 185.
34. Young, p. 100.
35. Playfair, p. 274.
36. Agar-Hamilton, p. 222.

Epilogue
1. Connell, p. 657.
2. Isham, pp. 311–12.
3. Bond, p. 17.

4. Parkinson, pp. 239–51.
5. Bond, p. 18.
6. Carver, *Dilemma*, p. 149.
7. Tunney, pp. 162–63.
8. Carver, *Dilemma*, pp. 148–49.
9. Maule, pp. 216–376.
10. Satterthwaite, p. 566.
11. Bright, p. 185.
12. Brett-James, p. 190.
13. Barnett, *Hitler's Generals*, p. xiv.
14. Ibid, pp. xiv–xv.
15. *New York Times*, 20 March 1950, p. 3e.
16. Keilig, p. 369; *New York Times*, 3 July 1982, p. 19.
17. Angolia, Volume 2, p. 46.
18. Keilig, pp. 35–36.
19. Ibid, p. 131.
20. Ibid, p. 354.
21. Alman, p. 280; Keilig, pp. 238–39; Angolia, Volume I, pp. 234–35.
22. Keilig, p. 171.
23. Ibid, p. 353.
24. Keilig, p. 62; Tessin, Volume 7, p. 51.
25. Absolon, p. 79.
26. Keilig, p. 232; Friedrich von Stauffenberg, personal interview.
27. Friedrich von Stauffenberg, "Panzer Commanders of the Western Front," unpublished manuscript in the possession of the author.
28. Keilig, p. 184.
29. See Luck.
30. Carlson, pp. 68–81; Keilig, pp. 221–22.
31. Martin Blumenson, "Rommel," in Correlli Barnett, ed., *Hitler's Generals* (London: George Weidenfield & Nicolson, Ltd., 1989; reprint ed., New York: Quill/William Morrow, 1989), p. 314.

Bibliography

Absolon, Rudolf, comp. *Rangliste der Generale der deutschen Luftwaffe nach dem Stand vom 20. April 1945.* Friedberg: Podzun-Pallas-Verlag GmbH, 1984.

Agar-Hamilton, J. A. I., and L. C. F. Turner. *Crisis in the Desert, May–July 1942.* Cape Town: Oxford University Press, 1952.

―――― *The Sidi Rezeg Battles, 1941.* Cape Town: OxfordUniversity Press, 1957.

Alman, Karl. *Panzer vor: Die dramatische Geschichte der Panzerwaffe und ihrer tapferen Soldaten.* Rastatt: Erich Pabel Verlag, 1966.

Angolia, John. *On the Field of Honor.* San Jose, California: R. James Bender Publishing, 1979. 2 Volumes.

Badoglio, Pietro. *Italy in the Second World War.* London: Oxford University Press, 1948. Reprint ed., Westport, Connecticut: Greenwood Press, 1976.

Barclay, C. N. *Against Great Odds.* Liverpool: Blake and Mackenzie, Ltd., 1955.

Barnett, Correlli. *The Desert Generals.* 2d Edition. Bloomington: Indiana University Press, 1982.

――――, ed. *Hitler's Generals.* London: George Weidenfield & Nicolson, Ltd., 1989.

Bergot, Erwan. *The Afrika Korps.* New York: W. H. Allen Publishers, Inc., 1975. Reprint ed., New York: Charter Books, 1975.

Birkby, Carel. *Saga of the Transvaal Scottish Regiment.* Cape Town: Howard B. Timmins, 1950.

Blake, Lord, and C. S. Nicholls, eds. *The Dictionary of National Biography, 1971–1980.* Oxford: Oxford University Press, 1986.

――――. *The Dictionary of National Biography, 1981–1985.* Oxford: Oxford University Press, 1990.

Blumenson, Martin. "Rommel." Correlli Barnett, ed. *Hitler's Generals.* London: George Weidenfield & Nicolson, Ltd., 1989 pp. 292–316.

Bond, Brian. "Auchinleck, Sir Claude (1884–1983)." Lord Blake and C. S. Nicholls, eds. *The Dictionary of National Biography, 1981–1985.* Oxford: Oxford University Press, 1990 pp. 16–18.

Brett-James, Antony. *Ball of Fire.* Aldershot: Gale & Polden, Ltd., 1951.

Bright, Joan. *9th Queen's Royal Lancers*. Aldershot: Gale & Polden, Ltd., 1951.

Cannistraro, Philip V., ed. *Historical Dictionary of Fascist Italy*. Westport, Connecticut: Greenwood Press, 1982.

Carell, Paul. *Foxes of the Desert*. New York: E. P. Dutton and Company, 1960.

Carlson, Verner R. "Portrait of a German General Staff Officer." *Military Review*, Volume LXX, No. 4 (April 1990), pp. 69–86.

Carver, Michael. *Dilemma of the Desert War: A New Look at the Libyan Campaign, 1940–1942*. Bloomington: Indiana University Press, 1986.

————. "O'Connor, Sir Richard Nugent, (1889–1981)." Lord Blake and C. S. Nicholls, eds. *Dictionary of National Biography, 1981–1985*. Oxford: Oxford University Press, 1990, pp. 302–03.

Churchill, Winston S. *War Memoirs*. Volume IV, *The Hinge of Fate*. Boston: Houghton Mifflin, 1950.

Collier, Richard, et al. *The War in the Desert*. Alexandria, Virginia: Time-Life Books, 1979.

Connell, John. *Auchinleck*. London: Cassell & Company, Ltd., 1959.

Davy, G. M. O. *The Seventh and Three Enemies*. Cambridge: W. Heffer and Sons, Ltd., 1952.

Farrar-Hockley, Anthony. "Nye, Sir Archibald Edward (1895–1967)." E. T. Williams and C. S. Nicholls, eds. *Dictionary of National Biography, 1961–1970*. Oxford: Oxford University Press, 1981, pp. 801–02.

Ferguson, Bernard. "Wavell, Archibald Percival, first Earl Wavell (1883–1950)" L. G. Wichham Legg and E. T. Williams, eds. *Dictionary of National Biography, 1941–1950*. Oxford: Oxford University Press, 1959, pp. 932–35.

Hart, B. H. Liddell. *History of the Second World War*. New York: G. P. Putnam's Sons, 1972. 2 Volumes.

Heckmann, Wolf. *Rommel's War in Africa*. New York: E. P. Dutton and Company, 1980.

Irving, David. *Trail of the Fox*. New York: E. P. Dutton and Company, 1977.

Isham, Gyles. "Gott, William Henry Ewart, 1897–1942." L. G. Wichham Legg and E. T. Williams, eds. *Dictionary of National Biography, 1941–1950*. Oxford: Oxford University Press, 1959, pp. 310–12.

Jackson, W. G. F. *The Battle of North Africa, 1940–43*. New York: Mason/Charter, 1975.

Jacobsen, H. A., and J. Rohwer, eds. *Decisive Battles of World War II: The German View.* New York: G. P. Putnam's Sons, 1965.

Keilig, Wolf. *Die Generale des Heeres.* Friedberg: Podzun-Pallas-Verlag, 1983.

Kippenberger, Howard. *Infantry Brigadier.* London: Oxford University Press, 1949.

"Kriegstagebuch Panzerarmee Afrika." Washington, D.C.: United States National Archives.

Law, Richard D., and Craig W. H. Luther. *Rommel.* San Jose, California: R. James Bender Publishing, 1980.

Legg, L. G. Wichham, and E. T. Williams, eds. *Dictionary of National Biography, 1941–1950.* Oxford: Oxford University Press, 1959.

Lewin, Ronald. *Rommel as a Military Commander.* New York: Ballantine Books, 1970.

Luck, Hans von. *Panzer Commander.* Westport, Connecticut: Praeger, 1989.

Mackenzie, Compton. *Eastern Epic.* London: Chatto and Windus, 1951. 2 Volumes.

Maule, Henry. *Spearhead General: The Epic Story of General Sir Francis Messervy and His Men in Eritrea, North Africa and Burma.* London: Odhams Press, Ltd., 1961.

McGuirk, Dal. *Afrikakorps: Self-Portrait.* Osceola, Wisconsin: Motorbooks International, 1992.

Mehner, Kurt, ed. *Die Geheimen Tagesberichte der deutschen Wehrmachtführung im Zweiten Weltkrieg, 1939–1945.* Osnabrück: Biblio Verlag, 1988. 12 Volumes.

Mellenthin, F. W. von. *Panzer Battles: A Study in the Employment of Armor in the Second World War.* Norman: University of Oklahoma Press, 1956. Reprint ed., New York: Ballantine Books, 1976.

Mitcham, Samuel W., Jr. *The Desert Fox in Normandy.* Westport, Connecticut: Praeger, 1997.

Mitcham, Samuel W., Jr., and Gene Mueller, *Hitler's Commanders.* Latham, Maryland: Scarborough House, 1993.

Mueller, Gene. *The Forgotten Field Marshal, Wilhelm Keitel.* Durham, North Carolina: Moore Publishing Company, 1979.

New York Times. Various Issues.

Packard, Reynolds, and Eleanor Packard. *Balcony Empire.* New York: Oxford University Press, 1942.

Parkinson, Roger. *The Auk:Auchinleck, Victor at Alarmein.* London: Hart-Davis, MacGibbon, Ltd., 1977.

Playfair, I. S. O., et al. *The Mediterranean and Middle East.* Volume III, *British Fortunes Reach Their Lowest Ebb (September 1941 to September 1942).* London: Her Majesty's Stationery Office, 1966.

Quilter, D. C. *No Dishonourable Name: The 2nd and 3rd Battalions Coldstream Guards, 1939–1946.* London: William Clower & Sons, Ltd., 1947. Reprint ed., London: S. R. Publishers, Ltd., 1972.

Rommel, Erwin. *Infantry in the Attack.* Vienna, Virginia: Athena Press, 1979.

———. *The Rommel Papers.* B. H. Liddell Hart, ed. New York: Harcourt, Brace & Company, 1953.

Satterthwaite, R. G. "Messervy, Sir Frank Walter." Lord Blake and C. S. Nicholls, eds. *The Dictionary of National Biography, 1971–1980.* Oxford: Oxford University Press, 1986, pp. 566–67.

Schmidt, Heinz Werner. *With Rommel in the Desert.* London: G. Harrap & Co., 1972; reprint ed., New York: Ballantine Books, 1972.

Simpson, B. G. *History of the Rand Light Infantry.* Cape Town: Howard Timmins, 1965.

Stauffenberg, Friedrich von. "Panzer Commanders of the Western Front." Unpublished manuscript.

———. Personal interviews.

Strawson, John. *The Battle for North Africa.* New York: Bonanza Books, 1969.

———. "Cunningham, Sir Alan Gordon (1887–1983)." Lord Blake and C. S. Nicholls, eds. *Dictionary of National Biography, 1981–1985.* Oxford: Oxford University Press, 1990, pp. 103–04.

Tessin, Georg. *Verbande und Truppen der deutschen Wehrmacht und Waffen-SS im Zweiten Weltkrieg 1939–1945.* Osnabrück: Biblio Verlag, 1979. 14 Volumes.

The Tiger Kills. London: Her Majesty's Stationery Office, 1944.

Tuker, Sir Francis. *Approach to Battle.* London: Cassell, 1963.

Tunney, Christopher. *A Biographical Dictionary of World War II.* London: J. M. Dent and Sons, Ltd., 1972.

United States Army Military Intelligence Service. "Order of Battle of the Italian Army." Washington, D.C.: Military Intelligence Service, 1943. Available on microfilm at the U.S. National Archives, Washington, D.C.

Warlimont, Walter. "The Decision in the Mediterranean." H. A. Jacobsen and J. Rohwer, eds. *Decisive Battles of World War II: The German View.* New York: G. P. Putnam's Sons, 1965.

Williams, E. T. and Helen M. Parker, eds. *Dictionary of National Biography, 1951–1960.* Oxford: Oxford University Press, 1974.

Williams, E. T. and C. S. Nicholls, Eds. *Dictionary of National Biography, 1961–1970.* Oxford: Oxford University Press, 1981.

Wilson, Maitland. *Eight Years Overseas.* London: Hutchinson and Co., Ltd., 1950.

Yindrich, Jan. *Fortress Tobruk.* London: Ernest Benn, Ltd., 1951.

Young, Desmond. *Rommel: The Desert Fox.* New York: Harper & Row, 1950.

Name Index

Subject Index